America's Top Internet Job Sites

By Drs. Ron and Caryl Krannich

BUSINESS AND CAREER BOOKS AND SOFTWARE

101 Dynamite Answers to Interview Questions
101 Secrets of Highly Effective Speakers
201 Dynamite Job Search Letters
America's Top Internet Sites
Best Jobs For the 21st Century
Change Your Job, Change Your Life
The Complete Guide to International Jobs and Careers
The Complete Guide to Public Employment
The Directory of Federal Jobs and Employers
Discover the Best Jobs For You!
Dynamite Cover Letters
Dynamite Networking For Dynamite Jobs
Dynamite Resumes
Dynamite Salary Negotiations
Dynamite Tele-Search
The Educator's Guide to Alternative Jobs and Careers
Find a Federal Job Fast!
From Air Force Blue to Corporate Gray
From Army Green to Corporate Gray
From Navy Blue to Corporate Gray
Get a Raise in 7 Days
High Impact Resumes and Letters
Interview For Success
Job-Power Source CD-ROM
Jobs and Careers With Nonprofit Organizations
Military Resumes and Cover Letters
Moving Out of Education
Moving Out of Government
Re-Careering in Turbulent Times
Resumes & Job Search Letters For Transitioning Military Personnel
Savvy Interviewing
Savvy Networker
Savvy Resume Writer
Ultimate Job Source CD-ROM

TRAVEL AND INTERNATIONAL BOOKS

Directory of Websites For Overseas Job Seekers
International Jobs Directory
Jobs For People Who Love to Travel
Mayors and Managers in Thailand
Politics of Family Planning Policy in Thailand
Shopping and Traveling in Exotic Asia
Shopping in Exotic Places
Shopping the Exotic South Pacific
Travel Planning on the Internet
Treasures and Pleasures of Australia
Treasures and Pleasures of China
Treasures and Pleasures of Egypt
Treasures and Pleasures of Hong Kong
Treasures and Pleasures of India
Treasures and Pleasures of Indonesia
Treasures and Pleasures of Italy
Treasures and Pleasures of Morocco
Treasures and Pleasures of Paris and the French Riviera
Treasures and Pleasures of the Philippines
Treasures and Pleasures of Rio and São Paulo
Treasures and Pleasures of Singapore and Bali
Treasures and Pleasures of Singapore and Malaysia
Treasures and Pleasures of Thailand
Treasures and Pleasures of Vietnam

America's Top Internet Job Sites

The Click and Easy™ Guide to Finding a Job Online

Ronald L. Krannich, Ph.D.
Caryl Rae Krannich, Ph.D.

IMPACT PUBLICATIONS
Manassas Park, VA

Library of Congress Cataloguing-in-Publication Data

Krannich, Ronald L.
   America's top internet job sites: the click and easy guide to
finding a job online / Ronald L. Krannich, Caryl Rae Krannich
      p. cm.
   Includes bibliographical references and index.
   ISBN 1-57023-165-6
   1. Job hunting–Computer network resources. 2. Internet.
I. Krannich, Caryl Rae. II. Title

HF5382.7 .K69 2001
025.06'331702–dc21   2001026453

Publisher: For information on Impact Publications, including current and forthcoming publications, authors, press kits, online bookstore, and submission requirements, visit Impact's website: *www.impactpublications.com*

Publicity/Rights: For information on publicity, author interviews, and subsidiary rights, contact the Media Relations Department: Tel. 703-361-7300, Fax 703-335-9486, or email: *info@impactpublications.com*.

Sales/Distribution: All bookstore sales are handled through Impact's trade distributor: National Book Network, 15200 NBN Way, Blue Ridge Summit, PA 17214, Tel. 1-800-462-6420. All other sales and distribution inquiries should be directed to the publisher: Sales Department, IMPACT PUBLICATIONS, 9104 Manassas Drive, Suite N, Manassas Park, VA 20111-5211, Tel. 703-361-7300, Fax 703-335-9486, or email: *info@ impactpublications.com*

Contents

Preface . . . . **vii**

1 The World of Internet Job Sites **1**
- Facing a Daunting Task 2
- More Than Just the Alphabet 3
- Being Effective and Staying Focused 4
- A Click and Stupid Approach 4
- A Focused Job Search Approach 6
- Structuring Benefits Around Eyeballs 7
- Coming Up 8

2 Getting Started in the Right Direction **11**
- Use Your Time Wisely 11
- Basic Skills and Guidance 12
- A Library and an Orchestra 13
- Search Engines 16
- Search Agents 18
- Directories 18
- Most Popular Search Engines 19
- Employment Site Comparisons and Ratings 22
- Saving Time and Effort 26

3 Virtual Job and Career Communities **27**
- Information Communities 27
- Usenet Newsgroups 29
- Mailing Lists 32
- Message Boards of Websites 33

4 Gateway Employment Sites **37**
- Gateways As Website Directories   37
- Gateways With Wisdom and Judgment   39
- Other Useful Gateways   44

5 Mega Employment Sites and Databases . . **49**
- Managing Resumes, Job Boards, and Traffic   49
- Old Wine in New Electronic Bottles   50
- Structure and Process   52
- Too Busy to Job Search?   54
- Viewing Classifieds (Postings) Online   55
- 35 Peripheral Services and Features   55
- The Top 10   58
- 61 Favorite Employment Sites   65

6 Assessment and Testing Sites **83**
- Doing First Things First   84
- Beware of 21st Century Snake Oil   86
- Online Assessments   86
- Contacting a Career Professional   99

7 Education and Online Learning Sites **101**
- Distance Learning   101
- Major Online Educational Programs   105
- Useful Associations and Companies   109
- Traditional Education Programs   109

8 Career Information, Advice, and Research Sites **111**
- Career Information and Advice   111
- Career Research   117
  - Business Resources   118
  - Public Records Resources   121
  - Association and Nonprofit Resources   122
  - Online Employment Resources   124
- Declining Companies   124

9 Resume and Cover Letter Sites **127**
- Paper Resumes Becoming Nuisances   127
- Resumes and Cover Letters   128
- Resumes Play a Renewed Role   128

- The Hunt For Resumes   129
- The New Resume Entrepreneurs   130
- Resume and Letter Writing Tips   130
- Professional Resume Writers   131
- Resume Distribution Services   133
- Do It Right   137

10 Networking, Mentoring, and Q&A Sites 139
- Networking Sources, Skills, and Strategies   139
- Associations As Networks   141
- Women's Networks   142
- Alumni Groups For Networking   143
- Locators For Re-Building Networks   144
- Military Locators and Buddy Finders   145
- Job Search Clubs and Support Groups   145
- Mentors, Career Coaches, and Q&A   146

11 Interview, Salary, and Relocation Sites . . . 149
- Interviews Count the Most   149
- Interview Preparation and Practice   150
- Useful Job Interview Sites   151
- Salary Negotiation and Compensation Sites   154
- Relocation Sites   159

12 Career Counseling and Coaching Sites 163
- Self-Starters and Wishful Thinkers   165
- A Season For Everything   166
- Career Management Firms   166
- Certified Career Counselors   170
- Commercial Career Coaching   170

13 Employer and Recruiter Sites 175
- Executive Recruiters and Candidates   175
- Staffing and Employment Firms   182
- Model Employer Sites   185

14 Specialty Occupational and Job Sites 187
- Finding Your Specialty   187
- Academia and Education   189
- Airline Industry   193
- Architecture   195

- Arts, Entertainment, and Media   197
- Business   199
- Computers and Information Technology   202
- Construction   205
- Engineering   206
- Health Care   208
- Hospitality and Travel   211
- Law   214
- Science   217
- Sports and Recreation   220

15 Niche Sites For Special Job Seekers 223
- College Students and Recent Graduates   223
- Military in Transition   227
- Executive-Level Candidates   231
- Women   232
- Minorities and Diversity   234
- People With Disabilities   237
- Government and Law Enforcement   239
- Nonprofit Sector   243
- International Job Seekers   250
- Part-Time, Temporary, and Contract   253
- Freelancers and Telecommuters   255
- Spooks, Spies, and Intel Specialists   257
- Ex-Offenders in Transition   258

Index **261**

The Authors **269**

Career Resources **271**

Preface

FINDING A JOB TODAY IS BOTH EASIER AND MORE difficult than ever before. It looks and feels easier because of the wealth of employment information and free services readily available to job seekers on the Internet, 24 hours a day and with just a click of a mouse. At the same time, it can be more difficult and frustrating because you may become overwhelmed with the information, you may have difficulty choosing quality resources, your competition may be using the same online resources, and employers may demand more evidence of performance from a larger pool of qualified candidates. If you want to become a savvy job seeker, you need to wisely integrate the Internet into your job search and clearly communicate to employers that you have the requisite skills and abilities to do the job.

While the Internet should play an important role in your job search – from researching companies to applying for jobs online – it should never substitute for the job search itself. Indeed, too many job seekers become preoccupied with conducting an online job search rather than organizing an overall effective job search that includes both online and offline elements. Not surprisingly, many digital-oriented job seekers would rather sit behind a computer screen searching for job listings and applying online than picking up the telephone or meeting with individuals about their job search.

We wrote this book because we saw a need to approach both the Internet and the job search from a different, and hopefully more balanced, perspective. Too often, too much misplaced emphasis and hype is given to conducting a job search on the Internet. While we believe the Internet can play a critical role in any job search, we also believe it should be fully integrated into a well organized and purposeful job search process – from beginning to end. However, during the past few years, numerous employment websites, primarily funded by employers and recruiters, have promoted a questionable job search model that primarily benefits employers, recruiters, and website entrepreneurs rather than individual job seekers. Operated as free job boards for job seekers, these sites coach visitors to enter their resumes online and search for job listings. Essentially a "classified ad and resume submission" approach to the job search, many of these sites work especially well for employers who can now use the Internet to inexpensively and effectively cast a much wider net for locating, persuading, screening, and recruiting candidates. But this approach is not necessarily in the best interests of many job seekers who also should be engaged in several other job search activities *before* submitting their resume online, surveying job listings, and applying for jobs.

> *The truth is that employers know how effective websites are in the hiring process because they pay for effectiveness. Ironically, no one really knows, beyond anecdotal success stories, how effective these same sites are for job seekers.*

America's Top Internet Job Sites is primarily written for job seekers rather than for employers, recruiters, or Internet entrepreneurs who operate employment websites. From beginning to end, we organized the book around one key question – *How can job seekers best benefit from using the Internet or particular employment websites in their job search?* We're talking about *using the Internet in your job search* rather than *conducting an Internet job search* – an important distinction for organizing this book and assessing individual websites. Our single-minded pursuit of this *benefit question* for job seekers meant organizing the book around the *job search* rather than focusing on identifying, classifying, and judging the superficial visual elements or the "traffic" rates of employment websites. The truth is that employers know how effective employment websites are in the hiring process simply because they are the ones who pay for effectiveness; if a site doesn't deliver the goods – qualified candidates – they take their business elsewhere. Consequently, most websites are primarily designed for employers and recruiters who financially support the sites and secondarily for job seekers who must be motivated to use them for free.

From the perspective of employers, recruiters, and webmasters, these are *recruitment websites*. From the perspective of job seekers, these same sites are *job search websites*. The differing perspectives arise from the differences in expected benefits. Ironically, no one really knows, beyond a few anecdotal success stories, how effective these same sites are for job seekers. In fact, many job seekers remain frustrated in using these sites. They complain of receiving few if any invitations to job interviews based on their Internet activities. Yet, few job seekers really know how to conduct an effective job search either online or offline. The widespread presence of job boards on the Internet may actually increase the frustrations and ineffectiveness of job seekers who should be spending their time more wisely on activities other than working the job boards.

For us, as well as many experienced career professionals, *effectiveness for job seekers* is found in following a clearly defined job search process in which the Internet plays an important, but not an all-encompassing, role. It all begins with self-assessment and goal setting – not with resumes, letters, and applications. We believe you are best served by a book that integrates the Internet into each sequential step of the job search – assessment, goal setting, research, networking, resume and letter writing, interviewing, and negotiating compensation and terms of employment. Rather than focus primarily on the largest and most popular employment websites, we identify websites that can play important roles in each step of your job search. For in the end, the most critical steps in this whole process take place offline – job interviews and salary negotiations. After all, employers don't hire people off the Internet – they only screen them for interviews, which take place in face-to-face settings. The Internet can help you get to and prepare you for the job interview, but from there you are essentially offline and on your own.

One technical note as you use this book. In most cases we have shortened URLs by dropping the www prefix. If your browser is Internet Explorer, our shortened URLs should work fine. However, in some cases Netscape browsers require inserting the www prefix. If you get an error message when using Netscape, just insert the <u>www</u> prefix and it should work.

At the same time, you may discover that several of our website addresses no longer work. That would not surprise us since so many websites come and go or change URLs as they become absorbed into other sites. After all, these are "new economy" businesses that may have a very short life-span or become "cob webs" with little or no expensive maintenance (see page 125 for a related story). If you can't connect to some of our sites, chances are they've gone out of business. We expect 20 to 30 percent of our sites will disappear within three years. Keep in mind that most of these websites are dot-com businesses with very shaky financials. Many are venture capital experiments which may not survive beyond an initial two or three years of funding. In fact, it's surprising that so many of these sites have thus far survived for so long on so little support. Even some of the large and popular employment websites may be in for a thunderous fall in the near future, especially when unemployment increases and fewer and fewer employers need to use these online recruitment services.

We wish you well with your online job search adventure. You'll find an absolutely incredible amount of employment information and services on the Internet which can become very seductive and time consuming. Whatever you do, approach the many websites with the wisdom of someone who understands how the online information and services can best be integrated into your job search. While anyone can find a job, your single-minded goal should be to find a job that you do well and enjoy doing – one that allows you to pursue your passion. The Internet should help you find the perfect "fit" between your interests, skills, and goals and the needs of employers. May you find your perfect job and career fit with the help of the many websites identified in the following chapters.

Ron and Caryl Krannich

www.impactpublications.com
www.winningthejob.com
www.veteransworld.com
www.contentforcareers.com
www.contentfortravel.com
www.ishoparoundtheworld.com
www.greentogray.com

America's Top Internet Job Sites

monster.com
Work. Life. Possibilities.

Employer Log-In
Post A Job
Get Monster
Hiring Solutions [NEW]

 FIRST TIMERS START HERE  **SEARCH JOBS** **POST YOUR RESUME**

Monster Admin/Support

- Search Admin/Support jobs
- Get expert advice on networking, training, certifications and more
- Start advancing your career NOW!

ChiefMonster
Senior Executives, qualify and search for executive jobs now

MonsterTRAK
College Students, build your career today!

Monster Moving
Relocating?
Visit Monster Moving now

Monster Talent Market™
Free Agents start here Employers search for contract talent

Site Tools
Help
Privacy Index

 **Search Jobs**
Find the job you're looking for from the Monster Network® Search over **1,000,000** job postings now.

 **My Monster**
Job seekers: **post** your resume & **manage** your personal career account

Featured Employers
Research companies and find out more about today's top employers
▷ Foreign Service Exam, Register by 9/29.
▷ The Leadership Center, New Possibilities.
▷ Email a Resume to 1000s of Recruiters with Zapreo

Global Network
Explore the Monster Network

🇦🇺 AU 🇧🇪 BE 🇨🇦 CA 🇩🇪 DE 🇪🇸 ES
🇫🇷 FR 🇭🇰 HK 🇮🇪 IE 🇮🇳 IN 🇮🇹 IT
🇳🇱 NL 🇳🇿 NZ 🇸🇬 SG 🇬🇧 UK 🇺🇸 US

About Monster
Check out 18 Monster **job opportunities**
Use our handy **Site Tools** to learn more about Monster.com

CAREER CENTER
Search 2,000 pages of career advice, resume help and cover jobs

Find a job in...
Career Levels
Special Interests
Check Out

Monster Poll
Which would be best for your career advancement?
○ Attending industry seminars and conferences
○ Enrolling in career-related learning
○ Switching jobs
○ Spending more time at the office

[**Results**]

Sponsored by:
Belcan

Free Career Newsletter
(Over 467,755 Subscribers)
Subscribe Now

Communicate
Network with thousands of members or ask our experts about dozens of topics.
→ View Chat Schedule

 Monster Confidential Resumes **All NEW AOL 6.0** monster.com

 PRIVACY BBBOnLine

1

The World of Internet Job Sites

MOST JOB SEEKERS AND EMPLOYERS ARE WELL advised to incorporate the Internet in their job search and hiring activities. Indeed, by some estimates, more than 100,000 non-employer websites now focus on employment. Many of these sites manage nearly 4 million online resumes for connecting job seekers with employers. These range from dozens of mega employment sites designed for both employers and job seekers, such as Monster, CareerBuilder, Hotjobs, and Headhunter, to highly specialized websites that test, coach, or assist job seekers in blasting their resumes to thousands of employers, such as CareerHub, AskThe Employer, and ResumeBlaster. If you also include employment information found on the websites of employers, the number of job-related websites may well increase to over two million!

Welcome to the wonderful and seemingly chaotic world of employment information, an electronic world of great promises and numerous pitfalls. Easily accessible, the quality and usefulness of this world is by no means certain. It's a world worth exploring and incorporating in your job search. Exploited intelligently, this world can greatly enhance each step of your job search.

Facing a Daunting Task

So, you're well advised to incorporate the Internet in your job search, but where should you go once you're on the Internet? How can you best use this resource without wasting a great deal of time on random activities that may generate false hopes with few useful outcomes? What expectations should you have when using the Internet for finding a job? For job seekers, the ultimate goal or outcome should be to connect with the right employer who invites you to a job interview and offers you a job. Unfortunately, many job seekers get lost along the way as they wander aimlessly in a chaotic click and sound-bite arena. Lacking clear goals when using the Internet, they easily become distracted as they lose focus on what's really important in conducting an effective job search. Jumping from one "interesting" website to another, they forget there is indeed a forest amongst all the trees they've been having fun swinging from. The forest is the job search, which involves a very well defined series of steps in the process of finding a job. While the online experience may not result in connecting with an employer who invites you to a job interview, it should result in many other positive outcomes that can enhance your job search – from assessing your skills and abilities to acquiring tips on writing resumes, researching employers, networking, interviewing, and negotiating salary and benefits.

Size does seem to count as more and more people gravitate to the larger sites which, not surprisingly, get the most hits.

Given the continuing proliferation of employment-related websites, with dozens of new ones launched each month, individuals face a daunting task of determining which sites can best assist them. Should you, for example, frequent the same sites most other job seekers and employers visit, or would you be better off striking out on your own and finding sites that best meet your particular needs, especially the many "boutique" or niche sites that have developed during the past couple of years? Many people use search engines and directories to identify such websites, while others rely on periodic lists of the "Top 10," "Top 100," "best" or "most popular" sites as determined subjectively by self-appointed Internet or employment gurus or objectively by the number of "hits" each site receives. In the end, size does seem to count as more and more people gravitate to the larger sites which, not surprisingly, get the most hits. But if you follow such paths to locating the best of these websites, you may miss many small gems along the way. Worst of all, you may be on a very crowded highway involving high competition for low stakes. You may end up joining the growing chorus of frustrated online job seekers who discover that many employment sites basically function like classified print ads – generate lots of ad revenue from employers but result in few responses for job seekers. In other words, what works well for employers (accessing numerous resumes) does not necessary work well for job seekers (getting invited to job interviews).

More Than Just the Alphabet

Most examinations of Internet job sites, in either print or electronic form, use one of two approaches. The first approach primarily focuses on the process of using the Internet to find a job and is often designed for first-time users. Writers offering this approach include insights, advice, and tips on how to best use the Internet, with special reference to using search engines, posting resumes online, and sending email. They also include examples of major websites relevant to job seekers.

Using the Internet can be a great time waster – if you do not understand, nor stay focused on, what online activities are really important to your job search.

The second approach is more website-specific and results in producing a unique directory of employment websites. The primary focus here is to identify and annotate the best or top Internet employment sites. Writers using this approach usually provide an alphabetical listing of the largest and most popular websites – as measured by the number of visitors to the sites – which also may be cross-indexed by different classifications, such as occupation, industry, and job specialty. Individual sites are more or less annotated in terms of various user criteria – orientation, services, location, and costs. Since no one has evaluated such websites in terms of their effectiveness for either job seekers or employers, questions concerning outcomes are curiously absent. Indeed, users are left with the impression, as well as an unwarranted assumption, that since these sites are large, popular, and featured by the writer, they are probably the most effective employment websites. Welcome to potentially disappointing and frustrating employment websites!

Being Effective and Staying Focused

As in other volumes of the Click and Easy™ Series, we focus primarily on the interests of the individual rather than on the needs of organizations. Cutting through a lot of the first generation "revolutionary" true-believer Internet hype, we've organized this book around the notion that Internet information should be easily accessible, purposeful, and effective. Furthermore, the Internet should play a role in, or be a part of, your overall job search. It should never be equated with the job search, nor play the primary role in finding a job. If you mainly rely on the Internet to find a job, you will most likely be disappointed with the results.

> *If you mainly rely on the Internet to find a job, you will most likely be disappointed with the results. It's all about conducting a well focused and effective job search.*

We make no claims about the effectiveness of any websites featured in this book. Anyone who does make such claims is probably greatly exaggerating the truth. Rather, our goal is to make sure you use these sites to conduct your own effective job search, regardless of effectiveness claims of any particular site. As such, our central focus is on the *job search*, with employment websites being treated as *useful tools* for conducting a well organized job search.

We're especially concerned that you keep focused on what's really important in getting a job – following a step-by-step process that leads to desired outcomes. Above all, you should not waste valuable job search time engaged in Internet activities that have little or no payoff in terms of getting job interviews and offers, such as randomly clicking from one site to another or visiting numerous message boards to read about others' ineffective job searches or to receive amateur advice from self-appointed career experts. While such sites may look "cool" and appear "interesting," you may quickly discover there is much less available through these sites than what initially meets the eye. If you want to be effective, you must disengage from such random activities and become more focused and oriented to outcomes.

A Click and Stupid Approach

Like mass mailing hundreds of resumes and letters to employers, using the Internet in your job search can be a great time waster – if you do not understand, nor stay focused on, what online activities are really important to your job search. Devoting a great deal of time to conducting an Internet job search can quickly give you a false sense of making progress because you are putting so much Internet time in on your job search. As you will quickly discover in using the Internet in your job search, motion with your mouse does not equate momentum with employers. Indeed, the frequent lament of many job seekers is that they spend so much time on the Internet looking for a job, but nothing ever happens. Forget for a moment what you're really supposed to be doing – generating invitations to job interviews – and your online job search may well be lost in cyberspace!

> *Motion with your mouse does not equate momentum with employers.*

We understand the many promises and pitfalls of using the Internet in a job search. Not surprising, this electronic communication medium often gets confused with the message. Although the Internet promises to save time, generate information, and yield key contacts you might not acquire through other mediums, if not put in its proper perspective and used wisely, the Internet with its thousands of employment sites also can lead you down the wrong job search path with false hopes, dashed expectations, numerous distractions, and a great deal of wasted time. While we believe you must incorporate the Internet into your job search, we are not true believers in the efficacy of the Internet for finding a job. There are many different ways to find a job which do not involve the use of the Internet, especially through interpersonal networking involving the telephone and face-to-face meetings. Like a good resume, letter, or informational interview, the Internet can enhance your job search if you stay focused on what's really important. In the end, regardless of all your Internet job search activities, your next job may come from contacts unrelated to your Internet efforts. Be sure to use the Internet in your job search but do so with a healthy sense of skepticism.

A Focused Job Search Approach

Given our particular view of how the Internet should be integrated into an effective job search, we have chosen a **special directory approach** that is linked to a **process approach** for making better sense and use out of individual websites you will encounter. For us, incorporating the Internet into a job search is the old proverbial forest/tree dilemma: the job search is the forest and individual websites are particular species of trees that make up one important segment of the larger forest.

Our first assumption is that most users already know how to use the Internet. If not, they can quickly get started by using the resources identified in Chapter 2. Our second assumption is that most users do not know how to organize an effective job search. Failing to do first things first, like many users of Internet employment sites, most job seekers are often too quick to start their job search by writing a resume. Many of the large Internet employment sites, which primarily seek to increase the number of resumes in their databases as well as encourage more online traffic (advertising "eyeballs"), perpetuate a seriously flawed job search approach reminiscent of the traditional classified ad approach to finding a job. They encourage job seekers to post their resumes online before these individuals have a chance to do important preliminary job search work, such as assessment and research, for creating a powerful employer-centered resume. The result is often employment websites with lots of bells and whistles for people who do not know how to conduct an effective job search. The resumes that get entered into the databases or emailed to potential employers do not reflect their major strengths and accomplishments.

Our approach is different. We examine websites that are most useful to job seekers in conducting an effective job search based upon a clear understanding of the job search process. Therefore, we've organized this book around key steps and issues in the job search process:

- assessment
- research
- networking

- resumes and letters
- interviews
- salary negotiations

We also include several other categories of websites that are essential to conducting an effective job search:

- education and training
- relocation
- career assistance

- employers
- occupations
- job seekers

As you will quickly see, the major employment websites tend to be preoccupied with connecting job seekers to employers through resume databases and job listings – our fourth job search step. Other steps in the job search process, especially the critical first step, assessment, are usually neglected or relegated to a few tips or advice from experts.

Structuring Benefits Around Eyeballs

As you incorporate the Internet in your job search, keep in mind how most major websites are structured and for whose benefit. Most sites are advertising operations that sell their services to employers and recruiters by "per thousand visitor rates" rather than by actual outcomes for end-users. Few, if any, websites are ideally designed to help the individual job seeker find his or her best job. In other words, they are not structured around the key elements in a successful job search. If they were, these sites would be designed very differently and with the best interests of the job seeker in mind. Instead, most employment websites are commercial operations that are designed around the interests of those who pay for these operations – employers. And employers have one basic interest in using such sites – hire the best quality candidates. Through a variety of user fees and advertising rates, employers finance these sites and thus largely determine the structure and content of the sites. Access to the typical employment website, for example, is free to job seekers who are encouraged to enter their resume into the site's database, browse job listings, and use other services provided by the site. Since you usually get what you pay for, the free services of these sites may not be very helpful. In other words, job seekers become the "eyeballs" for determining the number of "hits" the site receives. These "hits," in turn, determine how much the site will charge employers for advertising on the site.

> *Few websites are ideally designed to help the individual job seeker find his or her best job. Most sites are designed for those who financially support the sites – employers.*

For example, a typical employment site will charge employers $200 to list a job vacancy and another $300 to search the site's resume database for a month. Not surprising, employment sites are primarily structured to maximize advertising and user revenue – they are designed to please employers who are trying to recruit needed talent at about one-third the cost of traditional print classified advertising. The services provided to job seekers – refreshed job listings, employment tips, message boards, company profiles, success stories – are largely designed to motivate them to frequently return to the site and thus increase the number of "hits" the site receives in order to justify the advertising rates and user fees charged to employers.

Given the basic economics of most major websites, few are structured with the job seeker's best interests in mind. They are designed for those who pay the bills – employers in search of talent to staff their operations. Consequently, it is up to you to determine how you will best conduct an effective job search by using these relatively biased employment websites.

Coming Up

The following chapters are organized around the interests of individual job seekers – how to best conduct an effective job search that goes beyond the employer-centered revenue models of most major websites.

While we include many of the most popular employment websites, which primarily operate huge resume databases (Chapter 5), we also feature many other websites that fit into our model of an effective job search. Therefore, you'll find separate chapters on websites not normally covered in other Internet job books: career assessment, education and training, relocation, and career counseling.

Whatever you do, make sure you incorporate the Internet in your job search. But do so with a healthy sense of skepticism and with the knowledge that the Internet can be a valuable tool if used within the context of an effective job search. Don't just click around an alphabetical listing of the top employment websites. Instead, do first things first. Organize an effective job search that mines the Internet for key employment information. In other words, your job search should direct your Internet activities rather than the Internet directing your job search. If you do this, you will be well on your way to finding a job you do well and enjoy doing – one that is the perfect fit for pursuing a rewarding career. Better still, you'll fully use the power of the Internet to your advantage.

> *Always remember that your job search should direct your Internet activities – not vice versa!*

Google™

Search 1,387,529,000 web pages

[ ]	• Advanced Search
	• Preferences

[Google Search] [I'm Feeling Lucky]

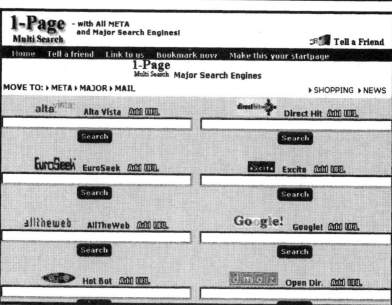

1-Page - with All META
Multi Search and Major Search Engines!

🔍 **Tell a Friend**

Home   Tell a friend   Link to us   Bookmark now   Make this your startpage

1-Page
Multi Search **Major Search Engines**

MOVE TO: ▸ META ▸ MAJOR ▸ MAIL   ▸ SHOPPING ▸ NEWS

alta vista   **Alta Vista** Add URL   directhit   **Direct Hit** Add URL

[Search]   [Search]

EuroSeek   **EuroSeek** Add URL   excite   **Excite** Add URL

[Search]   [Search]

alltheweb   **AllTheWeb** Add URL   Google!   **Google!** Add URL

[Search]   [Search]

HotBot   **Hot Bot** Add URL   dmoz   **Open Dir.** Add URL

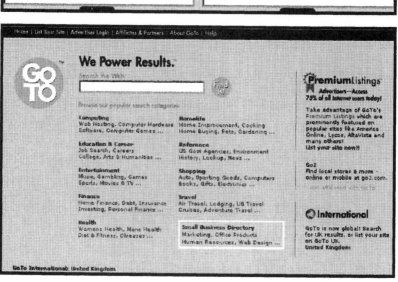

Home | List Your Site | Advertiser Login | Affiliates & Partners | About GoTo | Help

GOTO

We Power Results.

Search the Web
[ ] Find It

Browse our popular search categories.

Computing
Web Hosting, Computer Hardware
Software, Computer Games ...

Homelife
Home Improvement, Cooking
Home Buying, Pets, Gardening ...

Education & Career
Job Search, Careers
College, Arts & Humanities ...

Reference
US Govt Agencies, Environment
History, Lookup, News ...

Entertainment
Music, Gambling, Games
Sports, Movies & TV ...

Shopping
Auto, Sporting Goods, Computers
Books, Gifts, Electronics ...

Finance
Home Finance, Debt, Insurance
Investing, Personal Finance ...

Travel
Air Travel, Lodging, US Travel
Cruises, Adventure Travel ...

Health
Womens Health, Mens Health
Diet & Fitness, Diseases ...

Small Business Directory
Marketing, Office Products
Human Resources, Web Design ...

PremiumListings
Advertisers—Access
75% of all Internet users today!

Take advantage of GoTo's
Premium Listings which are
prominently featured on
popular sites like America
Online, Lycos, AltaVista and
many others!
List your site now!!

Go2
Find local stores & more
online or mobile at go2.com.

⚪ **International**

GoTo is now global! Search
for UK results, or list your site
on GoTo UK.
United Kingdom

GoTo International: United Kingdom

2

Getting Started and Staying Focused

CONDUCTING AN INTERNET JOB SEARCH IS RELA-
tively easy and rewarding as long as you have the proper
communication equipment, a willingness to learn, some
basic organizational skills, an ability to stay focused, and
time to explore the best of what the Internet has to offer job seekers.
In the end, *time and focus* may be your greatest challenges, especially if
you become addicted to the stimulating randomness of the Internet –
a common affliction of many Internet users who spend lots of time
going nowhere.

Use Your Time Wisely

The Internet is an extremely seductive medium that can easily eat up
hours of your time on activities that may have few if any discernable
outcomes. Use your time, both online and offline, wisely since time is
usually the scarcest resource in conducting an effective job search. In
fact, we normally recommend that you spend no more than 30 percent
of your job search time on the Internet. The other 70 percent should
be focused on offline job search activities, such as testing, conducting

research, compiling a portfolio, writing letters, and networking by telephone and in person. If, for example, you devote 30 hours a week to your job search, no more than 10 of those hours should be on the Internet; the other 20 hours should be on the telephone or literally in the streets meeting with important contacts and potential employers. If you find yourself spending more than 50 percent of your job search time on the Internet, you are probably wasting valuable time that could be better spent on other more high-impact job search activities. In fact, you may be avoiding more challenging offline job search activities by hiding behind your computer screen! Whatever you do, don't use the Internet to rationalize your lack of focus on what is really important to getting a job – making verbal contacts and meeting people face-to-face.

> *We recommend spending no more than 30 percent of your job search time on the Internet.*

Basic Skills and Guidance

Online job seekers quickly discover they basically need to do two things online – effectively use search engines and handle email. They also need to apply some *wisdom* to this process – know the promises and pitfalls of using the Internet in their job search. For the job search, the Internet is largely a search, retrieve, send, receive, and respond communication medium. Indeed, if there are only two things you learn about the Internet, make sure they focus on using search engines and email.

Regardless of your level of technical expertise or computer experience, the Internet is very easy to learn, with most people requiring only a few minutes of basic orientation. Really savvy Internet users invest a great deal of time in learning relatively sophisticated organizational and communication techniques, from using search engines to organizing files and sending email.

If you are an Internet novice, or need to brush up on using the Internet, you may want to pick up a basic book, written in plain English, on how to use the Internet. You don't need anything complex, cute, or expensive. Get a book that goes over Internet basics, such as setting your home page, bookmarking sites, saving and copying web pages, downloading files, using search engines, customizing web browsers, and using the Usenet, mailing lists, and email. Three good books that demystify the web with great brevity and clarity include:

> *Sams Teach Yourself the Internet in 24 Hours*, Ned Snell (New York: Macmillan USA Publishing, 2001)

> *Teach Yourself the Internet*, David Crowder and Rhonda Crowder (Foster City, CA: IDG Books, 1999)

> *The Rough Guide to the Internet*, Angus J. Kennedy (New York: The Rough Guides, 2000)

All three books complement each other. The first two are large texts. The third, by Kennedy, is designed as a small pocket-sized reference guide which is easy to travel with. In fact, one of the best kept Internet secrets is this: you can access the complete book online and use it free of charge, including hotlinks to hundreds of recommended sites, by going to this section of the publisher's website:

> *Job seekers need to know how to use two things on the Web – search engines and email.*

roughguides.com/internet/directory/index.html#tools

A Library and an Orchestra

There are two organizational/disorganizational dimensions to the Internet worth noting as you prepare to use the Internet: specific locations (URLs) and communities of interests (Usenet newsgroups, mailing lists, bulletin boards/forums). People go to the Internet to both find things (seek out specific locations by URL) and participate in discussions (join communities).

Imagine a library where millions of books are just thrown helter-skelter in one huge room. Or imagine an orchestra of amateur players without a director – where most participants are of questionable talent and are at times both in the orchestra and in the audience – trying to play a coherent tune or compose a score. In this chapter we'll examine the case of the library in need of classification, labeling, and location codes. In Chapter 3 we'll look at the case of the orchestra of amateurs without a director (virtual communities).

In the case of the library, nothing is labeled nor classified – even the covers are missing! While you may wander through the mess and serendipitously find an interesting resource, chances are you will be lost, confused, and frustrated about where to start and what you can expect to find along the way. You may just give up and decide this type of library is not for you. Without some form of organization and classification these millions of resources may be meaningless to you.

> *The Internet is like an orchestra of amateur players without a director who are trying to play a coherent tune or compose a score without knowing what their fellow players are up to.*

The Internet is like a huge library where few things have been classified and put on the shelves. In addition, it lacks objective gatekeepers who would normally assess the quality of information and recommend the inclusion or exclusion of resources. It's rich with information but chaotic in terms of organization and quality. While this book classifies employment sites and identifies specific resources by name and location (URL), the Internet also includes a variety of organizational elements – variously called search engines, search agents, and directories – that enable users to access resources in a relatively coherent manner. Not one, but hundreds of search engines, agents, and directories are available for exploring the Internet. Indeed, gogettem.com alone identifies over 2,600 search engines and directories! Creating a high level of redundancy, this multiplicity of search elements is extremely functional for anyone interested in accessing useful information on the Internet. The redundancy is often created by the fact that many search engines use the same databases (several use the Inktomi database system) and are powered by affiliate programs or parent companies which operate other search engines. Not surprisingly, a search conducted on one search engine may produce nearly identical results as the same search conducted using an ostensibly different search engine.

While most of the sites identified in this discussion are often subsumed under the general category of "Search Engines," we've broken them into three categories of search elements:

- Search engines
- Search agents
- Directories

These are important distinctions because they can lead to different approaches to using the Internet and thus yield different qualities of information for enhancing your job search. In the end, your searches are only as good as the quality of your questions. The sooner you improve the quality of your questions, the sooner you will generate quality information on the Internet and more efficiently use your Internet job search time.

Once you begin using these various search elements, you'll start noticing some major differences in how you query various sites and how databases are organized and information presented. **Search engines**, for example, use software with "spiders" to literally crawl the Internet for keywords, phrases, addresses, and page titles that you specify should be part of your search. On the other hand, **search agents** appear to be search engines but with one major difference – they explore various search engines simultaneously so that you get the benefit of multiple searches. **Directories** consist of compilations of websites, usually done by individuals, which are classified under a variety of subject headings. More targeted and judgmental than search engines and agents, directories typically identify the most popular sites relevant to a particular subject.

When you use a search engine or search agent, you are basically asking a question, in the form of keywords and phases, for which you desire an answer. When you use a directory, you are presented with a list of sites, by subject category, with little relevance to any particular questions; directories merely expose you to lots of popular sites which may, in turn, raise questions in your mind. If you have many questions for which you seek answers, by all means perfect your keywords and phrases and use search engines and search agents. But if you're not sure what questions to ask, you may want to start with directories that expose you to many different related sites. After examining several sites in the directory, you should have a better idea of the types of questions you would like to ask of the search engines and search agents.

Please note that many search engines also incorporate elements of search agents and directories, and vice versa. In these cases, you should be aware that the search element functions very differently from the directory element.

Search Engines

An essential starting point for Internet users are the various search engines that enable them to literally search millions of Web pages for information relevant to their particular interests and queries. Entering keywords and phrases into a search engine's query form, the search engine quickly returns a list of "hits" based upon your defining criteria. If, for example, you're interested in finding a computer job in Seattle, you might enter "computer jobs in Seattle" in your favorite search engine in the hopes that you will get lots of good "hits" that will help you determine the best places to take that big leap.

However, not all search engines are equal. Some have larger data-bases than others. Some use more sophisticated software than others. Some are much faster than others. And some are simply more intelligent and user-friendly than others. You may find, for example, that one search engine will only yield two references to computer jobs in Seattle whereas another search engine will give you over 20 such references. Since the quality and depth of various search engines differ, you are well advised to use more than one search engine when looking for resources on the Internet. Indeed, we regularly switch back and forth with five of our favorite search engines with often dramatically different results. Our current favorite is no-nonsense Google which has proved very reliable and yields some of the best sites: google.com. A few of our other favorite search engines include iWon, GoTo, Northern Light, and HotBot:

- iWon   iwon.com
- GoTo   goto.com

- Northern Light   northernlight.com
- HotBot   hotbot.com

In our example of "computer jobs in Seattle," our five favorite search engines recently yielded this number of "hits":

google.com	205,000
iwon.com	106,907
goto.com	240
northernlight.com	273,733
hotbot.com	139,700

You'll discover numerous other search engines for exploring the Internet. Going beyond our favorite five, these search engines also should prove useful for conducting searches:

- AltaVista   altavista.com
- AOL Anywhere   search.aol.com
- C4.com   c4.com
- CEO Express   ceoexpress.com
- Debriefing   debriefing.com
- Excite   excite.com
- FAST Search   alltheweb.com
- Go   go.com
- Looksmart   looksmart.com
- Lycos   lycos.com
- Microsoft Network   msn.com
- Netscape   netscape.com
- Searchbeat   searchbeat.com
- Webcrawler   webcrawler.com
- Yahoo   yahoo.com

However, after sampling numerous alternatives, you may conclude our top five, and especially Google and iWon, are the "best of the best" search engines.

One of the best websites for simultanously accessing over 30 search engines is **1-Page Multi Search**: bjorgul.com. We highly recommend bookmarking this site and using it as your main search site.

Search Agents

Also known as searchbots, search agents basically search a few key search engines and directories simultaneously in response to search queries. These search agents are not equal since each conducts simultaneous searches using a different set of search engines and directories. For example, MetaGopher simultaneously searches eight major search engines: Yahoo, Google, Spinks, Goto, HotBot, WebCrawler, Go Network, and AltaVista. MetaCrawler simultaneously searches Yahoo, InfoSeek, Lycos, Excite, and AltaVista. One of the stand-out sites, which requires downloading special software, is Copernic. Some of the most popular and useful search agents include:

- Ask Jeeves   ask.com
- Copernic   copernic.com
- DogPile   dogpile.com
- Go2Net   go2net.com
- MetaCrawler   metacrawler.com
- MetaGopher   metagopher.com
- ProFusion   profusion.com

Directories

Several sites that primarily function as search engines also include a directory section. This section includes a unique set of sites under specific subject headings, such as autos, cities, games, money, parenting, real estate, shopping, and travel. The real star directory here is About.com which has a reputation for compiling one of the most comprehensive listings of sites by subject matter:

- About.com   about.com
- Ask Jeeves   ask.com
- Britannica   britannica.com
- DogPile   dogpile.com
- Excite   excite.com
- Go   go.com
- iWon   iwon.com

- Looksmart   looksmart.com
- Lycos   lycos.com
- Microsoft Network   msn.com
- Netscape   netscape.com
- Open Directory   dmoz.org
- WebTop   webtop.com
- Yahoo   yahoo.com

Most Popular Search Engines

But there are a lot more search engines, agents, and directories than the ones we've discussed above. In March 2001, for example, the following search engines were identified by Top9.com (top9.com/top 99s/top99_search_engines.html) as the most frequently used. Representing a combination of search engines, agents, and directories, many of these sites also are the most popular sites on the web with millions of visitors each week to searching for information and solve problems:

List Rank	Overall Web Rank	Search Engine	Unique Visitors (x000)
1	1	yahoo.com	65,415
2	3	msn.com	46,739
3	9	lycos.com	22,863
4	12	netscape.com	18,816
5	14	nbci.com (closes 9/01)	17,982
6	17	excite.com	17,452
7	18	about.com	16,291
8	19	iwon.com	15,350
9	21	altavista.com	14,128
10	22	google.com	13,747
11	29	go.com	12,097
12	34	goto.com	11,247
13	36	looksmart.com	11,115
14	84	go2net.com	6,313
15	100	directhit.com	5,728
16	128	gohip.com	4,996
17	129	dogpile.com	4,973
18	174	best20sites.com	3,753
19	190	search.com	3,753

20	199	clickheretofind.com	3,624
21	248	webcrawler.com	2,734
22	267	hotbot.com	2,584
23	275	bay9.com	2,841
24	288	bestoftheweb.com	2,744
25	329	mamma.com	2,448
26	373	found404.com	2,260
27	378	top50.to	2,241
28	370	metacrawler.com	1,984
29	465	centerfind.com	1,896
30	501	goclick.com	1,771
31	504	dotzup.com	1,762
32	505	megago.com	1,756
33	555	wordplanet.com	1,578
34	605	northernlight.com	1,462
35	662	pageseeker.com	1,351
36	711	blab.com	1,271
37	716	megaspider.com	1,266
38	727	4anything.com	1,250
39	735	popularcategories.com	1,232
40	765	searchcactus.com	1,189
41	861	bomis.com	1,087
42	875	www.com	1,071
43	904	37.com	929
44	1,053	homepageware.com	928
45	1,059	ignifuge.com	924
46	1,386	webhideout.com	748
47	1,458	yep.com	715
48	1,527	treasuresurfing.com	683
49	1,674	sureseeker.com	630
50	1,740	bol.com.br	607
51	1,862	findaroo.com	571
52	1,941	generalsearch.com	549
53	1,955	ah-ha.com	545
54	1,991	thesearchster.com	536
55	2,045	alltheweb.com	523
56	2,084	gotoworld.com	514
57	2,256	100searches.com	473
58	2,291	searchalot.com	467
59	2,382	findwhat.com	450
60	2,407	ezcybersearch.com	447
61	2,424	resoftlinks.com	443
62	2,496	companiesonline.com	432

63	2,532	suite101.com	428
64	2,662	jumpforce.com	407
65	2,663	turbofind.com	407
66	2,785	411web.com	387
67	2,908	ditto.com	372
68	2,971	iqseek.com	365
69	3,086	searchmagnifier.com	351
70	3,191	coolhits.com	338
71	3,389	myway.com	317
72	3,450	startingpage.com	311
73	3,532	looktown.com	303
74	3,574	search123.com	300
75	3,592	msn.co.uk	298
76	3,603	powersearches.com	298
77	3,735	searchforstuff.com	287
78	3,761	yahoo.ca	286
79	3,952	galaxy.com	272
80	3,991	yahoo.com.au	270
81	4,064	seekon.com	266
82	4,128	spray.fr	262
83	4,300	sprinks.com	252
84	4,312	techtarget.com	251
85	4,588	educationplanet.com	235
86	4,594	findology.com	235
87	4,627	7search.com	234
88	4,664	insider.com	232
89	5,032	ADULT	216
90	5,071	launchbase.net	215
91	5,105	100hot.com	213
92	5,138	oingo.com	212
93	5,202	boomerank.com	209
94	5,305	msnusers.com	205
95	5,322	efamily.com	204
96	5,330	searchbound.com	204
97	5,418	search.vu	200
98	5,587	niftyguide.com	194
99	5,656	ixquick.com	192

In addition to the key search engines, agents, and directories we identified in previous sections, you may want to explore the job or employment capabilities of the many additional search engines identified in this list of 99 top search engines.

For information on even more search engines, as well as tips on how to best use them, we recommend visiting Search Engine Watch:

searchenginewatch.com

This site also includes a comprehensive listing of search engines for identifying search engines, such as directoryguide.com, searchiq.com, allsearchengines.com, and gogettem.com.

Employment Site Comparisons and Ratings

While most web directories identify the most popular sites by category, other sites actually rank sites by popularity. If you're interested in the most popular job and employment sites, be sure to periodically visit these three sites, which provide monthly rankings of various employment-related websites:

Top9   Ratings
top9.com/careers_education/general_employment.html

If you're interested in identifying the most popular career websites based on the number of visitors, as well as in seeing how each site ranks in comparison to all websites, be sure to bookmark Top9. It ranks the top nine websites for 12 different career and education categories:

- Universities
- General Employment
- Education Resources
- Universities – International
- Home-Based Employment
- University Education Resources
- K-12 Education
- Depts/Schools of Education
- Career Info and Services
- Specialized Employment

- Financial Aid
- Community and Technical Colleges

In addition, it identifies nine up-and-coming hot websites as well as related sites for each category. Under "General Employment," for example, in March 2001 it identified these sites as being the top nine:

General Employment Sites	Unique Monthly Visitors
Monster.com	6,951,000
Jobsonline.com	6,486,000
Hotjobs.com	4,280,000
Careerbuilder.com	1,933,000
Headhunter.net	1,850,000
Jobs.com	842,000
Flipdog.com	837,000
Joboptions.com	829,000
Nationjob.com	342,000

Up-and-coming general employment sites to keep an eye on included:

Employmentwizard.com
Ajb.org
Hire.com
Freecommunity.com
Jobsleuth.com
Jobcontrolcenter.com
Careerweb.com
Employment 911.com
CollegeRecruiter.com

Under "Specialized Employment," the following websites ranked in the top nine in March 2001:

Dice.com
Net-temps.com
Computerjobs.com
Jobdirect.com
Brassring.com
Gmac.com
Internshipprograms.com
Officeteam.com
Summerjobs.com

These nine sites are ranked at the top for "Career Information and Services":

Salary.com
Brainbench.com
Careercast.com
Careermag.com
Wetfeet.com
Brainbuzz.com
Vault.com
Careerexplorer.net
Isearch.com

Ranks   **Ratings**
ranks.com/home/lifestyle/top_job_search_sites

This site offers three categories of employment-relevant sites – job search, career resources, and freelance and consulting. Within each category it alphabetically lists nine to 26 sites. While it includes a few surprises, in general it confirms what most Internet job specialists recognize as the top sites. For example, it recently included these sites under the three separate categories:

Job search: BrassRing.com
                             CareerBuilder.com

Careermag.com
FlipDog.com
Headhunter.net
HotJobs.com
Monster.com
WantedJobs.com

Career resources:

Brainbench.com
CareerJournal.com
Quintcareers.com
Salary.com
Vault.com
WetFeet.com

Freelance and consulting:

Bullhorn.com
Ework.com
Guru.com
Talentmarket.monster.com
Smarterwork.com
Sologig.com

100Hot   Ratings
100hot.com/list.gsp?category=business&keywords=jobs

This site includes a mixture of popular job-related websites along with affiliate websites. In July 2001, it included 40 "hot" job sites including these top 10:

1. Home.earthlink.net
2. Gaapjobs.com
3. Careerbuilder.com
4. Adtagger.com
5. CareerMag.com
6. Healthjobsusa.com
7. Promoteyourresume.com
8. Resumebroadcaster.com

9. Adulthelpwanted.com
10. Media8.de

Saving Time and Effort

Getting started with job finding on the Internet can be a very laborious and disorienting process if you primarily rely on search engines, search agents, and directories for identifying useful job sites. While such organizational helpers are unquestionably useful, they also can be very time consuming and produce disappointing results because of the hit-and-miss nature of such sites. At best these devices will identify the most popular sites in terms of the number of "hits" they receive on a monthly basis. Such popularity may reflect more on the size of a site's advertising budget, publicity efforts, and marketing prowess – by seeding their site with keywords and META tags – than on the actual quality and usefulness of the site's content.

> *Many exceptional quality sites, especially boutique or niche sites, may appear low on the standard search engines.*

For example, while Yahoo is the most popular search engine, we find Google, which ranks tenth in search engines, to be much more useful.

In the pages that follow, we identify specific employment sites that we have found especially useful for conducting an effective job search. Many of these sites, especially boutique or niche sites, are of exceptional quality. Some may seldom appear, or they appear very low, on the standard search engines. You may want to sample these sites before venturing into the world of search engines, search agents, and directories. Indeed, you can save a great deal of time and effort by going directly to several of the gateway employment sites we identify in the next chapter. Once you locate quality sites, be sure to bookmark them and return to them often. In so doing, you may discover your time is better spent going directly to the special employment sites identified in subsequent chapters than in using the search engines, search agents, and directories identified in this chapter. Whatever your choices, you will at least be heading in the right direction for using the Internet to plan your job search.

3

Virtual Job and Career Communities

T
HE INTERNET IS MUCH MORE THAN A COLLECTION
of websites from which to access employment information
and services. It's first of all a *community of individuals and
organizations* that come together because of common interests,
goals, and expected benefits. You use the search engines in Chapter 2,
for example, because you are looking for something very specific, such
as resume databases, specific companies, salary information, and career
advice, or because you wish to explore new opportunities, from career
fields to employers and job listings. In so doing, you may encounter
individuals and organizations that can assist you. Hopefully you will
make many new friends and gain useful advice along the way.

Information Communities

While most of this book focuses on the organizational players on the
Internet – companies that have websites, staffs, commercial operations,
and perhaps venture capital subsidizing their efforts – the Internet also
is made up of thousands of individuals who have formed specialized

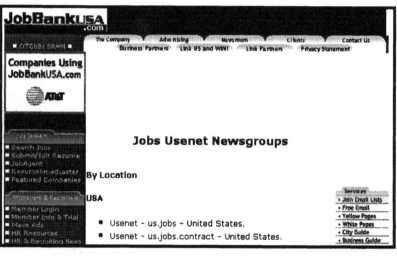

JobBankUSA.com

■ OTOBBi SRHN ■

The Company | Advertising | Newsroom | Clients | Contact Us
Business Partners | Link US and WIN! | Link Partners | Privacy Statement

Companies Using JobBankUSA.com

AT&T

Job Seeker
■ Search Jobs
■ Submit/Edit Resume
■ JobAgent
■ Resume Broadcaster
■ Featured Companies

Employers & Recruiters
■ Member Login
■ Member Info & Trial
■ Place Ads
■ HR Resources
■ HR & Recruiting News

Jobs Usenet Newsgroups

By Location

USA

- Usenet - us.jobs - United States.
- Usenet - us.jobs.contract - United States.

Services
• Join Email Lists
• Free Email
• Yellow Pages
• White Pages
• City Guide
• Business Guide

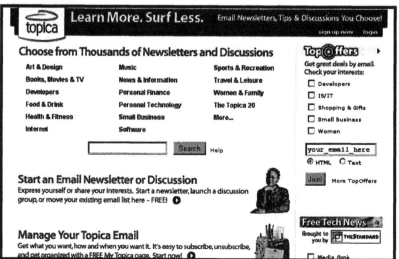

topica

Learn More. Surf Less.

Email Newsletters, Tips & Discussions You Choose!

sign up now | login

Choose from Thousands of Newsletters and Discussions

Art & Design	Music	Sports & Recreation
Books, Movies & TV	News & Information	Travel & Leisure
Developers	Personal Finance	Women & Family
Food & Drink	Personal Technology	The Topica 20
Health & Fitness	Small Business	More...
Internet	Software	

[_____] [Search] Help

Top Offers
Get great deals by email.
Check your interests:
☐ Developers
☐ IS/IT
☐ Shopping & Gifts
☐ Small Business
☐ Women

[your email here]
⊙ HTML ○ Text

[Join!] More TopOffers

Start an Email Newsletter or Discussion
Express yourself or share your interests. Start a newsletter, launch a discussion
group, or move your existing email list here - FREE! ▸

Manage Your Topica Email
Get what you want, how and when you want it. It's easy to subscribe, unsubscribe,
and get organized with a FREE My Topica page. Start now! ▸

Free Tech News
Brought to
you by THE STANDARD
☐ Media Grok

communities that are focused on information rather than commerce. Most such communities are very loosely structured for exchanging information and advice. They are virtual networks designed for information, advice, and referrals. Some are linked to commercial websites, whereas others are independent nonprofit community websites or they reside elsewhere (Usenet) on the Internet. Individuals can easily join and leave such groups. Held together virtually by the Usenet and email, these communities are a mixed bag for job seekers. Some are very useful while many others are dreadful wastes of time. Some stay together for many months whereas others may only last a few weeks, depending on the quality of their participants and the benefits they dispense to their "members." Few such communities will last more than a couple of years.

These virtual communities are a mixed bag for job seekers. Some are very useful while others are dreadful wastes of time.

You should be aware of your community options before you explore specific employment sites on the Internet. You will normally find three types of communities in three different places on the Internet:

- Usenet newsgroups
- Mailing lists
- Message boards of websites

While each of these communities has limitations, all potentially offer some very important employment information and advice. If you participate in these communities, you'll most likely come away with some very timely information – especially job search street smarts – that cannot be found from other sources on the Internet.

Usenet Newsgroups

If you are used to communicating with others by email, you know the importance and timeliness of such communication. Indeed, many people now have a hard time living without their email. At the same time, many people have discovered the communication advantages of newsgroups. Some become addicted to them – representing a unique combination of voyeurism and advice.

Newsgroups are one of the most interactive aspects of the Internet. Also known as Usenet, this is the virtual community aspect of the Internet – the largest electronic public discussion forum in the world. In fact, nearly 40,000 newsgroups currently function on the Internet. These are loose communities of shared interests where members or participants ask questions, share experiences, post alerts, review subjects, introduce new activities, spread gossip, and sometimes create mischief. Depending on the nature of the subject and the particular mix of participants, many of these groups are fun, educational, and exciting to join; others lack energy and are often boring, stressful, and useless. Newsgroups tend to live and die based upon the quality of the participants, ongoing communication dynamics, and benefits offered to the group. While not all the so-called "news" of these groups is fit to print, some of it is useful. For job seekers, newsgroups can be very educational and timely, especially as networking forums for acquiring useful information, advice, and referrals.

> *Usenet newsgroups function as the largest electronic public discussion forum in the world – nearly 40,000 newsgroups currently operate on the Internet.*

Similar to the many discussion and chat groups found on the major employment sites, newsgroups function like public bulletin boards. Someone posts a message which can be read by everyone who accesses the newsgroup. Viewers, in turn, post replies within the community for all to read or privately send an email to the individual who originally posted the message.

The Usenet is one section of the Internet, separate from the World Wide Web, which has its own networks, servers, and routers for handling newsgroups. In order to participate in newsgroups, you must have special software, called a newsreader, installed on your browser. Netscape Navigator and Microsoft Internet Explorer browsers come with this software pre-installed.

Newsgroups are an especially rich resource for individuals who wish to join communities of like-minded people with similar interests.

Discover what they are talking about, including many of their major career concerns.

For information on how to best use newsgroups, as well as tips on which newsgroups might best meet your needs, visit these useful sites:

- **Cyberfiber** — www.cyberfiber.com
- **JobBankUSA** — jobbankusa.com/usejobs.html
- **Google (DejaNews)** — groups.google.com (dejanews.com)
- **Topica** — topica.com
- **Usenet Info Center** — metalab.unc.edu/usenet-i/home.html
- **Questions** — xs4all.nl/~wijnands/nnq/grouplists.html

A good source for identifying newsgroups relevant to conducting a job search in the United States, Canada, and a few other countries and regions (Australia, Bermuda, Denmark, Europe, Ireland, Israel, Ukraine, United Kingdom, and South Africa) is CareerInternetworking:

careerkey.com/newsgroups.htm

You'll find several newsgroups on the Internet. However, you'll need a specialized search engine to find newsgroups related to your particular career interests. The largest and most popular such search engine is Deja News (dejanews.com) which recently became part of Google.com (groups.google.com).

Google	Newsgroups
groups.google.com	

This is the granddaddy directory of newsgroups (DejaNews). It includes useful search engines for finding discussion groups by subject and name. For example, if you search for "Employment" under "Miscellaneous," you'll find the following discussion forums:

misc.business
misc.entrepreneurs
misc.job
misc.jobs

Cyberfiber	Newsgroups
www.cyberfiber.com	

This site includes a comprehensive listing of newsgroups that deal with all types of employment questions. Most are job listings or resume postings. Not all links remain active.

JobBankUSA	Newsgroups
jobbankusa.com/usejobs.html	

The "Jobs Usenet Newsgroups" section of this mega employment site includes one of the most comprehensive listings of newsgroups in North America and abroad. It also includes newsgroups by career field and for universities. Most of the groups consist of job listings and resume postings.

Topica	Newsgroups
topica.com	

This popular site is a major center for nearly 100,000 newsletters, mailing lists, and discussion groups. You can easily start your own newsletter or discussion group by following the easy online instructions. Like Google, Topica's search engine allows you to type in your interests and then it lists all relevant mailing lists.

Mailing Lists

Mailing lists are another useful way to access travel information on the Internet. Unlike spontaneous newsgroups that require you to take initiative in posting your own messages and/or checking on other publicly posted messages, mailing lists are more structured and are often moderated by the individual who initially created the list. While most are open to the public, many also are private – only certain individuals who meet membership criteria can join. At the same time, mailing lists have the potential of automatically driving tons of email to your address. Indeed, with mailing lists you become a "member" or "subscriber" to the list by giving the group your email address. When messages are posted to the group, you automatically receive copies of the messages. Subscribe to a few active mailing lists and you may see a dramatic increase in your daily email volume. You'll no longer feel lonely with only receiving two or three messages a day – you could easily end up with 50 messages a day. After a while, you may think your membership is an exercise in self-directed spam!

The purpose of most mailing lists is to disseminate information and/or encourage the exchange of ideas amongst members who have a common interest in the same subject. Some lists are excellent forums for acquiring useful news and information, whereas others wander off on the deep end as they generate lots of useless email from individuals who need to get a life. For example, if your passion is being a travel guidebook writer or web designer, you should consider joining the relevant newsgroups found on Topica:

- Travel guidebook writers   topica.com/list/tgw
- Web designers   topica.com/lists/web-design

For a complete listing of current mailing lists and newsletters available through Topica, check out this URL:

topica.com/dir/cid=561

The long-term viability of mailing lists depends on the quality of the information. Members tend to come and go ("subscribe" and "unsubscribe") by completing online subscription forms that officially put their email into the mailing list. Many mailing lists become defunct because of the lack of time and interest on the part of the creator.

If you are interested in participating in mailing lists, a good starting point is the following site which serves as a useful directory to more than 7,500 mailing lists:

Publicly Accessible Mailing Lists   paml.net

You can search the directory by keyword or go directly to an alphabetical index of mailing lists by names and subjects.

If you are interested in creating your own mailing list – which would be a great way to focus attention on a particular career – check out these four sites:

- **Coollist**   coollist.com
- **Google**   groups.google.com
- **Topica**   topica.com
- **Yahoo! Groups**   groups.yahoo.com

Using these sites, you can easily organize a free mailing list. For example, if you are graphic designer, you might want to create a mailing list that focuses on career advice for graphic designers. Your list might attract many other graphic designers who have an interest in networking for information, advice, and referrals.

Because mailing lists have the potential of creating such high volumes of email, you may want to consider unsubscribing if you travel for a lengthy period of time. If not, you may be overwhelmed trying to sort through your email when you return from your trip. And you probably don't want to access such email while you are traveling since it can be very time consuming.

Message Boards of Websites

Message boards are similar to newsgroups but with one major exception – they are found on websites. Numerous employment websites include a community section which is variously called "community," "forum," "message board," "discussion group," or "chat group." Most are free-flowing forums (anyone asks and answers questions) whereas others may be periodically hosted by career experts. These sections enable visitors to ask questions in anticipation of receiving responses from other site users or hosts. Most such message boards are relatively static – you must revisit the message board to look for replies. However, a few sites provide automatic email responses from message boards. In other words, if you leave a message, all responses will autonomically appear on the message board as well as be routed to your email.

Some of the best, and most active, message boards for job seekers are found on Monster:

<u>community.monster.com/boards</u>

We prefer the message boards of this website to the more general newsgroups and mailing lists because of Monster's large number of messages received for a variety of career interest fields.

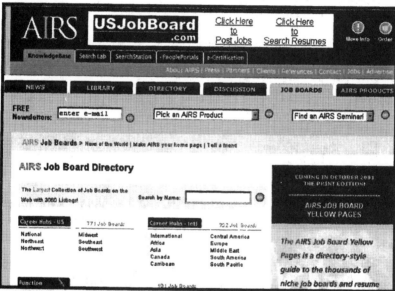

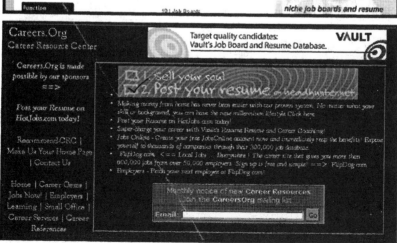

4

Gateway Employment Sites

S EARCH ENGINES, SEARCH AGENTS, NEWSGROUPS, and mailing lists have their limitations when it comes to identifying key websites with useful employment information and services. Fortunately, several websites function as gateways for locating thousands of employment-related websites. They include specific websites for a variety of career fields as well as websites relevant to particular job or career interests and processes: careers, employee screening, executive search, freelance specialist, internships, job search, recruiters, resumes, and staffing services. The sites identified in this chapter outline the rich variety of websites available for job seekers. These sites literally function as gateways to the world of online jobs and employment.

Gateways As Website Directories

Many of the search engines identified in Chapter 2 include directory sections which list hundreds of thousands of websites by interest category. "Jobs," "Employment," and "Careers" are either separate categories or subsumed under "Business" or "Work and Money." Some of the same sites also include affiliate career centers and job boards for posting resumes and searching for job vacancies. The directory sections of the following websites are well worth visiting:

➤ **Yahoo**
  dir.yahoo.com/Business_and_Economy/Employment_and_Work

➤ **About**
  home.about.com/careers/index.htm?PM=59_0222_T

➤ **AltaVista**
  altavista.com/sites/dir/search?pg=dir&tp=Work_.26_Money/Jobs&crid=317865

➤ **AOL Anywhere**
  search.aol.com/cat.adp?from=SEARCHHOME&id=71

➤ **Dmoz**
  dmoz.org/Business/Employment

➤ **C4.com**
  c4.com/opendir.html?get=/Business/Employment

➤ **GoTo**
  goto.com/d/searc/?Keywords=Job+Search&did=207&_requestid=4072623

➤ **Hotbot**
  dir.hotbot.lycos.com/Business/Employment

➤ **Excite**
  excite.com/careers

➤ **Webcrawler.com**
  www.webcrawler.com/careers

> Searchbeat
  outlet.searchbeat.com/jobs.htm

Several of the most popular web portals and search engines also offer career centers with information, advice, resume databases, and job boards. However, most are powered by a few of the major mega employment sites with which they have affiliate relationships. You may want to go directly to the mega employment site. For example, the following major portals and search engines have affiliate arrangements with the mega sites to power their employment sections:

Portals and/or Search Engines	Employment Section Powered By
Yahoo.com	headhunter.net
MSN.com	careerbuilder.com
Netscape.com	monster.com
Excite.com	monster.com
Lycos.com	net-temps.com
Looksmart.com	net-temps.com

Looksmart.com also powers the search directories of the major portals on the web, such as msn.com, excite.com, altavista.com, iwon.com, and cnn.com.

Gateways With Wisdom and Judgment

Six of the best gateway sites primarily focus on compiling the most useful career resources for job seekers, employers, and recruiters. The first three sites are essentially gateway directories to job boards – websites that primarily offer searchable job postings and resume databases for employers. The remaining three sites are each operated by leading career specialists – Richard N. Bolles, Margaret F. Dikel, and Dr. Randall Hansen – who understand the job search process and who are primarily job seeker-oriented rather than employer-oriented. These gateway sites provide a refreshing balance to what is often "Internet hype" found on many other commercial employment websites. These are "must visit" sites for anyone planning to use the

Internet in their job search. Each of the sites approaches the Internet differently, from user judgment calls of Richard N. Bolles to the huge number of career categories and linkages of Margaret F. Dikel and the useful content of Dr. Randall Hansen. It's well worth spending at least 30 minutes exploring each of these fine sites. You'll be a much wiser job seeker – both online and offline – for having done so. They will add one of the most important ingredients to your online job search efforts – *wisdom*! The other sites offer a huge range of recommended career resources for launching an online job search. Using these sites may simply overwhelm you with so many online career choices.

MyJobSearch   Gateway
myjobsearch.com

This is one of the more intuitive and useful employment sites on the Web. Its "Job Board" section takes visitors to three types of job boards: general, regional, and specialty or niche sites. The site even goes one step further – includes a unique "Classifieds" section linked to hundreds of newspapers throughout the U.S. that offer online versions of their classified ad sections. Just click on to the state map and the site will direct you to various newspapers in your targeted state. From there it's up to you to find the classified section from the newspaper's home page. If you're primarily interested in reviewing job vacancy announcements on the Internet, it doesn't get much better than this gateway site to job postings, with perhaps the exception of our next site, the AIRS directory.

AIRS   Gateway
airsdirectory.com/jobboards

No need to mess with those print classified ads that appear in newspapers after visiting this site. Here's the ultimate directory to the electronic classifieds which include millions of job vacancies. Indeed, this site claims to have compiled the largest collection of job boards – over 3,300 – on the web. And they are probably correct. This is wonderful a gateway site if you are primarily interested in identifying electronic classifieds or "job boards" – sites that include lots of job postings. Designed for employers who are interested in posting jobs, the site also is a rich resource for job seekers who are interested in identifying job boards in their particular occupational areas. The site includes hundreds of niche job boards that are often overlooked by job seekers. In addition to identifying 901 career hubs (general employment websites with job boards) in the United States, the site includes 352 international job boards, 868 industry job boards, 681 technical job boards, 160 healthcare job boards, and many others dealing with financial services (79), diversity (103), college and alumni (74), and free agents (77). The site also includes a search feature for locating job boards by name. You can easily spend hours playing around with this gateway site to the wonderful world of job boards.

CareerXroads	Gateway
careerxroads.com	

Brought to you by the authors of *CareerXroads* (Gerry Crispin and Mark Mehler), the annual directory to the best employment and recruitment websites (see order form at the end of this book), this site currently provides a searchable database to more then 600 information technology sites. Book buyers, who register on this site, receive free updates to the book. The site is updated monthly with new sites and changes to the database. It plans to soon expand the database to include websites in the fields of business and finance, education, engineering, retail and hospitality, sales and marketing, and science. Primarily designed for employers and recruiters, who pay subscription fees to use the database, CareerXroads is one of the most focused groups for identifying and reviewing employment websites. If you are interested in identifying websites in particular disciplines or employment fields, this is the perfect gateway site.

Quintessential Careers   Gateway
quintcareers.com

This is not your typical flashy employment website with lots of
job postings and a much hyped resume database run by lots of
inexperienced young techies operating with venture capital and
naive concepts of careers and the job search. Run by career
expert and author Dr. Randall Hansen, this is one of the richest
websites for career information, advice, and linkages to the
world of online employment. It's a smart site because it's
designed by a career professional who knows the key ingredients of an effective job search and reflects this expertise in
numerous sections throughout this user-friendly website. Well
organized with the needs of the job seeker in mind (most
commercial sites tend to be more employer-oriented because of
their primary revenue stream – advertising), the site unfolds
with a rich database of job search tools, articles, tips, advice,
and linkages. Definitely the work of a career professional who
understands the major ingredients – from self-assessment to
negotiations – that go into conducting a successful job search.

The Riley Guide   Gateway
www.dbm.com/jobguide (or rileyguide.com)

Margaret Riley (now Margaret F. Dikel) is every job seekers'
favorite online librarian – she knows where to find the "stuff."
This is her site, a testimonial to what one very persistent and
focused person can really do to create a useful gateway site to
employment information and services on the Internet. While it
is by no means complete and is sometimes helter-skelter, this
site attempts to be comprehensive and succeeds to a certain
extent. During the past seven years, Margaret Dikel has led a
one-person crusade to compile one of the largest databases of
career resources available anywhere. The result has been "The
Riley Guide," a major gateway to career resources on the

Internet. Consisting of thousands of employment-relevant websites and articles organized by hundreds of useful categories, this site catalogs who is doing what on the Internet related to jobs and careers. It's not a fancy website with lots of functionality designed to stimulate one's desire for appealing colors, graphics, and interactivity. Instead, it's a bare bones site that delivers exactly what most job seekers need and want when they initially incorporate the Internet in their job search – lots of useful information and linkages about jobs and careers. Since the site is designed to "deliver the facts," you'll have to make your own judgments about the relative usefulness and value of the various sites and information that get cataloged in The Riley Guide. Many of the sites appearing on this website also are featured in Margaret F. Dikel's popular Internet job search book, *Guide to Internet Job Searching* (see order form at the end of this book or online at www.impactpublications.com).

JobHuntersBible	Gateway
jobhuntersbible.com	

This site is ostensibly linked to the author's (Richard N. Bolles) bestselling career guide, *What Color is Your Parachute*. But it does much more. It's a good gateway site to the Internet for one major reason: it's organized according to sound job search principles (begins with testing/assessment and proceeds to make critical judgments about the "do's" and "don'ts" of being an online player). Unlike other sites that merely present the "facts" – list websites, present articles, and offer job search services – this one performs the ultimate service. It has opinions and makes judgments about the good, the bad, and the ugly aspects of this online business. That's very refreshing since most job seekers don't have enough knowledge and experience to make good judgments about the quality and effectiveness of online employment information and services, nor do they have the bigger picture about both online and offline job search activities that lead to success. Indeed, like the author's book, this website has "attitude." Reflecting the experience of a career professional who knows what works, Bolles makes judgment calls about using the Internet in one's job search as well as assesses the usefulness of various websites. Many job seekers will find these to be very sound judgments – not just a sterile presentation of Internet sites and facts. After all, using the Internet to conduct a job search requires using good judgment. When you get frustrated by using the Internet in your job search – you see few results and often feel disoriented – be sure to return to this site to review some sage advice on why things do not always work according to expectations and why you are probably wasting a lot of time on useless Internet activities that have few if any payoffs. Not surprisingly, putting job search time in on the Internet probably has little relationship to making progress with your job search! This site tells you why this is so and what you really should be doing to make your time more productive. Much of this information also appears in the author's Internet job search book, *Job-Hunting on the Internet* (see order form at the end of this book or online at www.impactpublications.com).

Other Useful Gateways

The remaining eight gateway sites outlined in this section also pull together a wealth of job search and employment websites. Each uses a different approach to compiling its lists of recommended websites.

Job-Hunt	**Gateway**
job-hunt.org	

This site focuses on identifying the best job sites on the Internet. It includes tips on maintaining online privacy along with an annotated listing of employment super sites, job sites by location (U.S. and international) and career specialty, resume banks, employee sites, hot sites of the week, and several other types of websites. One of the best organized sites for locating websites relevant to different job search phases.

Career Resource Gateway
careerresource.net

Nothing fancy here – just hundreds of useful web resources linked to online commercial job databases, specific employers, professional associations, government agencies, university career services, alumni services, and other job resource indexes. A personal project of Jasmit Singh Kochhar, it was started in 1994 when he was a doctoral student at Rensselaer Polytechnic Institute. Since this is more of a hobby than a full-time job, the site is only occasionally updated (6-10 month gaps). While many of the links no longer function, there is plenty here to make this a worthwhile gateway career site.

Catapult Gateway
www.jobweb.com/catapult

This is the resource section of the JobWeb site sponsored by NACE, the National Association of Colleges and Employers. Heavily oriented toward its university student audience, this site includes a listing of websites most relevant to its audience. It includes a comprehensive listing of university career offices in the United States, Canada, United Kingdom, and Australia. Many of these offices include rich databases of career information, advice, and linkages to useful employment-related websites, including alumni career services. Explore a few of the university career websites and you should learn a great deal about how to conduct an effective online job search. The site also includes a comprehensive listing, with linkages, of the major employment websites in the U.S. and abroad as well as many state and city career centers and employment offices and major websites specializing on particular career fields. A very rich selection of websites for directing your job search.

Careers.org   Gateway
careers.org

Discover hundreds of linkages to key career and employment
websites directly from the front page of this useful website.
Indeed, this is an in-your-face website with a rich selection of
online career resources. It includes the top career websites,
regional employment resources for both the U.S. and Canada,
self-employment resources, career services, career advice, employer directories, learning resources, and much more. You can
easily wile away hours exploring the major rich links found on
this site.

JobSourceNetwork   Gateway
jobsourcenetwork.com

Includes a wealth of linkages to employers, career fairs, recruiters, employment agencies, resume services, internships,
self-employment, job listings, and much more. Sponsored by
the publishers of the Job Source city employment directories.

University of London Careers Service   Gateway
www.careers.lon.ac.uk/links

This site includes thousands of online employment links with
a greater emphasis on international resources. Covers career
exploration, education, job hunting, regional and international
work, self-employment, volunteerism, career fields, professional
and trade associations, employer websites, and search engines.
Includes many new links each month.

JobBoard.net   Gateway
jobboard.net

This sites includes numerous links to Internet job boards and resume banks through both a keyword search engine and eight categories of links: general, business, technical, education, engineering, medical, health, and legal. By no means complete, it does include many of the major Internet employment sites.

MegaJobSites   Gateway
megajobsites.com

MegaJobSites includes links to hundreds of its specialized job boards that are organized by occupation, country, region, state, and city. Job seekers select a relevant site and then enter search data (job title, location, keyword, category, company name) to locate appropriate job postings. Includes useful relocation tools provided by other websites, such as homefair.com. Affiliated with the world's largest Internet recruitment training company, AIRS (airsdirectory.com).

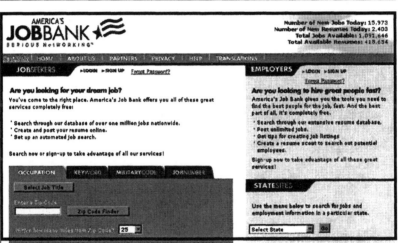

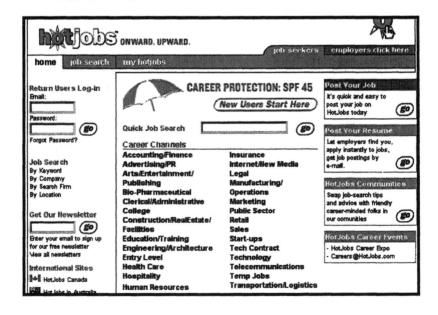

5

Mega Employment Sites and Databases

S OME OF THE MOST FREQUENTLY VISITED WEBSITES are several mega employment sites. Highly integrated, extremely competitive, and organized around an employer-centered advertising and user-fee model, these websites operate like huge classified ad operations. While some offer many useful services and features for job seekers – from message boards to job search tips and tests – their main focus is on delivering recruitment services for employers and recruiters through large resume databases and searchable job postings. Primarily functioning as online recruitment sites structured to meet the hiring needs of employers and secondarily to assist job seekers in finding a job, these sites present a very traditional job search approach – managing job listings and resumes – that best serves the needs of their paying clients.

Managing Resumes, Job Boards, and Traffic

The central focus of the mega employment sites is the searchable resume database and job board. Without a large resume database and

49

numerous job postings, these sites would not attract much operating cash. Financed by employers who post job listings, search resume databases, and/or advertise their company to job seekers through banners, buttons, and sponsored links – the three main employer-based financial streams supporting these sites – the primary goal of these sites is to attract a multitude of resumes and visitors ("eyeballs"), which in turn attract more and more paying customers, the employers and recruiters, who use these sites to screen candidates. The mega employment sites do a good job of attracting traffic to their sites because they offer numerous free peripheral services to job seekers. Finding new ways to sustain as well as attract more resumes and traffic is always a major challenge for these sites.

Old Wine in New Electronic Bottles

Despite all the fancy bells and whistles of the mega employment sites, the major job search and recruitment approach of these sites is very simple – connect employers and candidates by way of job listings and resumes. This is the highly formalized approach to finding jobs and recruiting candidates which was traditionally conducted through the classified ads in newspapers and magazines and personnel services of employment firms and headhunters. It's an approach that is useful for locating perhaps 25 to 50 percent of all job vacancies at any particular time. It's also an approach that leads to high competition for many uninspired jobs. If, for example, you anticipate making in excess of $75,000 a year, these sites may not be for you. Compared to classified ads and employment firms, one of the distinct advantages for employers in using such sites is the ability to search and retrieve by "keywords" through literally thousands of resumes found in a site's database. Two of the major advantages for job seekers are the ability to expose themselves, via their electronic resume, to hundreds of potential employers and to apply for jobs online.

> *The major approach of these sites is very simple – connect employers and candidates by way of job postings and resume databases.*

How effective these sites are in helping candidates find the perfect job and assisting employers in locating the perfect candidate is another question altogether, one that has yet to be determined. For job seekers, these sites tend to encourage a traditional, and much flawed, job search approach: focus on your resume and respond to advertised job listings. Self-assessment, research, and networking – the real hard work of conducting an effective job search – are hardly evident on these mega sites, although some are slowly recognizing the importance of these additional elements and encouraging job seekers to include them in their overall job search. Unfortunately, these sites may encourage job seekers to primarily focus their job search on using these sites rather than including them as one element in a larger job search. Indeed, such sites make the job search look quick and easy, which is not the case for most job seekers. In fact, many job seekers complain about the "ineffectiveness" of such sites: they get few, if any, "hits" that lead to job interviews and offers. If you primarily rely on such sites to find employers who might be interested in interviewing you for a job that really interests you, chances are you will be very disappointed. Employers usually have specific needs that are beyond the skill and experience levels of many online job seekers. Candidates with exotic hard-to-find skills and experience are most likely to benefit from these sites.

> *Many job seekers complain about the "ineffectiveness" of such sites: they get few, if any, "hits" that lead to job interviews and offers. Candidates with exotic hard-to-find skills and experience are most likely to benefit from these sites.*

In the meantime, the mega employment sites are large forums for conducting the business of connecting candidates with employers. They are huge screening arenas which are extremely cost effective for employers. In fact, employers who used to spend $5,000 to $10,000 on classified ads and employment firms over a 30-day period to find candidates to interview may now only spend $200 to $2,000 to locate candidates online within minutes by posting job listings or searching an online resume database. For many employers, these mega employment sites make economic sense because of the time and savings involved and the huge databases they can draw upon in searching for candidates. However, many employers also report that these sites tend to disproportionately attract job hoppers who are often more interested in playing the job search game (clever "keyword" writers) than in staying with an employer for more than 18 months. For job seekers, these sites make sense because they are free and offer the possibility of getting "hits" from a large range of potential employers. In other words, they are the ultimate free lunch – nothing to lose and perhaps lots to gain! For a new class of job hoppers, who get the 90-day itch, these are great places to explore new job and career opportunities – literally "test the waters" – 24 hours a day, even when they are ostensibly happily employed. Welcome to the new world of traditional employment where speed and economics play a central role in the employment process. In the end, job seekers should never forget who pays for these sites – employers – and what they want – your resume. They get resumes through two costly methods: buy advertising (job postings, banner and/or button ads, and sponsored links) and pay monthly user fees (for accessing a site's resume database). Therefore, the structure of these sites tends to be skewed toward the needs of the paying audience in search of resumes from which to identify possible candidates for job interviews.

> *The structure of these sites tends to be skewed toward the needs of the paying audience – employers in search of resumes for hiring candidates.*

Structure and Process

The mega employment sites offer job seekers numerous free services that can assist them with their job search. These services also motivate job seekers to constantly revisit the sites and thereby contribute to the site's carefully monitored monthly "hit" or traffic statistics. Take, for example, as we noted in Chapter 2, the top five employment sites which had the following number of unique monthly visitors in March 2001:

Website	Unique Monthly Visitors
Monster.com	6,951,000
Jobsonline.com	6,486,000
Hotjobs.com	4,280,000
Careerbuilder.com	1,933,000
Headhunter.net	1,850,000

A great deal of effort, including many subtle "tricks of the trade," goes into attracting such high levels of traffic to these sites. After all, the number of monthly visitors is the major determinant for setting advertising rates and user fees for these sites. The magical word "free" now encompasses a host of enticing job search services, including free email alerts and newsletters, that hopefully will constantly bring traffic back to these sites so they can further sustain and expand their high level of traffic and associated revenue streams.

Once you begin exploring the mega employment sites, you may become disoriented by so many free choices available to you. But let's look at the real nuts and bolts of these sites – where things are supposed to happen for both job seekers and employers. At the heart of these sites are two major elements for connecting job seekers and employers and keeping the traffic flowing:

1. **Resume database:** Job seekers register and then enter their resume online. Employers pay user fees to access this database for finding candidates that match their search criteria. If all goes well for job seekers, the lucky ones will get emails or calls from employers who discovered their resume in the site's database. If all goes well for employers, they will draw on a rich database of qualified candidates who cost their company less than $1,000 to find – a tremendous savings over the costly, slow, and cumbersome classified ads and recruiter approach, which used to be the major approach of human resources departments.

2. **Job postings:** Like classified newspaper ads, most mega employment sites require employers to advertise in order to have their jobs listed online. Often grouped into "channels,"

these job postings are usually organized by job fields or categories. Job seekers can search for appropriate job listings by a variety of criteria, such as keywords, company, or location, and then apply online by sending a resume and letter by email, fax, or mail, depending on the site's application instructions.

Too Busy to Job Search?

For job seekers, the **resume database element** is the most passive way of finding a job. It's also the one element where your participation is required for the overall health of the site. Indeed, some websites pose this motivational question up front to entice job seekers to register: *"Too busy to job search?"* Just enter your resume in the database and wait for employers to contact you with an invitation to interview for a job. You can even update your resume on a regular basis. What a great way to find a job, 24 hours a day, and even while you are currently employed! This really makes the job search quick and easy – if you can maintain your privacy, get lots of "hits," and convert a few of those hits into job interviews.

The real winners are employers who manage to inexpensively find candidates through such sites. The experience for job seekers is usually mixed – many get what they pay for, which is nothing.

Reality, however, is usually less than positive and often disappointing. Indeed, the experience of many job seekers is that they register and put their resume online but still do not get a single inquiry after 6, 8, or even 12 months. In addition to being frustrated, these somewhat naive job seekers switch over to the site's community forum section where they post some form of this question: *"What am I doing wrong – I haven't gotten a single hit after being registered for six months?"* Not surprisingly, they get similar complaints from other frustrated online job seekers who have not received responses even after 8, 10, or 12 months! Thinking they are doing something wrong, they review the "Career Tips" section or question an online "Career Expert" who invariably sends them to another section on the same website or recommends visiting other websites where they may experience similar online disappointments. The silver lining for the site is that traffic keeps coming back as job seekers repeatedly try to experience success. More traffic attracts more employers who pay higher advertising and user fees. The real winners are employers who manage to inexpensively find candidates through such sites. The experience for job seekers who use such sites for free is usually mixed – many get nothing.

Viewing Classifieds (Postings) Online

The **job posting element** requires job seekers to take a more proactive role in the online job search by periodically checking the latest listings in their particular career field. Some sites have even turned this element into a relatively passive activity by including a special email feature that automatically alerts the job seeker to new listings that fit their specific employment criteria. However, most of these sites require the email recipient to return to the site for information on how to apply for the position – an inconvenience for the job seeker but a clever way of increasing traffic for the site.

35 Peripheral Services and Features

Most mega employment sites include numerous peripheral services and features ostensibly designed to assist job seekers with their job search but which also serve as great traffic builders. You can usually expect to find some combination of the following 35 job search services and features on these sites:

- Job Search Tips
- Featured Articles
- Career Experts or Advisors
- Career Tool Kit
- Career Assessment Tests
- Community Forums
- Discussion or Chat Groups
- Message Boards
- Job Alert ("Push") Emails

- Company Research Centers
- Networking Forums
- Salary Calculators or Wizards
- Resume Management Center
- Resume and Cover Letter Advice
- Multimedia Resume Software
- Job Interview Practice
- Relocation Information
- Reference Check Checkers
- Employment or Career News
- Free Email For Privacy
- Success Stories
- Career Newsletter
- Career Events
- Online Job Fairs
- Affiliate Sites
- Career Resources
- Featured Employers
- Polls and Surveys
- Contests
- Online Education and Training
- International Employment
- Talent Auction Centers
- Company Ads (buttons and banners)
- Sponsored Links
- Special Channels for Students, Executives, Freelancers, Military, and other groups

> *The real value of these sites for most job seekers is found in the many useful peripheral services and features.*

Some sites, such as CareerBuilder, also include a "mega job search" feature that allows job seekers to simultaneously search for jobs on more than 75 different websites without leaving the CareerBuilder site. JobsOnline even provides an online skills training option for individuals who need to upgrade their technical skills. EmployMAX includes cutting-edge products for producing a multimedia online resume – EXPERTease™ multimedia resume and e-Vita™ interactive multimedia portfolio which showcases accomplishments and work samples. Such most of these services and features are free to job seekers, you are well advised to take advantage of such supports.

Theoretically, the resume database and job posting elements together should make the job search relatively quick, easy, and inexpensive for both job seekers and employers. But the economics of operating such sites are more complicated than what initially appears to be a good idea. One of the big issues for employers and job seekers is the aging or "freshness" of resumes and job postings in a site's databases. Since sites try to maximize the number of resumes in their databases as well as the number of job postings – the two elements that make their sites appealing to both employers and job seekers –

they often let the resumes and postings age beyond a safe two- to six-week period. Indeed, some databases may include resumes that are more than a year old. Sites that offer free job postings for employers may not automatically time-out the postings within a reasonable period of time. Consequently, some of the key data on these sites may be inaccurate or misleading.

> _Our advice is to create redundancy: use all of these sites by putting your resume online, surveying the job postings, and exploring the many special services and features._

In reality, employers are the primary beneficiaries since they quickly, easily, and inexpensively get what they want from such sites. Job seekers experience varying degrees of success and failure with posting their resumes and searching for job postings, similar to sending resumes and letters in response to classified ads in newspapers.

As you may quickly discover, the real value of these mega employment sites for most job seekers is found in the many peripheral services and features. Indeed, you'll discover a wealth of free and fee-based job search information, advice, and services which can strengthen each stage of your job search. Our advice is to use all of these sites by putting your resume online, surveying the job postings, and exploring the many special services and features. If you do this, you'll create a high level of online job search _redundancy_. It's this redundancy that should prove useful as you include an online component in your overall job search.

The Top 10

Our top 10 mega employment sites are no secret – they are the largest and most frequently visited sites as measured by the number of unique visitors each month. They also are some of the most attractive sites for users who find them engaging, relatively easy to navigate, and useful for job search information and advice. They attract thousands of employers who regularly access their databases and list job openings on the sites. Monster.com, for example, includes over 425,000 job postings on its site. While most of these sites attempt to give some evidence of effectiveness, usually with a testimonial of successful job seekers and satisfied employers, almost all such evidence is anecdotal to attract more visitors and employers to the site. After all, these are advertising and user-fee driven sites where "effectiveness" is primarily measured as "inputs" rather than "outputs," and for good reason (most advertising companies religiously avoid questions about outcomes, which threaten their operations, and instead focus on the number of "users" or "eyeballs"). In this case, effectiveness is primarily measured by traffic numbers relevant to employers rather than the number of individual "hits" both job seekers and employers actually receive. However, one suspects something must be happening since so many people are hanging around these sites. For job seekers, that "something" may be all the peripheral job search services and features that both entertain and enlighten job seekers who feel they are making progress with their job search by visiting and revisiting these sites.

Monster.com monster.com	Top Mega Site

Awesome! Impressive! Fabulous traffic numbers. But perhaps overwhelming and too big to get noticed among the masses. For job seekers, it simply doesn't get better in terms of job search services, features, and job postings. Boasting over 425,000 job postings and claiming nearly 6 million resumes in its database, Monster is the premier mega employment site. It includes a wealth of job search information and advice which is organized around several different interest and professional communities:

college students, senior executives, transitioning military, mid-career, nonprofits, self-employed, free agents, international, and work abroad. From career articles, a newsletter (450,000+ subscribers!), and a career assessment test to chats, message boards, resume and interview advice, salary calculator, relocation center, and bookstore, this site seems to have it all. You can easily spend hours exploring its many different sections. To further strengthen its position as the number one online employment site, in July 2001 Monster acquired HotJobs.com, the third largest online employment site. Claiming to be the world's leading career network, Monster operates a global network of employment sites in 14 other countries: Australia, Belgium, Canada, Denmark, France, Hong Kong, Ireland, India, Italy, Netherlands, New Zealand, Singapore, Spain, and the United Kingdom. No other site in the world comes near the depth and breath of Monster. Many job seekers make sure they post their resumes on this site, register for its email notifications, and return to the site frequently to check out the various postings and services. The site is perfectly structured to ensure a daily parade of new and repeat visitors who add up to nearly 7 million unique visitors each month. That's a lot of people looking for jobs! Many employers understand such numbers and buy into this site accordingly.

America's Job Bank	**Top Mega Site**
www.ajb.dni.us	

Don't miss this one – you've already paid for it. This site offers the perfect mix of online and offline employment services. Brought to you by your government (U.S. Department of Labor in partnership with the states and private sector organizations), this site represents what was once an ambitious attempt to create a free nationwide job bank for both job seekers and employers. While it didn't quite work out that way, nonetheless, this site includes a huge database of over 1.5 million jobs, a resume database for posting your resume online (includes over 400,000 resumes), and lots of great resources for conducting an effective job search and advancing your career. It includes a special military code finder for veterans. The site is linked to all public employment offices and career centers (One Stop Career Centers, Workforce Development groups, Employment Offices, Job Services, Veterans Assistance Centers), and many commercial career services. Special features include state-by-state employment information and job listings, a career information center (America's CareerInfoNet) for decision-making, an educational center (America's LearningExchange), and an employment and training service provider search center (America's Service Locator). Unlike many commercial sites which are primarily oriented to servicing employers who finance the sites, America's Job Bank is very job-seeker oriented with its emphasis on service providers. If, for example, you suddenly lose your job, just go to the service section of this site to find out what you need to do for assistance, from filing for unemployment compensation to attending job search workshops and getting one-on-one assistance in writing your resume. You can search for such free job services in your neighborhood by entering your zip code in the search engine. Often overlooked, this site is one of the best uses of taxpayers' money to help job seekers with their jobs and careers.

| Flipdog.com | Top Mega Site |
| Flipdog.com | |

We really like this site because of its rich database and great linkages to useful career-related sites – definitely one of the best on the Web. Indeed, this well organized site is a favorite of job seekers and employers alike who can explore a wealth of job search and recruitment resources through this one-stop portal. Unlike other sites that primarily compile job postings through paid advertising relationships, Flipdog literally crawls the web to find and compile job listings from employer websites. As a result, this site can claim to have the most comprehensive directory of jobs on the web – five times more than most other sites. Boasting a large database of resumes and job postings, the site also includes many useful resources under its "Resource Center": bimonthly newsletter, employer databases (links to key employment research sites, such as hoovers.com and wetfeet.com), employment outlook reports (monthly Job Opportunity Index), and career advice, tests, events, seminars, and training programs (through links with other sites). A rich site for exploring useful linkages to other career-relevant sites.

Jobsonline   **Top Mega Site**
jobsonline.com

This is one of the new kids on the block that began operating in July 1999 and has now skyrocketed to become the second most visited employment website with nearly 6.5 million unique visitors each month. Compared to Monster, Jobsonline is a much simpler site to navigate. While it lacks the depth and breath of Monster, its career advice is much better organized and user-friendly. Its career resources section is well worth reviewing for sound job search advice: career fairs, company research, cover letters, interviewing, relocation, resumes, and salaries. It also includes a unique online training section, weekly tips, a contest, survey information (from Salary.com), and testimonials.

HotJobs.com   **Mega Site**
hotjobs.com

Noted for its aggressive marketing, including its famous and expensive Super Bowl ads, HotJobs.com has been successful in becoming one of the most popular employment websites for both employers and job seekers. Acquired by Monster in July 2001 for over $450 million, it will remain a separate operation for at least another year. The site enables job seekers to search by keyword, company, and location. Individuals can view job postings by various career fields or "channels." The site also includes a newsletter, several communities, chats, industry resources, relocation information, salary and job search tips, and office humor. One of the least thoughtful sections is "Job Search Tips" which consists of links to articles found on other sites, many of which are superficial and mediocre. The site also is linked to affiliate sites in Canada and Australia.

CareerBuilder.com **careerbuilder.com**	**Top Mega Site**

This is one of the smartest sites on the Internet – very simple but loaded with great content and focus. It provides access to one of the largest databases of job postings as well as numerous linkages to other employment websites. Acquired a couple of years ago by the Tribune and Knight Ridder and recently merged with CareerPath, CareerBuilder also powers the career sections of many other websites, such as MSN.com and USATODAY.com. A very user-friendly site, CareerBuilder offers numerous useful job search tips and tools, weekly features, polls and surveys, communities (campus and tech), and free and fee-based online testing. Special features of this site include receiving job announcements via email and being able to search more than 75 local and national job sites by location, job description, keywords, salary, and URL through its "Advanced Search" or "Mega Job Search" feature.

Headhunter.net **headhunter.net**	**Top Mega Site**

A long-time favorite of both employers and job seekers, Headhunter.net also powers the career sections of other major websites, such as Yahoo.com and NBCi.com. Like many of the other mega employment sites, Headhunter.net includes a resume database and job postings (nearly 250,000) searchable by field of interest. Job seekers also can search jobs by type, industry, company, and international location. Individuals can elect to have job postings sent directly to their email address.

They also can post up to five different resumes for optimizing their job search (not sure this is such a good idea since it begs the question whether the job seeker knows what he or she really wants to do!). Other useful features include a newsletter, online job fairs, and a resource center, which tends to be structured around sponsored links. Individuals who conduct an online job search on their employer's time will appreciate the "Boss Button" which quickly refreshes their screen when the boss is near!

Jobs.com   **Top Mega Site**
jobs.com

There's nothing surprising or complicated about this site. The primary goal is to get your resume online or search for job postings by category, employment type, and/or location. The site also includes several peripheral job search services and resources. Its "Communities" section covers several communities: military, healthcare, diversity, college, temp/contract, part-time, and intern/voluntary. Its resources section includes articles, advice, and audio/ video shows by career expert Martin Yate; free online career assessments (through assessment.com); and a variety of career tools offered through sponsored links, such as a reference checker through myreferences.com, an email resume distributor by resumeexpress.com, and an executive employment publication produced through Career Advancement Publications, www.jobreports.net. The main strength of this site is its job postings and resume database. The other elements should improve over time as the site becomes more focused on quality job search information and services.

JobOptions   **Top Mega Site**
joboptions.com

At one time known as AdNet and then E.span, in the early 1990s this site was one of the leading pioneers of online recruitment. As the new JobOptions, it continues to offer a large number of job postings and a huge resume database for thousands of job seekers and employers. Job seekers can search for jobs or employers by location (state), categories (or "channels"), and keywords. The "Career Zone" section includes a rich selection of job search tips, career advice, career coaching, articles, self-assessment tests, online education and training, career fairs and trade shows, industry and business research, relocation information, a fun section (a career horoscope, bloopers, and workplace stories), and a free email service for maintaining job search privacy. Offers one of the most comprehensive and selective career resource centers. Well worth a visit just to survey the peripheral job search services and features.

Career.com   Top Mega Site
www.career.com

Not your traditional cluttered employment website with a very busy in-your-face, stretch-your-eyes, and scatter-your-mind front page design. Its clean and modern look is very user-friendly and focused. This is one of the web's oldest and most innovative online recruitment firms which has operated since 1993. Job seekers can search for job postings by companies, hot jobs, keywords, locations, and disciplines. The site includes several unique features, such as CyberFair™, Jobdigger™, Job Hosting, and Hot Jobs™ for enhancing the effectiveness of employers in using this site for recruiting candidates. The site also includes a useful resource section for job seekers: articles, links to other sites, career counseling services, reference checks, women's resources, college resources, career publications, frequently asked questions, and resume writing tips. All in all, a very good site that focuses on what this electronic recruitment and job search process is all about – efficiently and effectively connecting employers to qualified job seekers.

61 Favorite Employment Sites

Several other employment websites also offer a wide variety of employment services, information, and advice. Most of these sites offer the obligatory resume database and job postings which are their revenue streams. Some offer extensive career resource and linkage sections (independent and sponsored). Our favorite sites include the following:

MyJobSearch	**Mega Site**
myjobsearch.com	

Offering hundreds of specialty job boards organized by 57 occupational fields, this site is rich with job postings – a virtual gateway site to the major job boards (online classifieds). It also include a Fortune 500 section which provides links to each of the Fortune 500 companies and their employment sections. A similar gateway concept is carried over to its other sections, especially career planning advice, job search tips (resume, interviews, networking, negotiations), and relocation. Includes a free monthly newsletter. A rich site for exploring many useful job search resources. Does not include a resume database.

EmployMax	**Mega Site**
employmax.com	

Starting with a slick flash page that showcases unique products and services (e-Vita Online™ and EXPERTease™) in animated form, this site offers job seekers links to training and education, self-assessment, career coaching, resume broadcasting, and other career-related services. It also offers numerous useful services (in addition to job postings and resume database) to its two main revenue streams – employers and search firms. Its EXPERTease™ multimedia resume and e-Vita™ interactive multimedia portfolio help showcase accomplishments and work samples of job seekers. Includes lots of useful links for job seekers. One of the few sites that seems to understand the "big picture" involved in both communicating qualifications to employers and recruiting candidates, from self-assessment and multimedia presentations to conducting interviews, checking references, assessing skills, evaluating credentials, and dealing with retention issues. One of the better conceived employment websites which could well serve as a model for other sites that primarily offer mindless resume databases and job posting services.

Nationjob.com   **Mega Site**
nationjob.com

Another favorite site for thousands of job seekers and employers. Primarily focuses on offering excellent job postings and quality resume database with very little other proprietary information and useful advice. Includes a free email service for privacy and some success stories. Handles most peripheral career information, advice, and services through sponsored linkages to other commercial sites, including a free "teaser" assessment (through the same commercial linkage available on other employment websites, assessment.com); online career training and education (three linkages); company and industry reports (through a linkage with wetfeet.com); resume writing advice and services (through career-resumes.com); reference checks (through Allison & Taylor's myreferences.com); salary and relocation information (links to three sites); and reciprocal links (to a strange combination of websites). Because of its sponsored-links business model (a totally biased approach), this site does not provide as much useful job search information and advice as you will find on several of the other mega employment sites, which have dealt with the career information and advice issues – and the needs of job seekers – in a more integrated and focused manner.

Employment Guide's CareerWeb   Mega Site
careerweb.com

Increasingly oriented toward technical jobs and community-based employment websites, this long-established site offers searchable resume and job posting databases. Owned by Landmark Communications and the Trader Publishing Company (yes, the publishers of the popular *Auto Trader*), the site includes featured employers and jobs as well as a job seekers newsletter, career advice, career resource center, affiliate sites, and a bookstore. It also includes a unique ResumeTrader option ($29.95) that allows job seekers to post their resumes to nearly 100 national job boards, including Headhunter.net, HotJobs. com, and CareerBuilder.com, and numerous recruiters specifically related to the job seeker's industry. Includes links to several of their other websites and to the many versions of their community-based employment print newspaper, *The Employment Guide* (over 3 million weekly circulation in major metropolitan areas across the United States).

CareerJournal   Mega Site
careerjournal.com

Operated by the *Wall Street Journal* previously known as careers.wsj.com, this site primarily focuses on top executive, managerial, and professional positions. It's also linked to related sites for college students, executive search (Futurestep operated by Korn/Ferry International), and international careers. In addition to operating the standard resume database and job postings, this site is rich with job search information and services: salary information, career news, job hunting advice, and tips for success. It also includes special sections with articles relating to executive recruiters and HR professionals through alliances/linkages with the Society for Human Resource Management, American Society for Training and

Development, and the International Personnel Management Association. If you enjoy reading lots of articles on a wide range of job search and HR subjects, many of which come directly from the pages of the *Wall Street Journal*, this is one of the best employment sites to visit.

Employment911	Mega Site
employment911.com	

Operating similar to FlipDog.com, this site searches over 350 major job sites which offer nearly 3 million job postings. It also includes its own resume database, which supposedly is accessed by thousands of employers, as well as its own job postings service. The "Career Tools" section includes many articles, stories, videos, and links to commercial job search services (resume blasting, online education, references – includes many of the same companies found on other sites). Special services for job seekers include free email for privacy, a free job search organizer, and a free personal web calendar.

EmploymentSpot	Mega Site
EmploymentSpot.com	

A surprisingly well organized and useful one-stop site. Offers job postings and a resume database along with a wealth of job search information, tips, and services through its linkages with other websites. Enables job seekers to search by location and job field. Includes three major sections that generate useful information and contacts: Reference Desk, Employment News, and StartSpot Network. Each section includes pull-down menus for further exploring key career topics. The Reference Desk includes one of the best organized and informative career advice/tip sections. The Employment News section generates numerous articles from a variety of print and electronic sources on what's happening in the employment field – a rich and comprehensive overview of topics and trends. StartSpot

Network section takes you to related "Spot" websites. Offers a free monthly employment newsletter.

JobFactory   **Mega Site**
jobfactory.com

You can't go wrong with the wealth of information and connections found on this site. This is another powerful spider operation – its search engine can access over 3 million job openings by job title and geographic area, and it links to over 23,000 employment sites with job postings. This site also reviews the top 250 career sites; links to classified ads in over 1,000 newspapers in North America, Asia, and Europe; includes nearly 4,000 hotlines with recorded job openings; and identifies over 1,000 recruiters with online job postings.

Vault.com   **Mega Site**
vault.com

This popular site oozes with venture capital to support its large selection of online employment information services and job postings, which do not generate much revenue at present for supporting this very ambitious site. Indeed, employers can post jobs for only $49 a month and most services are free. Similar in many respects to WetFeet.com, with its emphasis on syndicating career content, Vault.com offers lots of career content for researching companies and organizing an effective job search. The site includes inside information on what it's like to work for particular companies. It also encourages individuals to network with current employees. The site is rich with message boards, expert advice, salary and relocation information, career news, a student/campus center, and a bookstore. Definitely worth visiting for the job search information and advice, which can be overwhelming at times.

WetFeet.com   Mega Site
wetfeet.com

Unlike most other mega employment sites, WetFeet.com does not operate a resume database. Instead, its primary focus is on searching for job postings and offering both job seekers and employers useful information and numerous services. WetFeet specializes in conducting research and publishing reports which are available for online purchase and syndication. It also creates several products to assist employers with recruitment and hiring. Job seekers use this site for researching companies, surveying salaries and benefits, and acquiring job search advice and tips from online discussion boards, articles, and a free newsletter. WetFeet's proprietary "Insider Guides" to industries, companies, and job search skills are available as downloadable e-books ($14.95) or print reports ($24.95). The site also offers a special section for students on internships (powered by InternshipPrograms.com), which includes advice, discussion groups, and job postings.

Net-Temps   Mega Site
net-temps.com

If you're interested in a temporary position, be sure to visit this site. It includes nearly 100,000 temp jobs – both contract and direct – as well as over 6,500 recruiters. Most of the jobs are in the fields of accounting and finance, administrative and clerical, engineering, health care, legal, IT, management, marketing, and sales. Many of the jobs are for professionals and executives. Like other mega sites, this one permits job seekers to include their resumes in a resume database and search job postings online. Includes numerous job search tips and a weekly newsletter.

4Work   Mega Site
4work.com

This is primarily a job postings service for employers. Rather than operate a resume database, 4Work offers a "Job Alert!" service that notifies job seekers when they qualify for particular jobs which are posted in the site's database. It currently has nearly 300,000 subscribers. This approach ostensibly saves both job seekers and employers a great deal of time because the employer-candidate "matches" are much more targeted. Job seekers also will find job search information and advice. 4Work also operates one of the largest volunteer and internship networks (nearly 100,000 registered) through its other website – 4laborsoflove.org.

BestJobsUSA   Mega Site
bestjobsusa.com

Operated by Recourse Communications, Inc., an employment newspaper publisher (*Employment Review*) and job fair specialty group, this site includes hundreds of online job postings as well as a resume database. Since there's much more to this site than what may initially appear on the front page, this site is well worth exploring for its many resources. Includes many useful job search resources, from articles, job fairs, relocation (through homefair.com), and employment tips to the best places to live and work, career links, salary surveys, and America's top 500 employers. The site includes several state and local employment sites. Its "Best University" section includes career information and advice for college students. You also can view parts of the company's employment newspaper online. This is one of the better sites for useful career tips, advice, and information.

Management Recruiters International   Mega Site
brilliantpeople.com

Designed for recruiting executive-level talent, this site claims to be the world's largest executive search and recruitment organization (Management Recruiters International) with more than 1,000 offices and 5,000 search professionals in North America, Europe, and Asia. This site includes a resume database, job postings, MRI recruiters, and an online resume editing and an application tracking system. Career assistance comes in the form of an online training center, articles relating to the job search, and a salary wizard and relocation tools. If you see yourself as executive-level talent, you'll want to use this site to get your resume in the hands of recruiters who work with employer-clients.

Career Shop   Mega Site
careershop.com

Offers an insightful advertising line: "Where the Hunter Becomes the Hunted." This site includes three main features – a resume database, job postings, and a Personal Job Shopper for automatically emailing job matches to candidates. Special features for job seekers include career advice, a career doctor (Dr. Randall Hansen who links advice to his fine gateway career site, quintcareers.com), virtual job fairs, training, video conferencing, virtual resumes, testing, counseling, career links, relocation tours, and special emphasis on health, legal, and IT careers. The site also is linked to CareerTV.net for online video career information and tips as well as several career resource companies for relocation, resumes, and salary assistance. You can learn a lot about the job search by exploring this site's many useful features.

Job Sleuth   Mega Site
jobsleuth.com

Using spider software to search key websites, Job Sleuth claims to have access to over 4.5 million job postings. Indeed, by using this site as a one-stop shop to search for jobs that match one's job profile through the use of a meta search, it can save job seekers time. You also can post your resume on several sites by registering through its jobdirect.com connection, which is operated by Korn/Ferry International. The site includes several useful career tools relating to resumes, salaries, relocation, assessment, and references. Its "Career News" and "Career Sites" sections provide linkages to other career sites, such as USjobs.com and Vault.com. Its "Career Workshop" section includes job tips, trivia, horror stories, a checklist, and a weekly poll. It also includes links to other "Sleuth" sites, company sleuth.com and entertainment.sleuth.com, and databases of articles through Electric Library (encyclopedia.com).

Career City   Mega Site
careercity.com

Operated by career book publisher Adams Media, this site also uses spider software to search millions of online job postings. Includes its own resume database for employers, job postings, bookstore (published only by Adams Media), and job search tips. If you're not interested in working for someone else, you can visit the entrepreneur section, "Start-a-Business," and avoid all the resume and employer stuff. While this is not a particularly exciting site for job seekers (although it has garnered numerous awards), some real nuggets can be found by going over to the other side – the section for employers called the "HR Center." This area includes a few useful tools for recruiters, such as examples of job offer and rejection letters and sample interview questions for different job fields – worthwhile sections job seekers should explore to get a good idea of how interviewers and employers think about them. Indeed, you can learn a lot about the types of questions, from traditional to behavioral, you are likely to be asked by reviewing the sample questions outlined for employers.

Job Web   **Mega Site**
jobweb.com

Operated by NACE (National Association of Colleges and Employers), this site is specifically designed for college students and recent graduates. Its financial support primarily comes from companies interested in recruiting college graduates through member organizations – college career services or career centers. While this site does not operate a resume database nor post jobs, it does include a wealth of useful job search information and advice. Its "Catapult" section includes a list of college and university career offices, employment centers, online job search sites, relocation resources, assessment tools, job search guides, international resources, resume writing guide, graduate and professional schools, research centers, and international resources. The site also includes information on career fairs (online and off line), current job outlook for college graduates, employers, alumni networks, salaries, and publications (bookstore). Overall, this is one of the richest career information sites on the web with lots of useful tips, insights, and linkages not available on other websites.

JobTrak   **Mega Site**
jobtrak.com

Now part of the Monster.com empire, this site is primarily targeted to college students and recent graduates – those interested in entry-level positions and in need of financial assistance. As might be expected, it includes a great deal of information on making career decisions, developing an effective job search, and linking to the right networks. The site is connected to hundreds of college and university career centers and alumni groups. It includes a career guide that addresses various steps in the job search for college students, a major to career converter, salary center, internship checklist, resume center, and virtual interview. The site also includes chats and message boards which are integrated into the main Monster.com site. Its commercial section focuses on several financial issues affecting graduates – relocation, housing, mortgages, finance, insurance, auto purchases, credit, and shopping. Overall, a very focused site for college students and recent graduates.

JobOpps.net jobopps.net	Mega Site

Job seekers can review thousands of job postings by job category and location through this site's "Advanced Search" function. Includes many job search resources (commercial linkages) for assessing skills, writing resumes, interviewing, relocating, acquiring education and training, and attending job fairs. Also includes success stories for both job seekers and employers, career news, and featured "Top Jobs."

Brass Ring brassring.com	Mega Site

Viewing itself as "The Ultimate Technology and Information Career Portal," this site has been especially active in organizing job fairs (they call them "Career Events"). Be sure to check out their calendar of upcoming events, some of which may be located near you. Job seekers can post resumes online as well as review job postings. The site includes some job search information through its "Career Guidance" center: resumes, company research, and links to other career sites. Several resources also appear under the "WWW Resources" section. The site also includes a newsletter and CyberLibrary for conducting research on companies and topics. Not as intuitive as many other sites, this site requires more work than the average site. Indeed, you may need to spend some time here unraveling the many resources behind the many buttons. Keep in mind that the central thrusts of this site consist of a resume database for employers, job postings for job seekers, and "career events" for both job seekers and employers.

JobBankUSA	**Mega Site**
jobbankusa.com	

This is a very user-friendly site. Job seekers can post their resumes online as well as search job postings and broadcast their resumes to over 9,000 possible employers and recruiters through a linkage with resumebroadcaster.com (not a free service). Its extensive career resource, news, and partners sections include Fortune 500 jobs, occupational guide, industry associations, hot companies, newsgroups, career fairs, assessment tools, relocation tools, career articles, resume samples, news sources, and links to partner sites. At times the site appears too eager to broadcast your resume for a fee – a job search approach of questionable effectiveness.

CareerTV	**Mega Site**
careertv.net	

This unique site offers a wealth of online resources for conducting an effective job search. Representing a merging of broadcast television with the Internet, the site includes streaming video television shows relating to companies and the job search. Job seekers also can search for job postings and submit resumes online, as well as explore several other career tools, through the site's linkage to careershop.com.

Jumbo Classifieds   Mega Site
jumboclassifieds.com

Nothing fancy about this site. Job seekers can quickly post their resumes on this site as well as search for hundreds of job postings. The search engine allows job seekers to search by industry, job category, location, zip code, job title, city, and salary. Not much else included on this site to assist job seekers.

America's Preferred Jobs   Mega Site
preferredjobs.com

In addition to posting resumes and searching job postings online, job seekers can explore internships and employer profiles as well as acquire career advice, verify their references, and check out job fairs. The site also links to its partner for more job listings – careershop.com.

ProHire   Mega Site
prohire.com

Includes a resume database and job postings for searching hundreds of candidates and job openings. Can search for job postings by category, location, keyword, or company. Includes "Featured Employers" and "Question of the Day." Claims to have a career center but none currently found on this site.

CareerExchange   Mega Site
careerexchange.com

Focusing on technical positions, this site includes a resume database for employer searches and job postings for job seekers. It also includes an online poll, job hunting tools (through reciprocal links with numerous other career-related sites), and relocation tools (through links with <u>homefair.com</u>)

Career Magazine <u>careermag.com</u>	**Mega Site**

In addition to including the obligatory resume database for employers and job postings for job seekers, this site is rich with career resources to assist a wide range of job seekers, from students to executives. Includes direct links to employer websites, a job match agent, relocation services, list of recruiters by occupational field, consultants section, career articles, message board, career links, bookstore (primarily for employers/HR professionals), job search tools, products and services (includes an online learning center), and a college campus center.

Employers Online <u>employersonline.com</u>	**Mega Site**

This is a very focused, bare-bones site for employers interested in candidates with sales/marketing, engineering/technical, computer/informational technology, professional/executive, and medical/health care backgrounds. Offers employers relatively inexpensive job postings and resume database search services. Encourages job seekers to put their resume into the database and search for job postings. Includes links to several other career-related sites which offer a variety of services to job seekers.

WantedJobs <u>wantedjobs.com</u>	**Mega Site**

This site enables job seekers to search 310 websites which include over 3 million job postings by job category, location, and keywords. While the site does not include a resume database, it does incorporate several job seeker services which primarily consist of sponsored links to companies in the banking, insurance, entertainment, and wireless communication industries. The site also includes relocation, housing, and travel services as well as serves as the career development center for Hoovers.com.

MindFind	**Mega Site**
mindfind.com	

This is a bare-bones but well focused site. It encourages job seekers to post their resume or "quick profile" online as well as search job postings on over 200 websites simultaneously. You get nothing else from this site – just resumes and job listings. The site discourages abuses by recruiters, who may try to pose as job seekers by posting resumes of their candidates, by charging them $200 for each "illegally" posted resume.

JobExchange	**Mega Site**
employmentwizard.com	

This rather busy site (lots of flashing buttons and banners) encourages job seekers to submit their resumes online and search for job postings. The free "My Wizard" services allows job seekers to create an online resume and cover letter which they can update and submit to employers at any time. Includes links to several useful job search resources, such as company profiles, newspapers, employers, and career advice.

RecruitUSA	**Mega Site**
recruitusa.com	

Primarily offers a resume database for employers and job postings for job seekers. Can search job postings by company, title, keyword, and location. Includes linkages to numerous companies (difficult to search by alphabetical listing). Its "Get Local" section includes linkages to state sponsors and state employment services.

JobDirect	Mega Site
jobdirect.com	

A wholly owned subsidiary of executive search firm Korn/Ferry International, this site is primarily designed for college students and recent graduates. Includes sections on internships, co-ops, summer/holiday jobs, contract work, and job search tips. Site allows users to search job postings, enter resumes online, and receive email alerts of new job postings. Profiles "hot" employers. Offers a variety of services for college career centers, from resume software to virtual job fairs.

Other major employment sites which operate resume databases and/or job postings include the following:

- 1-Jobs.com   1-jobs.com
- 6FigureJobs   sixfigurejobs.com
- Advance Careers   advancecareers.com
- CampusCareerCenter   campuscareercenter.com
- Career Marketplace   careermarketplace.com
- CareerSite   careersite.com
- Classifieds2000   classifieds2000.com
- CollegeRecruiter   collegerecruiter.com
- ComputerJobs   computerjobs.com
- Craig's List   craigslist.com
- Dice.com   dice.com
- Employment Wizard   employmentwizard.com
- ExecuNet   execunet.com
- Experience.com   experience.com
- Free Community   freecommunity.com
- GotAJob   gotajob.com
- Guru.com   guru.com

- HireAbility   hireability.com
- HireStrategy   hirestrategy.com
- IT Careers   itcareers.com
- Job Anywhere   jobanywhere.com
- JobCircle   jobcircle.com
- Jobnet   jobnet.com
- JobStar   jobstar.org
- Netshare   netshare.com
- Washington Post   washingtonjobs.com
- Workopolis (Canada)   workopolis.com

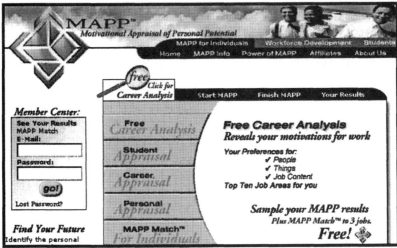

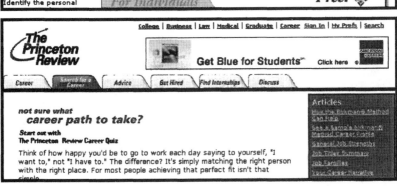

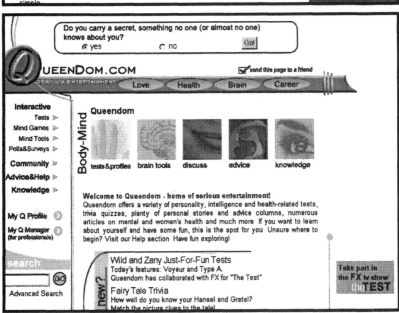

6

Assessment and Testing Sites

WHILE MANY OF THE MEGA EMPLOYMENT SITES include a self-assessment section under their "job tools" or "career resources" sections, in most cases this is a very weak and unenlightening section consisting of an entertaining interactive (self-scoring) quiz or a linkage to a commercial firm that sells career tests and related instruments. Keep in mind that the employer-centered financial structure of these sites has both intended and unintended consequences for job seekers. As we noted earlier – but it's well worth repeating – these sites are designed around an advertiser and user-fee model (employer focus) rather than a career planning and counseling model (job seeker focus). In other words, they are designed by advertisers in collaboration with employers rather than by career professionals in consultation with job seekers. They may or may not serve your best interests.

The major goal of these sites is to get you to visit and revisit them – initially post your resume and then return for surveying more job postings or using online job search tools or resources, from news to message boards. The more often you engage in these activities, the more "effective" these sites become (higher traffic) in the eyes of employers who advertise and pay user fees to support these online operations. These sites are not designed to help you conduct an intelligent job search that would use the best career advice and instruments available. Just the contrary. They are "dumbed down" to get you to use their free services and to return to their site again and again.

Doing First Things First

Few employment websites deal seriously with what professional career counselors consider to be the key to career success for job seekers – knowing what you do well and enjoy doing. In fact, if the sites focused on what really works for job seekers, they would have to de-emphasize the role of job postings – to increase traffic – on their sites.

Let's play devil's advocate for a moment. One major reason we believe so many job seekers are disappointed with their online experience is because they fail to do first things first – just as they do when conducting an offline job search, but to an even greater extent online. Skipping over the critical first few steps of the job search, they literally plunge into the job search with a poorly constructed and focused resume, often encouraged by automated online resume database forms, that doesn't really reflect what they do well and enjoy doing. Worst of all, they are unclear what they want to do other than land a job that they hope will be rewarding. If they really knew what they wanted to do, based upon a professional assessment of their interest, skills, and abilities, many would probably start this process over again to find a more rewarding job focus. The online "click and explore" experience often further exacerbates what is a problem from the very start – the lack of focus.

> *One major reason so many job seekers are disappointed with their online experience is because they fail to do first things first.*

But writing and distributing your resume via online resume databases and in response to listings found on job boards are things you should do only *after* you have had an opportunity to deal with career planning and job search *fundamentals*, such as conducting a self-assessment, formulating a clear objective, researching jobs and employers, and networking for information and advice. Rather than start your job search by posting your resume online or by searching and responding to job postings, you are well advised to do first things first. And the very first thing you should do in developing a powerful job search is to conduct a thorough self-assessment of your skills, abilities, interests, and values. You do this by *taking tests* which provide valuable information about who you really are, your values, and what you are most likely to do well and enjoy doing – your pattern of accomplishments. Armed with such information, you will be in a much better position to formulate a career objective and target your job search on particular jobs and employers with a powerful employer-centered resume that clearly reflects who you are and what you can do for the employer.

The most popular assessment instruments used by career professionals include the following:

- *Myers-Briggs Type Indicator®*
- *Strong Interest Inventory®*
- *Self-Directed Search*
- *Keirsey Character Sort*
- *Keirsey Temperament Sort*

While most of these tests are best administered by career professionals trained in the interpretation of the results for individuals, a few sites provide online versions of these and other career tests. In some cases, you must contact a career professional online in order to use the instruments. Since these are important proprietary instruments, most involve some fee for taking and interpreting the tests. Unlike most mega employment sites which offer a scattering of free online employment services to job seekers, many of the assessment sites charge user fees. As you will quickly discover, many of these powerful assessment instruments are well worth the price, especially since they can change the direction of your job search by putting you on a more productive path. Once you discover what it is you do well and enjoy doing, you'll be prepared to develop a well focused resume designed to clearly communicate who you are, what you can do, and what you want to do in the future. Best of all, you should be better prepared to handle the most important phase of the job search process – the job interview. For in the end, the whole purpose of the job search, whether conducted online or offline, is to get job interviews that result in job offers.

If you fail to do first things first, you will most likely wander in the job market looking for jobs that look interesting and which you think you might be able to fit into. Your goals should be to find a job that is fit for you, one that is compatible with your values and past patterns of behavior.

Beware of 21st Century Snake Oil

At the same time, one should also approach these testing and assessment approaches with a critical eye. Many of them still use 19th and early 20th century typological classifications and analyses, which sometimes border on being a form of 21st century scientific snake oil. Indeed, many career counselors prefer using self-directed assessment approaches to many of the professionally-administered assessment instruments. At the same time, many of these tests tend to be under-whelming, because they often discover the obvious which results in a temporary "Aha" response from job seekers who recognize in writing what they already know intuitively about themselves. In the end, a positive thinking and motivational approach – setting clear goals and pursuing them with passion – may be more useful to achieving career success than all the introspective data generated on "understanding" yourself and charting a course of action based on your past patterns of motivation and behavior.

Online Assessments

Several sites specialize in providing career testing and assessment services. While you can easily and inexpensively acquire such services through your community or junior college or through a professional testing and assessment center (you also may want to contact your local public employment office or career center by searching through America's Job Bank database: www.ajb.dni.us), you may want to exa-mine several of the following sites for acquiring these services online, or at least familiarize yourself with several important testing alterna-tives. If you enjoy taking self-assessment tests to probe your "inner self," you'll love many of the sites outlined in the remainder of this chapter. Some of the sites featured here offer relatively sophisticated fee-based tests whereas others offer free sample tests and quizzes. All of these sites are worth visiting just to discover what you should probably be doing, first.

MAPP	Assessment
assessment.com	

You can't miss this firm online since it has developed affiliate partnerships with several employment websites that directly link to this site as part of a revenue-sharing relationship. Known as MAPP (Motivational Appraisal of Personal Potential), this company offers a free online career analysis for sampling their assessment instruments. It also offers a variety of products in the form of assessment appraisals, profiles, and reports that focus on motivation and career interests: Student Appraisal, Career Appraisal, Personal Appraisal, and a MAPP Match™ for individuals. The MAPP Match™, for example, helps individuals explore different jobs and careers by matching their test results with over 1,000 jobs in the U.S. Department of Labor's O*NET database. The cost is $19.95, but the firm often runs online specials for $9.95. This company understands career planning and job search fundamentals when it states on its site that "Assessment testing is the first step to establish the learner's strengths and career goals." This could become your one-stop shop for career testing.

CareerHub	Assessment
careerhub.org	**Myers-Briggs Type Indicator®**

Welcome to a site operated by real career professionals with real career tools for organizing an effective job search. This is the closest you'll get to an online version of the _Myers-Briggs Type Indicator®_ – a sample test with interpretation. Operated by Consulting Psychologists Press (cpp-db.com), which has proprietary rights to the _Myers-Briggs Type Indicator®_, _Strong Interest Inventory®_, and the _Skills Confidence Inventory_, the site provides useful information on the career planning and decision-making processes, explains the various devices, and includes linkages to career professionals (through the National Board of Certified Counselors, www.nbcc.org) who are certified to administer the various inventories and tests produced by this company. This site also is linked to the publisher's new online training website, SkillsOne.com. If you want to get a good overview of what ingredients should go into sound career decision-making – from taking tests to using career counselors – be sure to visit this site. Indeed, this is a place you should visit before using any employment website that encourages you to post your resume online and explore its job board.

Keirsey Character Sorter and Keirsey Temperament Sorter keirsey.com	Assessment Keirsey Instruments

Based on the *Myers-Briggs Type Indicator®* and Dr. Kersey's two bestselling books, ***Please Understand Me*** and ***Please Understand Me II***, the Keirsey temperament approach classifies individuals into four temperaments: Guardian, Artisan, Idealist, and Rational. This site provides information on these two assessment devices, contrasting them with what they see as the less stable results of the *Myers-Briggs Type Indicator®*. Offers online questionnaires for taking tests in English, Spanish, Portuguese, German, Norwegian, Swedish, Bosnian, Czech, and Danish.

PersonalityType personalitytype.com	Assessment Type

This is the website of psychologists and bestselling authors Paul D. Tieger and Barbara Barron-Tieger (***Do What You Are***, ***Nurture By Nature***, ***The Art of Speedreading People***, and ***Just Your Type***). Using the popular personality type approach (based on the *Myers-Briggs Type Indicator®* and a whole school of "Type" psychologists who provide answers to all kinds of life challenges through their typological analyses), they offer an online quiz to help you identify your "Type." They claim this information will help you better deal with your career, love life, parenting skills, and communication with others – like a key to unlocking all of life's little and big problems. The site includes linkages to professional organizations and Type experts as well as FAQs, a store, and their books.

Personality Online   Assessment
spods.net/personality

This inviting site will really help you probe various dimensions of your personality. It includes nine self-scoring personality tests as well as information on analysis and resources relating to personal development. Several of the tests have implications for career decision-making: Keirsey Temperament Sorter, The Enneagram, Personality Profile, The Geek Test, The Nerd Test, and the Maykorner Test. The site also includes a few fun tests: The Love Test, The Colour Test, and The Purity Test. The site is especially noted for the Enneagram, a popular self-discovery device, which measures personality along nine different scales and which are linked to several personality traits; it includes 180 questions, resulting in the user being classified into nine different types: Perfectionist, Giver, Performer, Tragic Romantic, Observer, Devil's Advocate, Epicure, Boss, and Mediator (for more information on the Enneagram, visit ennea.com). The 80-statement Personality Profile measures users on 14 different profiles or "types" which are related to personality traits.

Self-Directed Search   Assessment
self-directed-search.com

This is the home site for John Holland's popular *Self-Directed Search (SDS)* which is used by millions of students and job seekers each year. The SDS classifies individuals into six categories: Realistic, Investigative, Artistic, Social, Enterprising, and Conventional. A proprietary self-assessment device produced by Psychological Assessment Resources (PAR), the SDS has influenced the thinking of many career counselors and is the basis for much of Richard Bolles's self-assessment devices, including his popular *Quick Job Hunting Map*. This site explains the SDS and provides an example of an SDS report for someone with an ESC Holland code. Visitors to this site can take an online version of the SDS and have the results printed out (8-12 page report) for $8.95 (takes credit cards online). The site also includes information on selecting a career counselor, along with linkages to the National Career Development Association (ncda.org) and the National Board of Certified Counselors (www.nbcc.org).

Birkman Method	**Assessment**
Princeton Review Career Quiz	
review.com/career/article.cfm?id=career/car_quiz_intro	

This 24-question quiz is designed to help users determine their most likely interests and work style for making better career choices. After registering and taking this free online quiz, you receive lots of information on jobs and careers relating to the analysis of your answers. Much of the same information is found in the book, *The Princeton Review Guide to Your Career*. A popular quiz that often provides surprising results for both job seekers and career counselors.

Analyze My Career	**Assessment**
analyzemycareer.com	

This site offers numerous tests and assessment devises for job seekers through its Test Center – aptitude, personality, occupational interest, and entrepreneurial index. It also includes a "suite" – an integrated report called "Expert Opinion." While this site includes a free sample section, most tests are fee-based.

This is an excellent one-stop shop for meeting several testing needs.

U.S. Department of Interior	Assessment
www.doi.gov/octc/typescar.html	**MBTI Career Chart**

For a good example of how the *Myers-Briggs Type Indicator®* relates to specific jobs and careers (without having to take the test) visit this useful page which includes 16 personality types with corresponding jobs and careers linked to each. If, for example, you are an ISTJ type, chances are you will enjoy being an engineer, stock broker, police officer, or real estate agent.

Career Services Group	Assessment
careerperfect.com	

Offers information and advice on various types of career inventories and tests: career interest, values, skills, and personality. Includes a self-scored "Work Preference Inventory." Also includes three software programs which can be purchased through the site's store: *CareerDesign* ($49.95), *The Right Job Fit* ($34.95), and *InterviewSmart* ($9.95).

Personality and IQ Tests	Assessment
www.davideck.com	

This site is jam-packed with linkages to a variety of personality, IQ, love, health, career, and other fun tests. Each test is rated on a scale of 0 to 4. The personality test section includes the IPIP-NEO (competitor to the *Myers-Briggs Type Indicator®*), Enneagram, Quizbox.com Personality, LuscherColour, King-domality Personality, Keirsey Temperament, Keirsey Temperament Sorter II, MayKorner Personality, Goofy Personality, and more than 20 other tests. The career test section includes the Microsoft Online Skills Assessment (for fitting into the IT industry), Typing Test, Are You a Risk Taker?, Situation Maker or Taker?, The Entrepreneur Test, Panhandling Effectiveness Survey, Birkman Method Career Style Summary, and The Career Key.

QueenDom   Assessment
queendom.com

Test junkies will enjoy exploring this site. It includes numerous personality, intelligence, and health-related tests and questionnaires. "Test junkie" section includes linkages to several career-related tests on the Internet.

Tests on the Web   Assessment
2h.com

This bare-bones site includes a variety of IQ, personality, and entrepreneurial tests found on the World Wide Web. The tests are listed by title and accompanied by a short description and the amount of time to complete each one. The personality test section includes 23 tests, including PROFILER, Keirsey Temperament Sorter, VALS, Kingdomality, Power Test, Stress-O-Meter, Life Style Test, Type A Personality Test, Communication Skills, The MayKorner Personality Test, Self-Esteem Test, Anxiety Test, Balance Test, and Are You Assertive?

Fortune.com   Assessment
fortune.com/careers/

Fortune Magazine's website offers eight free quizzes for employees and job seekers:

- *What's Your Ideal Career?*
- *How High Is Your Work EQ?*
- *Are Your Employees Ready to Change?*

- _Do You Deserve a Raise?_
- _Will You Be Promoted Soon?_
- _Is It Time to Switch Jobs?_
- _What's Your Charisma Quotient?_
- _Do You Have a Fear of Success?_

Profiler	Assessment
profiler.com	

The CISS (Campbell™ Interest and Skill Survey) online assessment is designed to help job seekers discover their right fit in the world of work. The CISS report compares test results with people who are successfully employed in the same fields. Costing $17.95, the personalized report covers nearly 60 occupations and includes a comprehensive career planner for interpreting results.

CareerLab.com	Assessment
careerlab.com	

Operated by career advisor and author William S. Frank, this site includes a lengthy paper and pencil self-discovery exercise on "How to Create Your Career Blueprint or Vision." The exercise is divided into three parts:

- Likes and Dislikes
- Career Blueprint
- Ideal First Month

The "Testing and Assessment" section of this site lists several instruments which can be purchased online and includes 30 minutes to two hours of personal consultation:

- _Campbell Interest and Skill Survey (CISS)_
- _Strong Interest Inventory_
- _Myers-Briggs Type Indicator (MBTI)_

- *Myers-Briggs Type Indicator - Step II*
- *16-Personality Factors Profile*
- *FIRO-B*
- *California Psychological Inventory (CPI)*
- *The Birkman Method*
- *Campbell Leadership Index*

This section of the site includes good descriptions of each instrument, especially the use of the highly respected Birkman Method.

College Board   **Assessment**
myroad.com

Presented by the College Board, the tests offered on this specialty site help students get a better understanding of themselves for planning their college and career. Includes career assessments, personality type, *QuickStarts*, and the *ORA Personality Profiler*.

CareerLeader™   **Assessment**
www.careerdiscovery.com/careerleader

CareerLeader™ is a comprehensive business career development tool designed to help individuals discover their best career in business. Developed by Drs. James Waldroop and Timothy Butler, directors of MBA Career Development Programs at Harvard Business School, it's an interactive, online program used by over 120 top business and MBA programs in the U.S. and Europe to guide students and help companies retain employees. It includes three tests that focus on business-relevant interests, values, and abilities to help individuals with their business careers. The resulting profiles recommend the best career path matches. Comes with a full money-back guarantee within seven days of purchase.

Careers By Design®   Assessment
careers-by-design.com

This company offers four popular assessment devices online followed by telephone counseling sessions for interpreting results:

- *Strong Interest Inventory®*
- *Myers-Briggs Type Indicator®*
- *FIRO-B™*
- *The 16 Personality Factors Questionnaire*

Since the site does not reveal prices for these instruments and consultation services, you'll need to call this company at 562-424-0527 for pricing information.

Career Interests Game   Assessment
http://web.missouri.edu/~cppcwww/holland.shtml

Based on Dr. John Holland's *Self-Directed Search*, this quick and easy game is designed to demonstrate how different interests and skills might best relate to various career areas as well as programs of study at the University of Missouri. A very clever use of the SDS which illuminates its many appealing features.

The Career Key   Assessment
ncsu.edu/careerkey

This site is developed as a free public service through the College of Education at North Carolina State University. Using Dr. John Holland's *Self-Directed Search*, the site is designed to help users make better career decisions through self-assessment. Includes online exercises.

Futurestep   **Assessment**
futurestep.com
(futurestep.com/cndt12/sign_in/sample_main.asp)

This site is operated by the executive recruiting firm of Korn/
Ferry International and the *Wall Street Journal*. It includes
sample results from two assessment devices used by Korn/Ferry
International:

- *Career Style Feedback*
- *Desired Job Characteristics*

GSIA Carnegie Mellon   **Assessment**
www.gsia.cmu.edu/afs/andrew/gsia/coc/student/assess.html

Developed for students in the Graduate School of Industrial
Administration (GSIA) at Carnegie Mellon University, this is
a paper and pencil self-assessment exercise that generates a
great deal of information on the individuals. It asks such
questions as *"Describe yourself in one sentence," "What challenges
you the most?," "How have you set yourself apart from the crowd?,"*
and *"What are the 10 most important things you are looking for in a
job?"* Includes a link to the CareerLeader™ program at Harvard
University (careerdiscovery.com).

Interest Finder Quiz   **Assessment**
myfuture.com/career/interest.html

This online quiz helps users decide whether to go to college or
look for a job and what are the best jobs for them. Includes a
checklist of 60 "like" items which are scored. Analyzes answers
and assigns the test taker to two of six work groups related to
Dr. John Holland's SDS: Realistic, Investigative, Artistic,
Social, Enterprising, or Conventional.

The Highlands Program   Assessment
highlandsprogram.com

Includes three online interactive career and life planning quizzes that deal with several important career questions:

- *Are You a Victim of the Lemming Conspiracy?*
- *How Big is Your Vision?*
- *How Satisfied Are You At Work?*

Jackson Vocational Interest Survey   Assessment
jvis.com

Enables visitors to take an online version of the Jackson Vocational Interest Survey. The survey provides a detailed picture of an individual's career interests. It includes 289 pairs of job-related activities. The cost includes a detailed report showing your career interest patterns with related matching occupations.

Emotional Intelligence Quotient   Assessment
www.utne.com/azEq2.tmpl

Daniel Goleman's book, *Emotional Intelligence: Why It Can Matter More Than IQ for Character, Health, and Lifelong Achievement*, is the basis for this self-scoring instrument. Includes 10 multiple choice questions which yield a score that is translated into your emotional quotient.

OnlineProfiles   Assessment
onlineprofiles.com

This site includes four different instruments for making career choices:

- *Career Advantage*
- *Improving Performance at Work*
- *Communication and Problem Solving*
- *Understanding Others at Work*

Emode	Assessment
www.emode.com/emode/careertest.jsp	

This fun site includes several types of tests relating to personality, romance, relationships, health, careers, and other aspects of life. The career section includes 15 tests relating to everything from leadership and risk-taking to IQ, identity, and stress.

Humanmetrics	Assessment
humanmetrics.com	

This Israel-based company offers a free online version of the Jung-Myers-Briggs typology for identifying your personality type. Also offers a few other assessment devices, such as Small Business Entrepreneur Profiles and Rick Attitudes Profiler

Quick Personality Test	Assessment
http://users.rcn.com/zang.interport/personality.html	

It doesn't get much quicker than this form and color test – just click onto the most appealing of 9 shapes. The results sound very similar to your daily horoscope, which may actually yield better results!

Inner Self Personality Test	Assessment
www1.wiwo.nl/innerself	

This 60-question test, which takes about 20 minutes to complete, is designed for those who want to improve their life by better understanding their personality. Includes one question per screen. Generates an online score. Yields an abbreviated and extensive analysis of one's personality.

Contacting a Career Professional

If you feel you need the testing and assessment services of a professional career counselor, especially someone you can meet with to administer and interpret test results, you should explore the many resources found on these five websites for career professionals:

- **National Board of Certified Counselors, Inc.**   www.nbcc.org

- **National Career Development Association**   ncda.org

- **Career Planning and Adult Development Network**   careernetwork.org

- **Career Masters Institute**   cminstitute.com

- **Professional Resume Writing and Research Association (PRWRA)**   prwra.com

For additional resources on career professionals who might be able to assist you with testing and assessment, please explore several websites identified in Chapter 12 on career counseling and coaching.

Microsoft
eLearn
Microsoft

eLearn Home | What the industry is saying |

LRN & LRN 2.0 Toolkit
LRN FAQs

Download the **LRN**2.0
Toolkit now...

Resources for Online Learning

Welcome to Microsoft eLearn

Welcome to the Microsoft eLearn site. Here you will find the latest information about online content, and resources available today from Microsoft and our eLearning vendors. By providing the enabling technology, content, and services in eLearning – our goal is to enable anytime, anywhere access to information for knowledge workers. Whether you are an educator, trainer, solution provider, global company, or just interested in what Microsoft is doing in the area of eLearning—we have something for you.

Enabling anytime, anywhere
access to information

University of Phoenix

WHY U at PHX?   WHAT CAN I STUDY?   WHERE CAN I STUDY?   HOW DOES IT WORK?

THE UNIVERSITY OF PHOENIX.
A LEADING UNIVERSITY FOR WORKING ADULTS.

University of Phoenix

Contact Us
Campuses
Online Education
Mission Statement
Library
Student Services
Emporium Online
Publications
Search

Call Us Toll Free:

YES YOU CAN DO THIS

At University of Phoenix, we make it possible for busy adults to earn their college degree or professional certificate while maintaining their career and personal life. Specifically designed for working professionals, our innovative format provides a valuable, real-world education in the most convenient and efficient way possible.

We offer bachelor's, master's and doctoral degrees, as well as professional certificate programs in several areas, including: Business, Administration, Accounting, Management, Technology Management, Information Systems, Education, Counseling and Nursing.

Classes are offered at the times and places that work for you,

---

hobsons
CollegeView
Your College Search & Financial Aid Solution

members login

IN PARTNERSHIP WITH:
XAP YOUR WAY TO
xap.com

College Search
Scholarship Search
Test Prep Center
Virtual Tours
Financial Aid Office
Electronic Apps
Career Center
Campus Bookstore
Guidance Office
Game Room
Bulletin Board
Search/Help
CollegeView News

Key Features

Search from over 3,000 colleges to find your perfect fit

Study at a Historically Black College or University

Discover the benefits of a Christian College

Sign up to win one of five $1,000 scholarships

Unlock the secrets of financial aid

Apply online to hundreds of schools at Xap.com

Are you an international student interested in studying in the U.S?

Who's Who Students click here

Featured Schools

Take a virtual tour of hundreds of campuses - see the featured schools below for some great ones!

ARCADIA UNIVERSITY

AUDREY COHEN

Briarwood College

Capitol College

Chatham College

Clemson University

Iowa State University

SAINT JOSEPH'S COLLEGE OF MAINE

THE UNIVERSITY OF ALABAMA

7

Education and Online Learning Sites

O NE OF THE BEST WAYS TO JUMP-START AS WELL as advance your career is to acquire more marketable skills through formal education and training. On-going education and training are facts of life in today's workplace. Indeed, the skills you use today may become obsolete within the next few years. Staying marketable means constantly acquiring more education and training. While many employers operate in-house training programs, you are well advised to identify your own education and training needs in reference to your long-term career goals. Few people have valid excuses – other than avoidance – for not upgrading their skills given today's numerous educational and training opportunities. Many of these opportunities are low cost and available online.

Distance Learning

If you lack marketable skills, wish to upgrade your skill level, or need to acquire new skills to change careers, you'll discover numerous websites available to assist you with all your education and training needs. Most of these educational institutions or training groups offer courses and degrees online. Almost every major university or college now offers some type of distance learning, distance education, continuing education, and/or Internet or online education. But one of the real innovators has been the once much criticized but now high-flying University of Phoenix (phoenix.edu), which enrolls over 70,000 students (the largest private university and often called by its jealous critics the "K-Mart of private business schools") and offers over 50 percent of its undergraduate and graduate degree and certification programs online, with students never having to set foot on a traditional college campus. Even traditional institutions, such as the University of Maryland University College (umuc.edu/gen/virtuniv.html), have become pioneers in developing separate online undergraduate, graduate, and certificate programs. Many up and coming university programs, such as the highly targeted American Military University (www.amunet.edu), offer 100 percent online bachelors, masters, and certification programs which are fully accredited.

Many of these education and training institutions and programs can be found by visiting the following gateway sites:

Peterson's   **Education**
petersons.com

Peterson's, which is now part of the Thomson Learning empire, remains the leading publisher and distributor of information on educational programs. In fact, no one does it better than Peterson's, given its long history as well as recent merger with Thomson Learning, in compiling one of the most sophisticated and reliable educational databases. This site offers information on just about every type of education and training program available. It allows users to access a fabulous database on the following education and training programs and institutions:

- Colleges and Universities
- Graduate Programs
- Information Technology Programs
- Adult/Distance Learning Programs

- Training and Executive Education
- Private Schools
- Career Education and Guidance
- Summer Opportunities
- Study Abroad Programs

This site also is rich with information on college selection and includes online chats with education counselors. If you visit only one site for exploring education and training opportunities, make sure it's Peterson's.

America's Learning Exchange   Education
alx.org

This site represents your tax dollars at work for you – well worth visiting for its database (6,000 training providers and 350,000 programs, seminars, and courses) and functionality (great search capabilities). It also is included on its sister U.S. Department of Labor employment site – America's Job Bank, www.ajb.dni.us (all part of America's Career Kit). The site assists individuals and organizations in locating educational and training programs most appropriate for their needs. The search engine allows users to identify educational and training programs by subject (30 major categories), state, and delivery method. This latter search category should prove useful to many individuals who seek educational and training opportunities outside the traditional classroom. This search function currently identifies eight major delivery methods:

- Classroom
- Computer Based/CD-ROM
- Conferences
- Customized Training
- Distance (TV, Satellite, Cable)
- Media-based (Audio, Video, Print)
- Self-Study/Correspondence
- Web Based/Asynchronous Training Network

Distance Learning on the Net	Education
hoyle.com/distance.htm	

Operated by distance learning guru Glenn Hoyle, this site functions as a directory to all types of distance learning programs, products, and services on the Internet. The database includes adult education and continuing education programs, training and development programs for business and industry, colleges in North America and abroad, conferences and events, courses and classes, distance learning portals, K-12 education programs (including home schools), associations and agencies, teaching resources, technical and vocational programs, and vendors offering products and services.

International Distance Learning Course Finder	Education
www.dlcoursefinder.com	

Education and training are truly borderless once you explore this site. Claiming to be the world's largest online directory of e-learning courses, this site includes over 55,000 distance learning courses and programs offered by universities, colleges, and companies in 130 countries. You can search the site by keyword or course name, subject, country, or institution name. Also includes a list of distance learning associations by regions.

MindEdge	Education
mindedge.com	

This e-learning database and education infrastructure company contains thousands of education courses from hundreds of educational producers that offer distance and local learning programs. This site allows users to search nine ways for numerous distance learning programs and courses. Users also can search for courses that are only offered over the Internet.

The Distance Education	Education
and Training Council	
detc.org	

Formerly known as the National Home Study Council, this is the professional association and clearinghouse for the field of distance study/correspondence. Its 61 accredited members offer hundreds of courses in a variety of different distance learning formats and disciplines, from military training and truck driving courses to hospitality and hypnosis programs. Since many business schools and correspondence programs are controversial (often diploma mills operating on the edge with government educational assistance monies), you are well advised to visit this site for information on accreditation and members. Includes a directory of accredited institutions, subjects taught, degree programs, and useful resources.

| Bear's Guides | Education |
| www.degree.net/books/bearsguide.htm | |

Two leading experts on distance learning, John and Mariah Bear (authors of _Bears' Guide to Earning Degrees by Distance Learning, College Degrees by Mail and Internet, Best MBAs by Distance Learning,_ and _Best Computer Degrees by Distance Learning_), offer advice on distance learning programs. The site also includes information on 100 of the top distance learning programs (click on to the "Schools" button at the top) and links to information on the distance learning arena (click on "Links").

Major Online Educational Programs

Leading educational institutions, publishers, and technology companies have gone into the online education business within the past few years. Five of the major players include the following:

University of Phoenix   Education
phoenix.edu

This is one of the real innovators in developing online education and distance learning programs. It has surprised many traditional universities as it has become the largest university in the United States even though it has no central campus. With over 70,000 students enrolled in its many programs, the University of Phoenix grants traditional undergraduate and graduate degrees as well as offers certificate and special training programs at more than 90 learning centers across the country and via the Internet. This site outlines its many programs and services for students, faculty, corporations, and other parties.

Capella University   Education
capellauniversity.edu

Started in 1993, this innovative online university offers more than 400 courses relevant to undergraduate and graduate degree programs in 40 areas of specialization. Currently offers degree programs through the schools of business, education, human services, psychology, and technology. Offers special programs for military personnel, community colleges, and corporate employees. Includes a quiz to find out if you fit the profile of a successful online learner. A well organized site that will give you an up-close look at what an online university is all about – from a virtual library to alumni links.

Kaplan Colleges   Education
kaplancollege.com

This is a sleeper site – a lot more to what initially appears to be just another company offering online educational services. This is big and it's getting bigger. Kaplan Colleges, which has been in the education business since 1937 and is now owned by the Washington Post Company, delivers educational programs via the Internet. As part of Kaplan, Inc. (kaplan.com), it's a leading provider of educational and career services, especially test prep and college admissions books and software. It also is the largest shareholder in Brass Ring (brassring.com), which appears as the career resource link for Kaplan Colleges. Offers several schools and programs of study: Kaplan College, College for Professional Studies, and Concord University School of Law (based in California). Under Kaplan College, these programs include AS, BS, and MS degrees and certificates in business and information technology. Under the College of Professional Studies, students can pursue studies in paralegal studies, legal nurse consulting, and criminal justice. Includes assessment tests for various programs. Operates an office/campus in Davenport, Iowa. Recently acquired Quest Education Corporation, a leading provider of post-secondary education with more than 13,000 students in 20 schools located in 11 states. Also is linked to education services provided by Dearborn Financial Services (www.dearborn.com) which is a division of Kaplan Professional (www.kaplanprofessional.com). Kaplan continues to be a major and growing player in the online education and career business, given the continuing integration of its various education and career businesses.

Harcourt Learning Direct   Education
harcourt-learning.com

Now part of the Thomson Learning publishing empire, this company has been providing distance learning services around the world for more than 100 years. It offers over 60 courses in six countries (U.S., Canada, United Kingdom, Australia, New Zealand, and the Netherlands). The courses cover the fields of administration, building trade, computers, creative/design, education, electrical/electronics, engineering, English, legal/medical, management, mechanical, security, and travel and hospitality. They also offer a U.S. high school diploma and ASB (Associate in Specialized Business) and AST (Associate in Specialized Technology) degrees. Also provides links to its other distance learning programs: California College for Health Sciences (www.cchs.edu) and Business and Industrial Training (primarily computer-based training courses) for corporations (harcourt-learning.com/b_and_i/cbt_courses.html).

Microsoft eLearn   Education
microsoft.com/eLearn

Microsoft Corporation has entered the education field in a big way. In fact, this is Microsoft's online learning site which is linked to several of the employment websites we identified in Chapter 5. It offers numerous web-based training programs for individuals and companies. As might be expected, most of these programs focus on using Microsoft IT products.

Numerous other websites offer an incredible number of online education and training opportunities. We recommend visiting the following sites for exploring various online courses and institutional options. Several of the non-university companies offer a wide range of courses and certification programs aimed at individuals in need of improving their technical skills:

- Brainbench, Inc.   brainbench.com
- Continuing Education
  University 4 You   ceu4u.com
- Cyber U   cyberu.com
- Entrinski   entrinsik.com
- Jacksonville University   www.ju.edu
- Mindleaders   mindleaders.com
- Quest Education Corp.   questeducation.com
- Regis University   www.regis.edu
- Saint Leo University   saintleo.edu
- Thinq   thinq.com

Useful Associations and Companies

For more information on distance learning and online education and training, visit the following associations and companies:

- America's Distance
  Learning Consortium   www.adec.edu
- Distance Education and
  Training Council   detc.org
- Distance Learning
  Channel   www.ed-x.com
- Distance Learning
  Resource Network   dlrn.org
- Educause   www.educause.edu
- International Association
  of Continuing Education
  and Training   iacet.org
- International Internet
  Learning Association   www.iila.net
- Learning Resources
  Network   lern.org
- United States Distance
  Learning Association   usdla.org
- University Continuing
  Education Association   www.nucea.edu
- World Association for
  Online Learning   waoe.org

Traditional Education Programs

Several websites focus on helping individuals locate colleges and universities which offer on-campus courses and programs. As noted above, Peterson's (petersons.com) includes a huge database on such educational institutions and programs. Two other websites also provide useful information on college selection and finance:

College Guide   Education
mycollegeguide.org

If you're looking for a traditional college or university campus for education and training, this site helps identify campuses that meet certain criteria, such as region, estimated annual cost, size of freshman class, surrounding community size, and school type. It also includes information about colleges and the two most important questions – how to get in and how to finance it all.

College View   Education
collegeview.com

If you're interesting in identifying the right college or university to meet your education needs, try the search features on this useful site. Users can search over 3,000 colleges by selecting 14 different criteria for finding the right "fit." The site also includes useful information on scholarships, test preparation, financial aid, and electronic applications, as well as includes a guidance office, career center, and bulletin board.

Career Explorer   Education
careerexplorer.net

This unique site is designed to help prospective students find information on career opportunities and select the right schools for pursuing educational and career goals. One of the few websites to focus on exploring both education and career opportunities. Includes both career and school search options, numerous links to educational institutions, articles on selecting the best vocational schools or colleges, financial aid tips, and career planning advice. Offers job postings, a resume database, a free scholarship search, aptitude and assessment tests, and links to *Cliffs Notes* and other resources.

8

Career Information, Advice, and Research Sites

W HILE MOST EMPLOYMENT WEBSITES FOCUS ON the needs of employers with resume databases and job postings, some websites are primarily designed to assist job seekers with various steps in their job search. Often operated by career professionals rather than advertisers and entrepreneurs, these sites include a great deal of useful information, tips, and advice on how to conduct an effective job search: assessment, research, resumes and letters, networking, interviews, negotiations, and career services.

Career Information and Advice

You can find a wealth of career information on the Internet in the form of articles, quizzes, and directories dealing with everything from employment trends to salary negotiations. The following sites are especially noted for their collection of career information designed to assist job seekers with various stages of the job search:

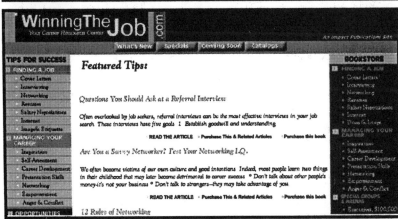

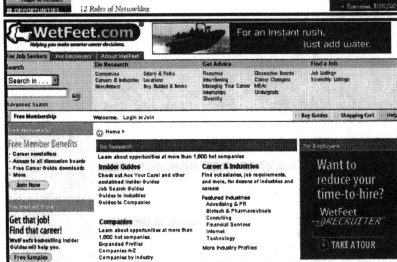

America's CareerInfoNet (ACINet)   Career Information
www.acinet.org/acinet

This is a really useful information-rich website designed to help job seekers, employers, human resource specialists, and workforce development specialists make smart career decisions based upon sound information about the job market. Once again brought to you by the government, ACINet is another U.S. Department of Labor career center linked to two other useful job centers – America's Job Bank (www.ajb.dni.us) and America's Learning Exchange (alx.org). This site focuses on providing useful career information. It includes occupational outlook data from the latest edition of the *Occupational Outlook Handbook* as well as information on the fastest growing and declining occupations and those with the most openings, largest employment, and highest pay. Its "Career Tools" section includes a unique section called "Employability Checkup" where users can get some sense of how difficult it would be to find a similar job at a similar wage if they became immediately unemployed. This section also includes a useful employer locator, licensed occupations, job description writer, financial aid advisor, and a career exploration area which also includes several downloadable videos on a variety of occupations. The "Career Resources" section includes a library of more than 4,000 links to resources (articles and videos) that deal with hundreds of career issues, from employment and wage trends to researching employers, exploring job and resume banks, and acquiring relocation information. You'll also find useful information on wages, job requirements (knowledge, skills, and abilities), and state-by-state labor market information.

Riley Guide   Career Information
www.dbm.com/jobguide (or rileyguide.com)

As noted in Chapter 4 on gateway employment sites, this site is the work of career librarian Margaret F. Dikel who clearly understands the job search process and has organized her massive database accordingly. It's presented around key categories that primarily relate to the needs of job seekers:

- What's New
- Prepare for a Job Search
- Resumes and Cover Letters
- Targeting and Researching Employers
- Executing Your Job Search Campaign
- Job Listings
- Networking, Interviewing, and Negotiating
- Salary Guides and Guidance
- Information For Recruiters
- A-Z Index

Each category includes annotated links to other sites that provide information, advice, or additional resources. For example, under Resumes and Cover Letters, the site includes a partial list of resume and cover letter books with links to the publishers as well as linkages to sites with information, advice, or services relating to CVs, portfolios, video portraits, and resume broadcasting. While never complete and with many absences, nonetheless, this site compiles a wealth of job search information from other websites. The A-Z Index has it all!

Quintessential Careers	Career Information
quintcareers.com	**and Advice**

You can see the fingerprints of a career professional all over this site, which is primarily designed to help college students get into college and conduct an effective job search based upon a sound understanding of what ingredients should go into the job search. The job and career sections also are relevant to all types of job seekers – not just college students and recent graduates. As a major job and career portal, this site includes over 1,000 pages of content with numerous helpful career articles and linkages to other employment websites. Most of the articles are authored by Dr. Randall S. Hansen and Katharine Hansen who also are authors of the book *Dynamic Cover Letters* (see order form at the end of this book). The site also includes a "Career Doctor" Q&A section (with Dr. Randall S. Hansen and also found on careershop.com), a career tutorial section, and a free online newsletter. You'll want to bookmark this site and refer to it several times during your job search.

Vault.com	**Career Information**
vault.com	**and Advice**

This is a very busy site that takes some time to figure out what it actually does, which is a lot of different things related to employment, job seekers, employers, and recruiters. You can easily get lost in its multiple channels and sections. Developed by the unsuccessful offline publishers of the *Vault Reports*, this flashy online venture capital operation is trying to be all things to everyone. In so doing, it offers a wealth of resources in the form of information, advice, and research. You can browse numerous message boards, ask career experts questions, have someone review your resume, network with others, read career news, sample one of Vault Reports's career and industry guides (can purchase 15 different ones), and research selected companies ("Premium" and "Law Firms"). The site also has developed special communities dealing with law, finance, and consulting, as well as operates a bookstore. And, of course, the site includes a resume database and job postings. But it's an especially useful site for job seekers in search of information and advice on employers and various steps in the job search.

Wetfeet	**Career Advice**
wetfeet.com	**and Research**

This site specializes in providing a wealth of career information and advice to job seekers which it also syndicates to other employment websites. Consequently, you might find some of their articles on several websites we reviewed in Chapter 5. Wetfeet specializes in conducting employment research, producing short career news and job search articles. The "For Job Seekers" section of this site is divided to focus on the three actions job seekers need to take:

- Do Research
- Get Advice
- Find a Job

Its "Do Research" section is especially useful for job seekers interested in researching companies, careers and industries, locations, salary and perks, and publications. The "Get Advice" section includes numerous short articles on resumes, interviews, managing your career, internships, diversity, career changers, MBAs, and undergrads, as well as discussion boards.

WinningTheJob	**Career Advice**
www.winningthejob.com	

This is our own career information, advice, and resource website. It's designed to provide job seekers and employees, from entry-level to CEO, with sound advice on finding jobs and managing their careers. Offering numerous tips for success in the form of one- to three-page articles, it includes expert advice on everything from developing a career objective, writing resumes and letters, networking, interviewing, and negotiating a compensation package for job seekers, to career development, empowerment, assessment, communication, stress management, and anger control for managing the day-to-day details of one's job. This site also is linked to our three other career websites that focus on career resources (books, videos, software) and syndicated career content:

- Career Bookstore   impactpublications.com
- Career Content   contentforcareers.com
- Military Transition   veteransworld.com

Several mainstream business magazines and newspapers offer excellent career articles and advice through their online sites. These four in particular are well worth bookmarking and visiting frequently:

- **Business Week**   businessweek.com
- **Fast Company**   fastcompany.com
- **Fortune**   fortune.com
- **Washington Post**   washingtonjobs.com

Several career experts, who have written books and/or write syndicated career columns for newspapers and magazines, also maintain their own sites or their content can be found on other sites that archive their many articles. In fact, you may find the tips and advice of these experts to be especially informative, since many are in a Q&A format and respond to current issues facing job seekers and employees:

- **Richard Nelson Bolles**   jobhuntersbible.com
- **Paul and Sarah Edwards**   paulandsarah.com
- **Dale Dauten**   dauten.com
- **Anne Fisher (Ask Annie)** fortune.com/fortune/careers
- **Andrea Kay**   andreakay.com
- **Joyce Lain Kennedy**   sunfeatures.com
- **Carol Kleiman**   chicagotribune.com/go/
                               kleiman
- **Ron and Caryl Krannich**   www.winningthejob.com
- **Hal Lancaster**   careerjournal.com/columnists
- **Fran Quittal**   careerbabe.com
- **Rob Rosner**   workingwounded.com
- **Barbara Sher**   barbarasher.com
- **Martin Yate**   careerbrain.com

Career Research

Conducting an effective job search requires doing a great deal of research on jobs, companies, employers, and salaries. While much of this research function gets carried out during the process of networking for information, advice, and referrals, much of it should also take place on the Internet. Indeed, numerous websites offer rich databases for conducting research. These include company directories, listings of associations and nonprofit organizations, financial reports of publicly held companies (through SEC), company profiles, business news, and key contact information, including names, addresses, phone/fax numbers, and emails of officers.

If your research skills are a bit rusty, or if you're not sure where to start online, you should visit Debbie Flanagan's very useful website, which is actually a tutorial on how to research companies online for free. She takes you step-by-step through the research process, as well as provides hot links to all the major databases and research sites:

http://home.sprintmail.com/~debflanagan/index.html

Business Resources

CEO Express	Research
ceoexpress.com	

We really like this site for its wealth of in-your-face information. It doesn't get much more intuitive than a front page that lays out all its resource possibilities. This is the type of site you'll want to bookmark and refer to daily for information, from newspapers and magazines to news feeds and search engines. Pay particular attention to a very small button near the top center – "Business Research." It will take you to an incredible number of resources for conducting research on all aspects of companies. The "Industry Center" delivers even more useful links to key resources. Be sure to spend some time exploring this gateway site. It's a remarkable research resource!

Hoovers	Research
hoovers.com	

This popular site includes a wealth of information on thousands of companies in Hoover's database. It's especially useful for job seekers who wish to conduct research on particular companies as well as link to their websites and employment sections. While much of the information on this site is free, other more detailed research information is by monthly subscription fees only. Hoover's database includes company contact information, profiles, financials, and a link to the company's employment section ("Company Job Openings"). The "List of Lists" section includes numerous articles that rank companies by various criteria – fastest growing, best to work for, worst performers, most layoffs, most admired, coolest, best locations, best for women. The "Career Development" section will take you to a searchable database of over 300 employment websites operated by wantedjobs.com. Includes a training center through a linkage with thinq.com. A rich research and information site for understanding corporate America.

| **CorporateInformation** | **Research** |
| corporateinformation.com | |

Operated by Winthrop Corporation, this is one of the best sites on the web for finding information on over 350,000 companies in more than 100 countries around the world. Includes a variety of search engines for locating companies in the United States and abroad. Nothing fancy – just good search features that deliver the goods. Includes business news.

| **@brint.com, The BizTech Network** | **Research** |
| brint.com | |

This is another excellent online resource for researching companies. It claims to be the premier business and technology portal and global community network for e-business, information, technology, and knowledge management as well as "Your survival networking for the brave new world of business." If any of these are your fields of expertise, you're well advised to explore the numerous linkages on this site. Includes numerous articles and the latest news on these cutting-edge fields.

AllBusiness   Research
www.allbusiness.com

This is one of the largest small business directories on the Internet with more than 700,000 companies in its database. It classifies businesses into nearly 9,000 categories. Includes numerous useful articles, forms, services, and checklists for eight major business categories: employment and HR; Internet and technology; office management; legal; sales and marketing; finance and accounting; business planning; and insurance. Offers a virtual gold mine of information for small businesses. In fact, it may motivate you to explore starting your own business rather than work for someone else! It's all here – sample business plans, legal advice, hiring/firing tips, financing, marketing, and lots more for developing a sound business.

BizWeb   Research
bizweb.com

This business guide includes 46,323 companies listed in 207 categories. Just click to any business category and you'll get an alphabetical listing of companies with short 4-15 word annotations. Includes keyword search engine. Links to Electric Library (elibrary.com) for conducting more advanced searches.

Business.com   Research
business.com

This high trafficked site (2 million visitors a month) focuses on developing one of the largest online directories for conducting business research. It currently offers over 25,000 categories and subcategories of businesses and more than 400,000 business websites. Includes a search engine, detailed profiles on 64,000 companies, an Industry Center on 58 industries, and business news aggregated from the *Financial Times*, *Industry Standard*, Dow Jones, and Reuters. Supported by McGraw-Hill, Cahners Business Information, and Pearson plc.

Thomas	Research
thomasregional.com	

One of the most reliable names in business directories offers free access to a searchable database of more than 550,000 distributors, manufacturers, and service companies in the United States. Users can browse over 6,000 product/services categories from a menu of over 100 main categories. Also covers events and trade shows, government resources, and industry and professional organizations. Includes numerous useful resources for conducting online business research.

Harris InfoSource	Research
www.harrisinfo.com	

Designed primarily for sales and marketing professionals, this website includes a searchable database with profiles of over 600,000 manufacturers and service establishments. Allows users to search by location, industry, company, size, and contact information.

Public Records Resources

EDGAR	Research
www.sec.gov/edgar.shtml	

This is the Filings and Forms (EDGAR) section of the U.S. Securities and Exchange Commission (SEC). The SEC requires that all public companies with assets in excess of $10 million and more than 500 shareholders must file registration statements, periodic reports, and other forms electronically through

EDGAR. This information can be accessed and downloaded for free from this site. Just follow the Quick EDGAR Tutorial and you'll be able to research the records of thousands of public companies. You also can access the annual reports of numerous publically traded companies through a commercial website with a similar name: edgar-online.com.

Search Systems	Research
pac-info.com	

This site includes 4,564 free searchable public record databases, organized by state and listed in alphabetical order. This is a rich database for researching various aspects of communities, from corporations and libraries to properties and registered sex offenders in your neighborhood.

Association and Nonprofit Resources

Associations on the Net	Research
ipl.org/ref/AON	

Part of the Internet Public Library, this is a gateway site to thousands of trade and professional associations, most of which are nonprofit organizations. If you are interested in working for an association or nonprofit or exploring opportunities with companies and organizations that belong to these associations (associations and nonprofits employ about 10 million people in the U.S.), this is a good site for locating such employers. The site primarily provides links to the associations. From there you can explore the associations. Many large associations maintain their own niche job banks and resume databases to service their member organizations. These are good sources for conducting research on member organizations and for exploring job postings. Many of the associations also maintain online links with their members and related groups and resources – a great source for exploring potential employers.

AssociationCentral   Research
associationcentral.com

This is another excellent site for locating associations appropriate to your particular career interests. Organizes associations by categories and includes a search engine. Each association is profiled along with contact information and a link to the association's website. Also includes a career center, in association with headhunter.net, for posting resumes and reviewing job listings. A second niche career center is linked to the American Society of Association Executives (www.asaenet.org) for finding a job with an association. These employment websites are two of AssociationCentral's strategic partners.

American Society of   Research
Association Executives
www.asaenet.org

The American Society of Association Executives (ASAE) is the professional association of association executives as well as the premier gateway site to over 6,500 associations. If you are interested in working for an association, you should belong to this professional organization. It has its own career center which includes a resume database, job postings, and several other job search services. Everything you ever wanted to know about careers in the association world can probably be found on this site. This also is a good site for researching who's who in the association world.

GuideStar   Research
guidestar.org

If you're interested in researching the world of nonprofit organizations, try this site. It includes a searchable database of over 700,000 nonprofit organizations. The site also includes numer-

ous resources – from articles and reports – for better understanding the nonprofit sector.

Online Employment Resources

JobFactory	Research
jobfactory.com	

Job seekers can access a great deal of information from this one
site. In addition to searching thousands of other employment
sites for job postings, JobFactory includes a list of 250 top
career sites; links to classified job advertisements in 1,067
newspapers in the U.S., Canada, Asia, and Europe; a list of
3,787 job hotline telephone numbers (these include recorded
vacancy messages); and links to employer websites.

Job Search Engine	Research
job-search-engine.com	

This site basically functions as a job search engine for
locating job postings on the Internet. It searches the top 300
U.S. and Canadian job boards to identify jobs by keywords
and location. Its "Resource Center" includes linkages to
career services and specialized job sites.

Declining Companies

While you can tell a lot about the financial health and growth
prospects of companies by examining the above databases, at the same
time you should beware of declining fortunes of many companies. As
the high flying dot-com world of 2000 suddenly discovered, fortunes
can quickly disappear in a volatile economy.

The following sites are worth visiting for tracking who's downsizing
and possibly going out of business. While at times truly raunchy and
filled with gallows humor, nonetheless, these sites may raise some
important questions that you should consider asking about the

financial health and growth of a company before you accept a job offer:

- **BankruptcyData**   bankruptcydata.com
- **Business 2.0**   business2.com
                                 ecompanynow.com
- **Dismal Scientist**   dismal.com
- **Downside**   downside.com
- **Failure Magazine**   www.failuremag.com
- **FuckedCompany**   fuckedcompany.com
- **The Industry Standard**   thestandard.com/trackers/
                                 layoff
- **The Street.com**   thestreet.com
- **Red Herring**   redherring.com

In late breaking news, the day this book went to press – August 16, 2001 – the once high-flying *The Industry Standard* magazine announced it would suspend publication immediately since it, too, had become a victim of the economic downturn, which saw the dramatic decrease (79 percent) in advertising revenues. Launched in 1998 at the height of the Internet business boom, the magazine got fat on dot-com advertising revenues, which went bust in 2001. Once a symbol of the new economy and the leading chronicler of the highs and lows of the Internet industry, the continuing survival of this popular award-winning weekly print and online magazine was in serious question. It would continue its online editorial coverage while it sought a buyer to bail it out. In the meantime, it laid off most of its staff (down from 150 to six) and began seeking Chapter 11 bankruptcy protection. Ironically, *The Industry Standard* became what it covered so well – another flash Internet business that rose dramatically with an initial infusion of venture capital and advertising revenue and then declined quickly as its two main revenue streams abruptly dried up. For some observers, the impending death of *The Industry Standard* was indicative that the so-called Internet industry was no longer an industry.

Career Masters Institute

Building Bridges Across The Careers Community

WELCOME TO THE CAREER MASTERS INSTITUTE™
Career & Employment Industry's First Global Training, Development &
Professional Networking Organization

Career Masters Conference
* Click Here For Details

Member Code of Ethics
* Click Here For Details

Credentialed Career Master (CCM)
* Our Industry's Most Prestigious

Our Members Receive:
* Tools Of The Trade
* Online Training Programs
* Networking Opportunities
* Exclusive Publishing Opportunities
* Discounts
* Job Postings For Your Clients

Leadership Team
Membership Directory
Member Benefits
Testimonials
I Want To Join CMI

Impact Resume & Career Services

We write resumes that get interviews.

Home
Company Profile
Resume Samples
Services & Pricing
FAQ-How to Order
Career Resources

HOW MUCH ATTENTION WILL *YOUR RESUME* RECEIVE?
Only 15 to 30 seconds on first review!

A resume written by a **Certified Professional Resume Writer** is the key that opens the door to employment opportunities. Don't gamble your career with a poorly written resume that does not *clearly* convey your job qualifications & accomplishments.

- Is your resume an **effective marketing tool?**
- Is your resume **achievement-based?**
- Does your resume **show what you can do** for a prospective employer?
- Is your resume **getting you interviews?**
- Are you using the most **effective job search strategies?**

---

e-resume.net™

Ranked *"best of the bunch"* -LA Times

August
8

| HOME | ABOUT US | ORDER ONLINE | PRICES | OUR PROCESS | SAMPLES | CONTACT US |

WELCOME

e-resume.net is a national resume writing company combining personalized attention with the speed of the Internet to deliver professional resumes.

TELL A FRIEND

If you are impressed with the convenience and service you've experienced here at e-resume.net, please tell your friends and associates. here

HOT TOPICS

How is your resume?

don't you wish
you were better
prepared ▶

RESOURCES

After e-resume.net writes your professional resume, visit **some of these sites** to try out your new

ORDER ONLINE

Order now to receive your professionally written resume delivered on high quality resume paper.

- Ⓐ The secure method. Get started today on your resume. You can easily attach your current information and we'll take it from there. (Prices)
- Ⓑ The standard method. Tell us your name, email and phone number and we'll take care of the rest. (Prices)
- Ⓒ Telephone us Toll Free: 1-888-277-6650
- Ⓓ International customers (Outside USA & Canada) Click Here

TIPS

9

Resume and Cover Letter Sites

RESUMES ARE THE BREAD AND BUTTER OF THE ON-line employment business. Ironically, only a few years ago many career experts were predicting the end of resumes and the rise of portfolios and other forms of job search communication and applications. But the resume has become the perfect medium for new online and scannable technologies as well as for email distribution systems. Without a dynamite electronic resume, your chances of being discovered in some faceless resume database are nearly zero. More so than ever, resumes have become a necessary evil for imperfectly screening candidates.

Paper Resumes Becoming Nuisances

Given the high costs of managing paper resumes, more and more companies prefer receiving resumes by email. Indeed, for many companies it is now much easier and more cost effective to receive, scan, share, store, and retrieve an electronic resume than to handle a paper resume. As a result, some companies now discourage candidates from either mailing or faxing their resumes. Take, for example, Dow

Chemical as reported in the July 18, 2001 issue of *Business Week*. As of January 2001, Dow Chemical streamlined its hiring process with a new software system that only accepts electronic resumes. All resumes received in the mail are now automatically returned to the sender with a note saying that the prospective candidate must use the company's website to apply online with an electronic resume. In so doing, Dow Chemical reduced its average hiring time from 90 to 34 days and lowered the average cost of hiring by 26 percent as well as downsized its number of in-house recruiters from 100 to 60. Dow Chemical is not alone. As company websites become more sophisticated, and HR departments further automate the application and screening processes, paper resumes – whether scanned or hand processed – will no longer be the norm for communicating qualifications to employers. They are becoming obsolete. The trend is very clear, at least for large companies that must handle thousands of applicants and their resumes each year – HR departments increasingly prefer electronic emailed resumes that are compatible with their hiring databases.

Resumes and Cover Letters

There's something mystical or magical about resumes. While they are job seekers' calling cards for getting job interviews, when placed online they seem to take on a different life. Job seekers enter them into a mysterious resume database and wait to be called for interviews. Somehow their electronic resume is expected to work its way up into the offices of hiring officials.

The same holds true for cover letters. Many career professionals note that a well crafted cover letter is often more important to landing a job interview than a resume. How both resumes and letters best get distributed is often the key to understanding effectiveness. In the meantime, the mystery goes on!

Resumes Play a Renewed Role

How technology has changed the role of resumes and given these documents renewed importance in the employment process! Indeed, the business model defining the structure of most major employment websites focuses on the key role of the electronic resume – sites are designed to attract job seekers' resumes into searchable databases as well as quickly transmit resumes to employers. The resume, whether in electronic or paper form, is the medium by which job seekers initially connect with employers. The important questions center around resume content and how to best distribute one's resume – whether passive or active – to potential employers.

The Hunt For Resumes

The larger the resume database, the more attractive a site becomes to employers who pay higher fees to search the larger databases. Sites must constantly recruit job seekers to their operations (just "Post Your Resume") and persuade them to enter their resume into the site's resume database – an all-seasons' "hunt for resumes." Sustaining, as well as in-creasing, the number of resumes in the database is by no means an easy task, nor is it cheap to do so. Resumes quickly become dated and thus must be updated or replaced by resumes of new job seekers.

> *As a job seeker, you are constantly being hunted by online employment sites.*

As a job seeker, you are constantly being hunted by online employment sites that offer free resume services in the form of entering your resume into their online database and managing it through various options:

- create and store multiple versions of the resume
- revise the resume(s) whenever necessary
- maintain privacy or anonymity through coding options
- incorporate a job search agent that automatically emails you when a new job listing matches your criteria

You write the resume and upload it into their database, or you enter information about yourself into a standardized online resume form. These sites want your resume because they, in turn, have paying customers – employers and recruiters – looking for resumes from which to select candidates for job interviews.

The New Resume Entrepreneurs

At the same time, you're also being hunted online by professional resume writers and entrepreneurial email distributors who charge you for their specialized resume services. Many of them have linkages on a site's career resource or links section, present themselves in banner or button ads, or maintain affiliate or partnership relationships with the site on a shared revenue basis. Their pitch is always the same – the quality of your writing and distribution can be greatly enhanced by buying into their resume services. Indeed, when it comes to dealing with resumes, there is always room for improvement!

Numerous entrepreneurs are in the online resume writing and distribution business. This is a big business, from offering professional resume writing services to persuading individuals of the efficacy of "shotgunning" or "blasting" their resume to thousands of employers and recruiters. For the most part, these are not certified career counselors nor trained career professionals; most are professional writers who primarily write and produce resumes for a living. Some belong to organizations that issue professional credentials in this area.

From writing to distribution, this is both a mysterious and lucrative business. In fact, being mysterious probably contributes to making this such a lucrative business. Services of a professional resume writer, for example, usually cost anywhere from $100 to $600, depending on the level of your position – executive-level resumes are the most expensive to produce. Signing up for the services of a resume distributor, who will blast your resume to a special list of employers and recruiters who supposedly want to see your resume, usually costs from $50 to $200.

Resume and Letter Writing Tips

Many employment websites will include tips on how to write winning resumes and letters. These often come in the form of short one- to two-page articles that list the "do's" and "don'ts" of both traditional and electronic resumes. Several sites maintain an inventory of such tips in the "Career Resources" or "Resource Center" section:

- Monster.com   resume.monster.com
- America's CareerInfoNet   www.acinet.org/acinet

- JobStar   jobstar.org/tools/resume
- CareerBuilder   careerbuilder.com
- Quintessential Careers   quintcareers.com
- Wetfeet   wetfeet.com
- Jobsonline   jobsonline.com
- WinningTheJob   www.winningthejob.com
- MyJobSearch   myjobsearch.com
- Resumesion   resumesion.com

A few sites, such as vault.com, even provide a free online resume review by a career professional. Other sites, such as headhunter.net ("Resource Center"), primarily include sponsored links to companies that offer fee-based resume and distribution services. Resume writing professionals, such as author Rebecca Smith, maintain their own websites (eresumes.com) with tips on writing an electronic resume.

Professional Resume Writers

You'll have no problem finding individuals who will help you write both conventional and electronic resumes. Many can be found through your local Yellow Pages. Others maintain websites which showcase resume writing tips, testimonials from satisfied clients, and examples of their work. Indeed, the Internet is a huge shopping mall for identifying professional resume writers.

Our experience with resume writing is confirmed by many other career professionals. While most individuals can benefit from reviewing resume writing principles and examples of outstanding resumes, when it comes time to actually write their resume, they fall short in producing a first-class document. Writing a one- to two-page resume is hard work and requires special talents. Contacting a professional resume writer, with the experience and skills to produce a resume that reflects your talents, may well be worth $100 to $600, especially if it produces expected results – attracts the right employers to you. If and when you feel you need to contact a professional resume writer, you should consider exploring the resume writing talent associated with the following associations that certify resume writers and other career professionals:

- Professional Association
  of Resume Writers and
  Career Coaches   www.parw.com

- Professional Resume
  Writing and Research
  Association   prwra.com

- National Resume
  Writers' Association   nrwa.com

- Career Masters Institute   cminstitute.com

For an online state-by-state directory of professional resume writers – which also includes a useful comparative chart for surveying service fees, years of experience, certification, samples, and free critiques – visit the NetWorker Career Services' (NCS) site:

careercatalyst.com/resume.htm

At the same time, check out some of these websites which are sponsored by professional resume writers. Most of them will give you a free resume critique prior to using their fee-based services:

- A&A Resume   aandaresume.com
- A-Advanced Resume Service   topsecretresumes.com
- Advanced Career Systems   resumesystems.com
- Advanced Resumes   advancedresumes.com
- Advantage Resume   advantageresume.com
- Best Fit Resumes   bestfitresumes.com
- Cambridge Resume Service   cambridgeresume.com
- CareerConnection   careerconnection
- Career Resumes   career-resumes.com
- CertifiedResumeWriters   certifiedresumewriters.com
- eResume (Rebecca Smith's)   eresumes.com
- e-resume.net   e-resume.net
- Executiveagent.com   executiveagent.com
- Free-Resume-Tips   free-resume-tips.com

- Impact Resumes   impactresumes.com
- Leading Edge Resumes   leadingedgeresumes.com
- Resume Agent   resumeagent.com
- Resume.com   resume.com
- Resume Creators   resumecreators.com
- ResumeMaker   resumemaker.com
- Resume Writer   resumewriter.com
- WSACORP.com   www.wsacorp.com

This is only a small sampling of the hundreds of professional resume writing services available to assist you with all your resume writing, and sometimes distribution, needs. We highly recommend using a professional at critical points in your job search, which may be here!

You also may want to visit a site that specializes in creating and managing unique interactive resumes – Resumesion. This site includes numerous job search tips, along with information on designing what they consider to be the most effective type of online resume, an interactive presentation that emphasizes accomplishments and qualifications. A great new idea whose time may, or may not, have come:

resumesion.com

Resume Distribution Services

Resume distribution approaches have always been controversial, whether offline or online. Indeed, career counselors usually caution job seekers about literally "throwing money to the wind" by shotgunning, or blasting, their resumes to hundreds of employers. This is usually the approach of unfocused, and often desperate and unrealistic, job seekers. The experience is usually the same: few if any worthwhile returns. Like direct-mail responses, one can expect less than a one percent return rate. If you mail your resume to 10,000 potential employers, chances are you'll get fewer than 100 responses and even fewer than 10 positive responses. There's also a good chance you'll get zero responses for all the time, effort, and costs involved in this unfocused "wishful thinking" approach to finding a job.

There's no reason to think that this direct-mail approach to the job search gets any better when you shift mediums – from snail mail to electronic mail – by blasting your resume to hundreds of employers and recruiters by email. Nonetheless, numerous resume distribution companies would make you believe this is an effective way to market your resume. They operate resume blasting businesses that usually charge anywhere from $50 to $200 to email your resume to hundreds of employers and recruiters; some may charge thousands of dollars for more specialized blasting services (visit executive-level search sites yourmissinglink.com and www.WSACORP.com). Many of them post testimonials from satisfied clients who claim great success using this approach. But as any direct-mail specialist will tell you, response rates are largely determined by the quality of both the mailing list and the

> *The old adage that you usually get what you pay for is equally valid for the job search. . . . To be effective with this approach, you need to be the perfect ($$$) candidate.*

mailing piece. When the two come together, expect a good response rate. The problem is that you never know the quality of the email lists of these companies until *after* you use them.

We still remain skeptical about using this approach to marketing your resume. In fact, we have yet to meet any employers who would subscribe to such a questionable service. While blasting your resume by email may make you initially feel good – because you are doing something and have high hopes of reaching many potential employers and recruiters – motion does not equate momentum. In the end, it may be a waste of time and money, accompanied by dashed expectations. Indeed, if you want to quickly experience the highs and lows of conducting a job search, this approach will surely provide such an experience. Resume blasting largely violates a key principle of conducting an effective job search that leads to an excellent job "fit" – target specific employers around your specific career goals, skills, and experience. Shooting a resume en mass to hundreds of employers and recruiters is not a very targeted approach. It's a "pot luck," and sometime desperate, approach to finding any job you think you might be able to fit into. We strongly recommend that you find a job that is fit for you. You do this with a more targeted approach.

Having said all of this as a cautionary note for taming your expectations, you may still want to blast your resume for under $100, just to see if you get any "nibbles" on this type of fishing expedition. At $69.95, you don't have much to lose and perhaps much to gain if you are an experienced professional who connects with the right job. But again, don't believe all the hype surrounding this approach and have realistic expectations of what you are likely to get for only $69.95, or even $3,000. The old adage that you usually get what you pay for is equally valid for the job search. Chances are your greatest success with this approach will come in having reached key recruiters or headhunters rather than specific employers – individuals who are primarily interested in marketing candidates who are skilled and experienced enough to make over $60,000, but preferably over $100,000, a year. These individuals are in constant need of new resumes to refresh their pool of fast-aging resumes and candidates who find jobs. Indeed, many recruiters and headhunters welcome the receipt of such blasted resumes which they, in turn, can "flip" to employers for hefty finders fees, if and when one of the candidates gets a job through their "recruiting" efforts. Their sourcing "commission" is usually 20 to 30 percent of the candidate's first-year salary, which is paid by the employer. In other words, you need to be the perfect candidate for this approach. If, for example, you are making under $50,000 a year, this approach is probably a waste of time and money. Most recruiters simply don't have time, nor a market, for such low-end candidates. This approach is one way to quickly reach hundreds of recruiters whom you might not reach by other means, such as putting your resume online with brilliantpeople.com or recruitersonline.com. Indeed, if you are a near or over six-figure job seeker, you can quickly rachet up your job search, as well as go global, by using these services to contact thousands of headhunters or executive recruiters who are always looking for high quality resumes and candidates they can market to their high-paying clients. The approach does work, but it works best for only certain types of candidates who fit the needs of recruiters and headhunters.

   If and when you decide to play this game – knowing full well the odds are probably against you – start by investigating the following fee-based resume distribution firms (your cyberspace "blasters"). Try to find out the relative mix in their database of recruiters versus actual employers who might be looking for someone with your qualifications.

These sites know the "mix" since they require employers and recruiters to sign up or register to receive "free" resumes from these services. For example, one of the largest such firms, Resumezapper.com, tells you up front that they only work with third party recruiters and search firms – no employers; they primarily appeal to candidates who prefer being marketed through an executive recruiter. The recipients of these free resumes usually specify filters, so they only receive resumes that meet their marketing criteria. Not surprisingly, most of these resume distribution sites will blast your resume to almost solely to recruiters or headhunters. Some sites, such as hotresumes.com, will blast your resume to numerous sites that have resume databases, thus saving time in entering your resume into each unique resume database.

- BlastMyResume — blastmyresume.com
- Career Masters Institute — cminstitute.com (same as yourmissinglink.com)
- CareerPal — careerpal.com
- Careerxpress.com — careerxpress.com
- E-cv.com — e-cv.com
- Executiveagent.com — executiveagent.com
- HotResumes — hotresumes.com (posts to multiple job boards)
- Job Search Page — jobsearchpage.com (international focus)
- Job Village — jobvillage.com
  - (Resume Agent) — (resumeagent.com)
  - (Resumeshotgun) — (resumeshotgun.com)
- Nrecruiter.com — nrecruiter.com
- ResumeBlaster — resumeblaster.com
- Resume Booster — resumebooster.com
- ResumeBroadcaster — resumebroadcaster.com
- Resume Carpet Bomber — resumecarpetbomber.com
- Resume Path — resumepath.com
- ResumeSubmit — www.careerxpress.com
- ResumeZapper — resumezapper.com
- ResumeXpress — resumexpress.com
- RocketResume — rocketresume.com
- See Me Resumes — seemeresumes.com

- Your Missing Link   yourmissinglink.com
- WSACORP.com   www.wsacorp.com

Do It Right

As many job seekers discover when incorporating the Internet in their job search, their resume plays a key role in the whole Internet job search process. Above all, employment sites, employers, and recruiters want your online resume. Therefore, make sure you produce and distribute a first-class resume that truly reflects your skills and accomplishments. As we've outlined in this chapter, you'll find numerous online resources to help you at every stage of developing and distributing your resume. Our advice: Make sure you also visit the many assessment and testing sites identified in Chapter 6, as well as perhaps visit a professional career counselor (Chapter 12), to help you focus your resume, and your job search, around what you do well and enjoy doing. If you do this, you'll find a job that best fits you rather than try to fit into a job description that may or may not be appropriate for you. The Internet is a great tool for connecting with employers. Just make sure you're making a quality connection with a top quality resume reflecting the real you.

Pick a State: **Alabama** [dropdown]   Click here to find your new apartment!   apartments.com

About | Create a New List | Join a New List | Contact | Help | Tour | Home

Owner Login | Member Login

Welcome to Coollist

New? What is Coollist?   About Coollist
Join a List   Help!

Join one of our mailing lists:

Coollist Directory

Arts & Entertainment
Movies, Music, Radio...

Reference
Books, World Records...

Business
Stock Market, Marketing...

Regional
North America, Europe, Asia...

Computers

Login

Owner Login ?

Member Login ?

Unsubscribe

Unsubscribe ?

10

Networking, Mentoring, and Q&A Sites

I F YOU'RE LOOKING FOR QUALITY JOBS AND WISH TO shorten your job search time, be sure to initiate an ongoing networking and mentoring campaign designed to acquire employment information, advice, and referrals. You'll find numerous networking and mentoring opportunities both online and offline. Many of the Usenet newsgroups listed in Chapter 3, for example, function as important networking arenas for asking and responding to questions and for acquiring useful tips. At the same time, numerous websites also serve as important centers for performing these same functions.

Networking Sources, Skills, and Strategies

As many career professionals emphasize, networking plays a critical role in the whole job search process, from beginning to end. While the most effective networking takes place in face-to-face situations, you also can do a great deal of e-networking on the Internet. As noted in Chapter 3, be sure to check out these Usenet newsgroups for online networking opportunities:

139

- Cyberfiber   www.cyberfiber.com
- Google   groups.google.com
- JobBankUSA   jobbankusa.com/usejobs.html
- Topica   topica.com
- Usenet Info Center   metalab.unc.edu/usenet-i/
                                home.html

Also, visit these six sites for finding, or creating, mailing lists related to your career interests:

- Coollist   coollist.com
- Google   groups.google.com
- Publicly Accessible
  Mailing Lists   paml.net
- Topica   topica.com/dir/cid=561
- Yahoo! Groups   groups.yahoo.com

Many of the mega employment groups we outlined in Chapter 5, such as Monster.com, have very active chat groups and message boards through which you can network for information, advice, and referrals. The Monster.com boards are among the best on the web:

community.monster.com/boards

Vault.com also offers several useful message boards for networking:

vault.com/community/mb/mb_home.jsp

If you're uncertain how to network, or if your networking skills are somewhat rusty, you are well advised to visit these websites for information and advice on how to sharpen your networking skills:

- MyJobSearch   www.myjobsearch.com/
                                networking.html
- WetFeet   wetfeet.com/advice/
                                networking.asp
- Monster.com   content.monster.com/
                                network

- Quintessential Careers   quintcareers.com/
                            networking.html
- Riley Guide   www.dbm.com/jobguide/
                            network.html
- WinningTheJob   www.winningthejob.com
- SchmoozeMonger   www.schmoozemonger.com
- Susan RoAne   susanroane.com/free.html
- Contacts Count   contactscount.com/articles.
                            html

While there are no good online substitutes for a well developed book on networking (see, for example, *Masters of Networking, Foot in the Door, How to Work a Room, Great Connections, The Power to Get In, Power Schmoozing, Power Networking, Smart Networking,* and *The Savvy Networker* – see order form available at the end of this book or online through www.impactpublications.com), these sites will get you started in the right direction.

Associations As Networks

One of the best networking sources is through membership and activities in professional and trade associations. Many professional associations, such as the American Society for Training and Development (www.astd.org) and the Society for Human Resources Management (www.shrm.org), have numerous active local chapters that provide excellent networking opportunities. They also operate niche online career centers – complete with resume databases, job postings, and career resources – for their members. To find a professional association most closely related to your professional interests, be sure to explore these gateway sites to the world of trade and professional associations as well as related nonprofit organizations:

- **Associations on the Net**   ipl.org/ref/AON
- **AssociationCentral**   associationcentral.com
- **American Society of**
  Association Executives   www.asaenet.org
- **GuideStar**   guidestar.org

Women's Networks

Several organizations are specifically set up to encourage networking among their members. Women, in particular, may belong to several organizations that encourage networking, from business and professional groups to alumni and social groups. Some of the major women's online networking groups include:

- Advancing Women   advancingwomen.com
- American Association of
  University Women   aauw.org
- American Business
  Women's Association   abwahq.org
- Business Women's
  Network Interactive   BWNi.com
- Federally Employed Women   few.org
- iVillage   ivillage.com
- Systers   systers.org
- Women.com   women.com
- Women's Wire   womenswire.com
                                           (women.com/iVillage.com site)

In the Washington, DC area, women professionally involved with the web development and design ("new media") have created one of the best networking organizations available anywhere – complete with discussions groups and job postings:

dcwebwomen.org

If you are female and travel a lot, you'll appreciate this very unique networking site for women who want to make connections in unfamiliar places – the ultimate web-based long distance networking tool:

HERmail.net

This site could also be used for establishing long distance networking contacts for purposes other than just travel.

Alumni Groups For Networking

If you are a college graduate, one of the best places to network is through your college alumni office. Many universities operate alumni networks ostensibly designed to raise financial support from alumni but which also offer excellent opportunities for graduates to make face-to-face contacts with fellow graduates for employment information, advice, and referrals. Alumni are often asked if they would be willing to speak with other alumni about career-related matters. If they agree, they are flagged in the alumni database as someone who would be willing to help fellow graduates network. Please check with your college career center or alumni office for such formalized networking opportunities. If, for example, you are a business school graduate, from one of the "elite" institutions, you may be associated with one of higher education's best organized alumni network groups. According to a *Business Week* study, the business schools at the following institutions had the strongest and weakest alumni links (see complete story at www. businessweek.com/1996/43/b349812.htm):

School	MBA Alumni (Percent Giving)	Average Gift	MBA Alumni Clubs
Strong Links:			
▪ Dartmouth	6,818 (63%)	$418	17
▪ Virginia	5,655 (47%)	610	18
▪ MIT	5,500 (37%)	350	16
▪ Stanford	22,172 (31%)	684	47
▪ Duke	6,521 (31%)	418	14
▪ Harvard	35,378 (30%)	1,860	110
Weak Links:			
▪ Berkeley	26,455 (10%)	$496	15
▪ Indiana	11,000 (11%)	134	3
▪ Thunderbird	28,442 (13%)	123	81
▪ Texas	9,350 (14%)	136	0
▪ Rochester	7,243 (15%)	100	1

Most of these universities, as well as many of their schools and departments, have dozens of local alumni chapters throughout North America and abroad where members occasionally meet to raise funds for programs, assist graduates, and develop and strengthen personal and professional contacts with one another. As recent studies have noted, it's often the quality of the networking experience at universities – rather than the content of the educational curriculum – that is the key determinant of career success (see Seth Godin's thoughts on this story at www.fastcompany.com/online/38/sgodin.html). Harvard and Stanford universities, for example, are noted for the important role networking plays in the careers of their successful graduates. These institutions first and foremost recruit smart people into their programs and then provide a unique networking environment where students work together and form lasting bonds that often play a critical role in their continuing career success even 10, 20, or 30 years after graduation. Magazines, such as *BusinessWeek Online* (business week.com), offer unique opportunities for business school students to network online. You also should explore a few alumni sites which provide access to thousands of such alumni networks around the world:

- **Alumni.net**   alumni.net
- **Alumniconnections**   bcharrispub.com/isd/alumni
                                                connections.html
- **Planet Alumni**   planetalumni.com

Locators For Re-Building Networks

What ever happened to your old friend John Nebor who you last saw in Minneapolis three years ago at your tenth high school reunion? Remember your favorite college professor who you worked with on a special marketing project in 1993 but who you heard moved to another university in 1997? No problem; they may be just a quick click away.

You can use the Internet to find old friends and acquaintances you may have lost contact with over the years but whom you want to contact for networking purposes. Include these sites in your "network finder" folder:

- Anywho   anywho.com
- Classmates   classmates.com
- InfoSpace   infospace.com
- KnowX   knowx.com
- Switchboard   switchboard.com
- The Ultimate White Pages   theultimates.com/white
- Whowhere Lycos   whowhere.lycos.com
- WorldPages   worldpages.com
- Yahoo   people.yahoo.com

Military Locators and Buddy Finders

If you are in the military or if you are a veteran, you can check on the location of your service buddies by going to these people finder sites, which include personnel locators and missing buddies bulletin boards:

- GI Buddies.com   gibuddies.com
- GI Search.com   gisearch.com
- Military.com   military.com
- Military Connections   militaryconnections.com
- Military USA   militaryusa.com

Job Search Clubs and Support Groups

Other networks involve displaced workers and over-40 job seekers who literally form job search networks, job clubs, or support groups for the purpose of conducting a job search based upon networking principles. Most of these groups are organized at the local level, especially in major metropolitan areas, and offer free or inexpensive job search assistance. Check these sites to see if there is such a group functioning in or near your community:

- 5 O'Clock Clubs   fiveoclockclub.com
- 40-Plus Clubs   40plus.org/chapters
- Chicago Jobs   chicagojobs/org/support.html
- ExecuNet   execunet.com
- Professionals in Transition   jobsearching.org

You also may find job search networks, clubs, and support groups associated with colleges and universities, women's centers, churches, YMCA's, and local social service organizations.

Mentors, Career Coaches, and Q&A

Online career advice comes in many different forms, from short one- and two-page how-to articles, to chart groups, bulletin boards, "Ask the Expert," "Job Doctor," and "Q&A" sections. Unfortunately, much of what goes on in relatively unstructured and amateur-driven chat rooms is noise that can be distracting, misleading, and frustrating to job seekers who readily admit that they must be "doing something wrong," because they are not getting expected results from their job search efforts. Such forms of advice are usually found within a "Job Resources" or "Career Center" section.

Our advice: Skip most of the amateur noise and accompanying anarchy – which is usually brought to you by people who don't have a clue what they really should be doing – and visit an experienced expert who knows what he or she is talking about. Some of the most valuable online career advice comes from experts or career profession- als who serve as a combination career coach and mentor. Recognizing that the job search is by nature a lonely, difficult, and at time ego- deflating experience – often filled with many rejections and dashed expectations – mentors extend a helping online hand as they assist job seekers in dealing with various aspects of the job search, especially the many bumps and bruises along the way. As coaches, they help provide structure to the process and reassure job seekers that this process does indeed work for those who are well organized, purposeful, talented, persistent, and enthusiastic. Numerous well established fee-based career management firms, such as Bernard Haldane Associates (jobhunting.com), R. L. Stevens and Associates (interviewing.com), and Right Management Consultants (right.com), serve as professional career coaches who lead job seekers through a very well defined and structured process, from career assessment to salary negotiations (see features on these firms in Chapter 12). Like a personal career coach, these experts provide job seekers with a structure as they help them stay focused on what's really important by using smart strategies and techniques that work.

When it comes to getting good career advice, be sure to visit some of the major sites we've already recommended:

- **CareerShop** careershop.com
- **Monster.com** monster.com
- **Quintessential Careers** quintcareers.com
- **Vault.com** vault.com
- **WetFeet** wetfeet.com

AskTheEmployer is an innovative site designed to promote career mentoring relationships. Using an e-mentoring approach that develops an interactive relationship between mentors and mentees, this site also includes Q&As, discussion boards, job search tips, and links to related sites. It allows users to search for an online mentor or register as a professional mentor:

AskTheEmployer asktheemployer.com

Numerous other mentoring resources are available on the Internet. For a directory to such sites, be sure to visit **Peer Resources** as well as explore **FindAMentor** and **MentorU**:

- **Peer Resources** peer.ca/mentor.html
- **Find a Mentor** findamentor.org
- **MentorU** mentoru.com

The **Women's Executive Network** (wxnetwork.com) attempts to link girls ages 16-19 with female executives who serve as role models.

Once on the job, a few sites offer mentoring services to deal with the day-to-day realities of work:

- **Career Systems International** careersystemsintl.com
- **Deliver the Promise** deliverthepromise.com
- **Delta Road** deltaroad.com
- **Employer-Employee** employer-employee.com

Home | Salary Wizard | Salary news | Salary advice | Salary Talk | Career resources | The lighter side | For H.R. professionals
SalaryTrax › Post a job

FIND A JOB Enter job title/keyword Go

Salary Talk with
compensation consultant
Erisa Ojimba

Salary Talk is a forum in which Salary.com's compensation consultants answer readers' questions about compensation and benefits.

Salary Wizard™

Select job category

Accounting

Enter location

Job Finder
Search Salary.com's new job database

Post your resume

Get in front of employers

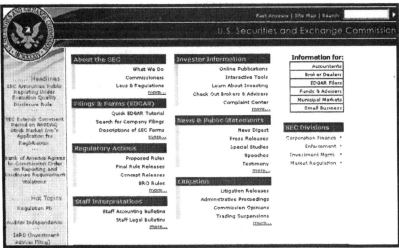

Past Answers | Site Map | Search

U.S. Securities and Exchange Commission

About the SEC
What We Do
Commissioners
Laws & Regulations
more...

Filings & Forms (EDGAR)
Quick EDGAR Tutorial
Search for Company Filings
Descriptions of SEC Forms
more...

Regulatory Actions
Proposed Rules
Final Rule Releases
Concept Releases
SRO Rules
more...

Staff Interpretations
Staff Accounting Bulletins
Staff Legal Bulletins
more...

Investor Information
Online Publications
Interactive Tools
Learn About Investing
Check Out Brokers & Advisers
Complaint Center
more...

News & Public Statements
News Digest
Press Releases
Special Studies
Speeches
Testimony
more...

Litigation
Litigation Releases
Administrative Proceedings
Commission Opinions
Trading Suspensions
more...

Information for:
Accountants
Broker-Dealers
EDGAR Filers
Funds & Advisers
Municipal Markets
Small Business

SEC Divisions
Corporation Finance •
Enforcement •
Investment Mgmt •
Market Regulation •

Headlines
SEC Announces Public Reporting Under Execution Quality Disclosure Rule

SEC Extends Comment Period on NASDAQ Stock Market Inc.'s Application for Registration

Bank of America Agrees to Commission Order on Reporting and Disclosure Requirement Violations

Hot Topics
Regulation FD

Auditor Independence

IARD (Investment Adviser Filing)

Job-Reviews.com®
Our job hunters help each other find the perfect job

Read a Job Review
- Salary
- Interview
- Job Position

Write a Job Review
Tough case question? Great job offer? Write a salary, interview, or job position review.

Subscribe to our Mailing List

What is JobReviews.Com?

How do I read a review?
How do I write a review?

Recent Salary Reviews (Find out how much people make!)

	Company	Date Posted	Page Views
1.	Greenburg Sports Complex	07-29-2001	56
2.	qwest communications	07-27-2001	70
3.	SBC Communications	07-23-2001	86
4.	chevy chase bank	07-23-2001	111
5.	Hatch	07-19-2001	38
6.	MyPoints.com	07-18-2001	59

11

Interview, Salary, and Relocation Sites

WHILE MOST EMPLOYMENT WEBSITES FOCUS ON connecting job seekers with employers through the use of resumes and job postings, a few other sites include useful information on the critical job interview, salary negotiation, and relocation steps of the job search. In fact, after experiencing the euphoria of being invited to a job interview, many job seekers quickly discover a new reality – the job interview is the most critical step in the whole job search process – no interview, no job offer, no job. If you handle the job interview well, you'll most likely receive a job offer as well as negotiate salary and benefits commensurate with your level of skills, abilities, and accomplishments.

Interviews Count the Most

Your resume may get you an invitation to the job interview, but it's your interview skills that will determine whether or not you will get the job. And it's usually during the final interview that you negotiate a compensation package that will influence the direction of your future compensation. Neglect these critical steps in your job search and you will be back to chasing down more employers with your resume to invite you to more job interviews.

If you review the many websites identified in this chapter, you should be able to better prepare for the job interview and salary negotiation steps. While none of these sites substitute for a good book on interviewing and salary negotiations (see the order form at the end of this book for recommended titles), they at least introduce you to many issues involved in this critical stage of your job search. You'll be a wiser, and hopefully more capable, job seeker for having visited these sites.

Interview Preparation and Practice

Many major employment websites, such as Monster, CareerBuilder, CareerCity, Vault, Wetfeet, Quintessential, and MyJobSearch, include information on job interviews. This is usually found in the resource center, career advice, or job tips section and comes in the form of one- to two-page articles on interview mistakes, sample questions, and interview preparation. Some sites may include a self-scoring interview quiz, a career coach dispensing interview advice, or an interactive practice interview which enables job seekers to select alternative answers (multiple choice) to a variety of questions often asked by interviewers. Most of the interview information and advice is free, although a few sites, such as WSACorp.com, charge for the services of an online career coach who assists individuals in preparing for the job interview. Such insights, advice, and practice sessions can help prepare you for the critical job interview. However, these online services should supplement, rather than substitute for, one-on-one interview preparation. While the Internet is a wonderful tool for initially screening candidates and employers, only a fool would hire someone over the Internet. In the end, the most critical step in the job search – the job interview, which could end up being four to seven interviews with the same employer – is conducted in face-to-face

> *While the Internet is a wonderful tool for initially screening candidates and employers, only a fool would hire someone over the Internet.*

situations where employers and recruiters have a chance to assess both your verbal and nonverbal interpersonal skills. In such encounters, where first impressions mean a lot, the final outcome may be determined more by your dress, handshake, eye contact, speech patterns, timing, and listening skills than by the content of your messages. In other words, the job interview is more about determining your likability and social competence than your technical qualifications. These are critical "job qualification" elements that cannot be determined through online communication.

Useful Job Interview Sites

In preparation for the job interview, we recommend visiting these websites which are primarily devoted to preparing job seekers for the critical job interview.

Monster.com   **Job Interviews**
interview.monster.com
content.monster.com/jobinfo/interview

As might be expected, Monster.com includes excellent sections on interview preparation. The first section offers practice interviews ("Virtual Interview") for a variety of occupational fields, including feedback on one's performance and tips on thank-you letters, second interviews, and negotiations. The second section includes tips on virtual interviews, questions to ask interviewers, using the telephone, and responding to tough questions. Taken together, these two sections offer some of the most useful interview preparation tips on the Internet.

JobInterview.net   **Job Interviews**
job-interview.net

This is a rich site for exploring numerous aspects of the job interview for both job seekers and employers. Includes numerous practice questions, mock job interviews, 900+ sample questions for 41 job functions, expert interview advice, a seven-step interview plan, and a downloadable ($16.95) interview preparation book. Interview advice for job seekers is provided by career authors Matt and Nan DeLuca (***Best Answers to the 201 Most Frequently Asked Interview Questions*** and ***More Best Answers to the 201 Most Frequently Asked Interview Questions***). In fact, much of what you will find in their interview books can be accessed for free through this site. Interview advice for employers and recruiters is provided by author Del J. Still (***High Impact Hiring***).

JobReviews.com **jobreviews.com**	**Job Interviews**

Immediately go to the "Recent Interview Reviews" section, which includes interview reviews of more than 500 companies (jobreviews.com/cgi-bin/getsection.pl?select+interview). This is a very useful site, especially if you are interviewing for a job with one of the featured companies. Includes inside information on various companies from job seekers who share their observations about what it was like interviewing at the particular company. Includes interview "stories" from the following categories of companies:

- Accounting
- Advertising
- Computer Hardware
- Computer Software
- Consulting
- Financial Services
- High Tech

- Internet/New Media
- Investment Banking
- Investment Management
- Law
- Semiconductors
- Telecommunications
- Other

This also is an excellent source for getting a feel for job interview realities – the types of situations encountered, questions likely to be asked, and potential problems one can expect to encounter – regardless of the particular company involved.

Joyce Lain Kennedy   **Job Interviews**
dummies.com/resources/jobquestions/default.htm

Popular career expert, author, and syndicated columnist Joyce
Lain Kennedy and her publisher include over 1,000 job interview questions on this site, which is dubbed the "World's
Biggest Job Interview Question Bank." While many of these
questions come from her book, *Job Interviews for Dummies*,
many others were not be included in the book because of size
limitations. This site classifies questions into nine categories,
ranging from questions about education and experience to
salary and inappropriate questions. If you want a handy list of
questions you may be asked, this is a good one-stop shop for
sensitizing yourself to a broad range of possibilities.

MeetIT   **Job Interviews**
meetit.com

Designed for information technology specialists, this site
includes two useful sections on the job interview. Includes
hundreds of questions candidates are likely to be asked along
with suggestions for positive answers. Also includes numerous
interview tips, from how to dress to post-interview behavior.

Interview Coach   **Job Interviews**
interviewcoach.com

Operated by "Interview Coach" Carole Martin, who also serves
as the "Interview Expert" on Monster.com, this site is designed
to assist job seekers in preparing for the job interview. Includes
practice interview questions to test your interview skills. Offers
an interview workbook and fee-based telephone and in-person
coaching services. If you need a professional interview coach for
one-on-one services, check out this site.

Virtualville	Job Interviews

virtualville.com/employment_agency/interviewing.html

This straightforward "interview tip" section provides useful advice on three major interview topics:

- The Do's and Don'ts of Interviewing
- Most Frequently Asked Questions
- Questions You Can Ask the Interviewer

Other good online sources for interview tips include these three gateway sites, which are loaded with a combination of articles and linkages to other interview and compensation sites:

- **MyJobSearch**   myjobsearch.com/
                                interviewing.html
- **Quintessential Careers**   quintcareers.com/intvres.html
- **Riley Guide**   dbm.com/jobguide/netintv.html

Salary Negotiation and Compensation Sites

Salary negotiations are one of the most important yet most neglected job search steps. In the end, it's your talent in exchange for salary, benefits, and perks. How well you negotiate your compensation package may well determine your long-term financial worth to this and other employers. However, few people are savvy salary negotiators. They often don't know what they are really worth in today's job market and are hesitant to talk about money. As a result, many job seekers accept the first salary offer, which may be 10 to 20 percent lower than what they could have gotten had they followed some very basic salary negotiation techniques.

Several books, including our own *Dynamite Salary Negotiations* and *Get a Raise in 7 Days*, outline how to best negotiate a compensation package to your advantage. At the same time, a few websites include tips from these books as well as important salary data for determining salary comparables. If you want to know what you are worth in today's job market, wish to better understand various elements in compensation packages, and need to hone your salary negotiation skills (what to say and when to say it), be sure to check out several useful websites that focus on this critical salary negotiation step in the job search. Some of the best salary negotiation sites to visit in preparation for addressing compensation issues include:

Salary.com   **Salary Negotiations**
salary.com

This site has quickly become the premier salary site during the past two years, and for good reasons. It includes a wealth of useful information for dealing with compensation issues. Its "Salary Wizard" provides quick access to salary comparables in numerous metropolitan areas and for hundreds of job categories and position descriptions – a good place to start researching what you are potentially worth in particular geographic areas. Numerous other employment websites incorporate Salary.com's Salary Wizard into their site for addressing questions concerning salary comparables. The site also includes salary news, salary advice, discussions, and career resources. Job seekers also can search for jobs through this site.

JobStar.org   **Salary Negotiations**
jobstar.org

Previously known as JobSmart.com, this site is operated by a library system in northern California. It includes one of the most useful linkage sections on salary surveys, which currently includes over 300 general and professional salary surveys found on the web (from "Accounting" to "Warehousing"). Also includes a "Salary I.Q." assessment test, tips on negotiating salaries, and linkages to salary articles. You also may want to explore other useful sections on this site related to resumes and career guides.

Wageweb   Salary Negotiations
www.wageweb.com

Primarily designed for employers, this HR salary service site includes compensation information on over 170 benchmark positions. Includes salary data on several categories of positions, such as Human Resources, Finance, Engineering, Healthcare, and Manufacturing. Organizations and consultants can join Wageweb for $169 and $219 per year respectively. Individuals can review some of the salary data as well as several job descriptions. The site also includes frequently asked questions and links to other HR websites.

Abbott-Langer   Salary Negotiations
abbott-langer.com

Another site primarily designed for HR professionals and compensation specialists in need of highly specialized, and somewhat pricey, compensation data. Abbott, Langer, and Associates, Inc. publishes salary survey information on over 450 benchmark jobs in information technology, marketing/sales, accounting, engineering, human resources, consulting, manufacturing, nonprofit, legal, and other fields drawn from data on more than 7,000 participating organizations. While the site offers free summary data for several positions, most of the reports cost $295 or more per report. The site also includes information on its HR and management services as well as a collection of useful HR articles.

Robert Half International   Salary Negotiations
www.rhii.com

Robert Half International claims to be the world's first and largest specialized staffing service. Focusing on staffing temporary, full-time, and project professionals in the fields of accounting and finance, administrative support, information technology, law, advertising, marketing, and web design, Robert Half International has 330 offices in North America, Europe, and Australia. The company is especially well known for its annual salary guides that cover the positions for which they provide staffing services. You can request complimentary copies of the various salary guides through this site's "Resource Center." Just complete the request form indicating which guides you wish to receive (the accounting and finance guide also can be downloaded in PDF format from this site). The site also includes useful resources on resumes, cover letters, interviewing, and links to other sites. Individuals can browse job openings and submit resumes online.

Securities and Exchange Commission **www.sec.gov**	**Salary Negotiations**

The U.S. Securities and Exchange Commission maintains compensation data on high-level executives through its EDGAR database. If you plan to earn in excess of $500,000 annually, you should visit this site for compensation information on companies registered with the SEC – those with more than 500 investors and $10 million in assets. Also see pages 121-122.

Monster.com **salarycenter.monster.com**	**Salary Negotiations**

Includes lots of useful information and linkages on key salary issues – research, negotiations, benefits, evaluation of an offer, relocation, education, self employment, and comparables. Includes a salary/money bulletin board and links to Robert Half International's salary database.

SalarySource.com   **Salary Negotiations**
salarysource.com

This site is rich with salary information and tips, including a database for assessing the market value of 350 benchmark positions by city. However, very little is free on this site. It costs $29.95 per inquiry to access the salary data. The site does include informative articles on compensation and lots of job descriptions.

Other compensation-related sites worth visiting for addressing various aspects of the job negotiation process include:

- BenefitsLink   benefitslink.com
- BenefitNews.com   benefitnews.com
- Bureau of Labor Statistics   bls.gov
- CareerCity   careercity.com/content/
                                    salaries/links.asp
- CareerJournal   careerjournal.com
- CompGeo Online   claytonwallis.com/cxgonl.
                                    html
- Employee Benefit
  Research Institute   ebri.org
- Homestore.com   homefair.com
- MyJobSearch   myjobsearch.com/
                                    negotiating.html
- Quintessential Careers   quintcareers.com/salary_
                                    negotiation.html
- Riley Guide   www.dbm.com/jobguide/
                                    netintv.html
- SalaryExpert   salaryexpert.com
- SalaryMaster   salarymaster.com
- Salary Surveys for
  Northwest Employers   salarysurveys.milliman.com
- Yahoo   careers.yahoo.com/careers/
                                    salaries.html

Relocation Sites

Much of life is a transition – moving from one location to another. Indeed, a large percentage of jobs require relocation. If you want to quickly advance your career – or change your life – you should seriously consider moving to a community that offers greater career and lifestyle opportunities. Changing your environment can have a major, and positive, impact on your career and life.

So, pull out a map and start dreaming about where in the world you would like to live and work. What are the comparative advantages and cost differentials of working in various communities, or even countries if you plan to become an expatriate? What do you know about the quality of schools and health care, the cost of housing, recreation and entertainment opportunities, and various community services and lifestyle opportunities available in other communities? When it comes time to consider relocation options, especially calculating the cost of relocating into a compensation package, you are well advised to visit several websites that address a multitude of questions relating to relocation issues – from calculating cost of living differentials to contacting a mover to take all your "stuff" to another location. Many of the sites outlined in this chapter include salary calculators useful to job seekers who need to know the differences in the cost of living between communities. These calculators basically indicate how much your salary in Community X is worth when compared to the cost of living in Community Y – information you need to know before accepting a job offer in a different community. After all, a $200,000 house in your present community may cost $350,000 in another community, which may effectively wipe out any salary gains you may think you are making by changing jobs. Each of these websites can provide useful information for making salary, relocation, and lifestyle decisions.

The following sites provide a wealth of information on relocating to thousands of communities in the United States and abroad. Use these sites for researching communities, locating housing, calculating the local cost of living, checking out schools and restaurants, investigating local cultural opportunities, and identifying community organizations and services.

Homestore.com   **Relocation**
homefair.com

This is one of the Internet's premier relocation sites which also powers the relocation section of many employment-related websites. Includes a wealth of information on dozens of important issues and questions affecting relocation decisions – cities, schools, crime, lifestyle, insurance, finance, employment, cost of living differences, planning, home ownership, professional movers, packing tips, storage, taxes, and moving to a new state. Includes a useful "moving through this life transition" section that includes sections on graduating, getting a job, getting married, raising children, getting promoted, emptying the nest, and retiring. If you've ever been reticent about pulling up stakes, this site will surely help in easing the transition.

Virtual Relocation   **Relocation**
virtualrelocation.com
monstermoving.com

Operated as part of Monster.com, this site addresses numerous issues relating to both domestic and international relocation. Includes sections on finding a home, shopping for a mortgage rate, finding a mover, changing addresses, planning and managing a move, and living and shopping in a new community. International section includes information on everything from visas to selecting an international moving company.

Relocation Central   **Relocation**
relocationcentral.com

There's a lot more to this site than what initially appears on a rather simple front page. The site includes relocation service information organized by state/city and category. If, for example, you select a specific city, you'll find a tremendous amount

of information on the community to help you plan your move
– from banks to weather. A good site for exploring numerous
aspects of various communities both before and after making a
relocation decision. Also includes numerous tools and tips,
relocation checklists, a human resources directory, international
relocation linkages, school comparison reports, roommate
services, an apartment directory, and much more.

Runzheimer International	**Relocation**
runzheimer.com	

Runzheimer is one of the oldest, largest, and most trusted
names in the international relocation and travel business.
Designed primarily for government agencies and corporations,
this site includes information on Runzheimer's many domestic
and international relocation services. Also includes a revealing
two-location cost of living comparison service (fee-based).

Job Relocation	**Relocation**
jobrelocation.com	

Designed for executive-level candidates and recruiters facing
critical relocation decisions that make the difference between
accepting and rejecting a job offer, this site includes several
useful free services and tools: cost-of-living reports, home-
selling assistance, relocation package, cost-of-living counseling,
and personalized recruiter and job candidate consultations.
Includes a few useful articles and links. Operated by salesman-
realtor-web designer-relocation specialist Steve Levine.

Homescape	**Relocation**
homescape.com	

This site primarily focuses on housing (finding and financing)
and the moving process. Includes sections on buying a home in

25,000 cities, applying for a loan, searching for an apartment, selling a home, and locating a moving company or truck rental firm.

For other useful relocation information, including tips from the U.S. Postal Service, a complete book on relocation (***Insiders' Guide to Relocation***), and international relocation services, visit these sites:

- 123Relocation.com   relo-usa.com
- **Employee Relocation Council**   erc.org
- **GMAC Relocation Services**   gmac-relocation.com
- **Insiders' Guide**   insiders.com/relocation
- **MoversNet**   www.usps.gov/moversnet
- Moving.com   moving.com
- MovingCost.com   movingprices.com
- **Relocate-America**   relocate-america.com
- Relocation-net.com   www.relocation-net.com
- **Wall Street Journal**   homes.wsj.com

12

Career Counseling and Coaching Sites

OME JOB SEEKERS ARE SELF-STARTERS WHO CAN pick up a job search book, follow each step in the job search process, and land their dream job within a few weeks. Bless them – they are true entrepreneurs who are focused on what works and they become successful despite encountering numerous rejections on the potholed road to job search success. However, the truth is that very few people are that entrepreneurial or successful on their own – perhaps five percent. However self-assured, positive, and talented they may be, most job seekers need some professional help.

But selecting and using a career professional can also lead to disappointments. The career business is populated by a very diverse mix of professionals and wannabees. Certification is often lacking or very lax. Some self-declared career professionals are known for engaging in fraud or taking advantage of vulnerable clients who are in desperate need of finding a job. If and when you decide to seek professional career assistance, you should do so based upon the information found in this chapter for identifying such services. For in the end, it should be your money in exchange for the very best career assistance talent you can buy.

163

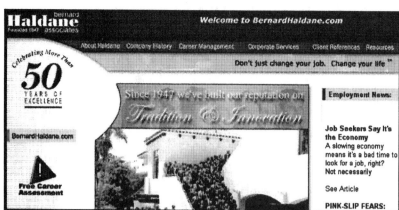

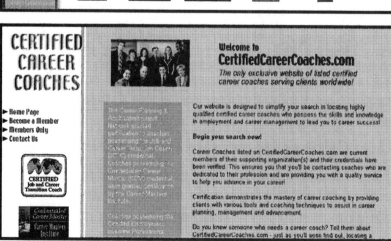

Self-Starters and Wishful Thinkers

Despite wishful thinking, most job seekers are not self-starters who can run with a self-directed book or put together a successful self-directed job search campaign based on tips from other people, including websites. Indeed, most job seekers get high on expectations but low on implementation. They may understand what they need to do in order to make the process work for them, but in reality they don't do it right. Their very first step should be self-assessment – discover what they do well and enjoy doing – but instead they start by writing their resume and then blast it to hundreds of potential employers and recruiters. Preoccupied with the trees rather than seeing the whole forest from start to finish, they never get back to basics by doing a proper self-assessment. Instead of making 25 new contacts this week (five per day), they only make two new contacts as part of their networking campaign, retreat to their computer to "surf the web" for jobs, and then complain about how difficult it is to find a job. They eventually land a job, but it's often not the right one, because they never really put together a well organized and implemented job search campaign focused around their major strengths. As in the past, they

Most job seekers get high on expectations but low on implementation. However self-assured, they need help.

become "accidental job seekers" who fall into jobs. They will most likely repeat this process in another year or two, once they discover they fell into a job that was not really a good fit for their particular interests, skills, and abilities.

Regardless of what other people might say about doing the job search on your own, most job seekers can benefit tremendously from the assistance of a career counselor, career coach, or other type of career professional who can provide you with a structure for organizing and implementing a well-targeted job search campaign. As you will quickly discover, a successful job search is all about structure and implementation. And that's where a career professional can play a critical role in helping you through what is often a difficult process – more difficult than you might ever imagine. Whatever you do, don't dismiss professional help in your job search. As many job seekers before you have discovered, a career professional may be your very best friend throughout this process. A professional may cost you some money, but he or she also may give you a tremendous return on your investment, which may be immediately reflected in your new salary which you negotiated with the assistance of your career professional.

A Season For Everything

There's a season for everything. In the case of the job search, you may quickly discover that it's the season to seek professional help for organizing and implementing a successful job search. After all, your next career decision will probably have important implications for your future income and lifestyle. Do it right, and you may be forever enriched with a job that is both financially and personally rewarding. Do it wrong, and you may soon be looking for another job which you hope will be better the next time. Look at it this way: the next job you accept will probably be worth $250,000 to $1 million, depending how long you stay. Is this the type of investment you want to make haphazardly on your own, or could you benefit from the expertise of a career professional who might be able to guide you into the right direction that could possibly double the worth of your next job?

Career Management Firms

Many executive-level candidates often use the services of professional career management firms which charge clients for career coaching services. These fees can run from $2,000 to $5,000, depending on the company and the services required. Most of these firms include one-on-one self-assessment, resume writing, and career coaching services. They work with clients, helping them develop effective marketing, networking, interviewing, and salary negotiation skills to ensure they are successful in finding a job; these are not employment or placement firms that find clients jobs. While many career counselors and job seekers may criticize these firms because they charge substantial fees for services that are available free through public sources (schools, community colleges, and community career centers), on the other hand, most of the free services are not geared toward executive-level candidates. Better still, many job seekers who use these fee-based career management services are thrilled with the outcome – they landed the perfect job that also paid far more than they could have received had they bootstrapped this process on their own. For example, they paid $4,000 for the career management services and ended up with a terrific job that paid $20,000 more than their last job. Conclusion: It was indeed a wise investment to contract with a professional career management firm to help guide them through this difficult process. They would not have achieved the same outcome on their own or through the many free career counseling services available through public sources.

Four of the most respected fee-based career management firms work with a variety of clients, from companies experiencing downsizing to individuals making $50,000+ a year. They include the following companies:

Bernard Haldane Associates   Career Management
jobhunting.com
bernardhaldane.com

This company represents the retail side of career management with its focus on individual job seekers who pay for a suite of job search services. Representing the oldest (50+ years) and one of the largest career management firms (600,000+ clients), Bernard Haldane Associates has pioneered much of today's leading career management, coaching, and counseling methods. Indeed, its founder, Dr. Bernard Haldane, is literally the father of modern career counseling. Beginning in the 1940s, his methods have been incorporated in most job search books (the basis for the popular *What Color Is Your Parachute?*) and career counseling practices. Such concepts as the information or referral interview, Success Factor Analysis, and "T" letters come from this source. Bernard Haldane Associates currently operates over 90 offices in the United States, Canada, and the United Kingdom. Clients work closely with a Career Advisor who coaches them through the job search process, from assessment to salary negotiations. Individuals can continue using these services at no additional charge for three years after finding a job through the Haldane organization. The job search methods used by this firm are outlined in five books published by Impact Publications (see order form at the end of this book): *Haldane's Best Resumes for Professionals, Haldane's Best Cover Letters for Professionals, Haldane's Best Answers to Tough Interview Questions, Haldane's Best Salary Tips for Professionals*, and *Haldane's Best Employment Websites for Professionals*. These books constitute one of the most thoroughgoing libraries for organizing and implementing an effective job search, including the use of the Internet. Many of the firms that compete with Bernard Haldane Associates use similar methods because many of their owners were once associated with the Haldane organization. The other firms, however, tend to focus on providing outplacement services to corporate clients who sponsor career management services for their departing employees. Only a few Haldane offices include corporate outplacement in their menu of services.

Right Management Consultants   Career Management
right.com

This international career management and human resources firm operates more than 200 offices worldwide. It provides career services to numerous corporate clients, especially those dealing with downsizing and requiring outplacement assistance. Most job seekers who work with Right Management Consultants receive free career management services because they are paid for by a sponsoring organization, which is most likely their employer who has just fired or "separated" them from the company. Right Management Consultants also provide customized online career management and outplacement services for their corporate clients through their proprietary website – online consulting, research tools, self-assessments, targeted job banks, and networking opportunities. This company also maintains an online database of resumes to market their clients' ex-employees.

Drake Beam Morin — Career Management
www.dbm.com

Drake Beam Morin (DBM) has been a leader in the fields of outplacement consulting and career transition services. It provides, for example, career transition services to the U.S. Olympic Team. It also hosts the popular gateway website, The Riley Guide. Operating 204 offices in 43 countries, including Vietnam, DBM primarily works with organizations that are downsizing their workforces and require the career management services of a firm such as DBM. They also work with HR professionals to enhance their hiring and retention programs. This site includes lots of informative sections on DBM's services, articles, tips, resources, and a bookstore of DBM publications. The fastest way to navigate this site is to go directly to the site navigation button on the left.

R. L. Stevens & Associates — Career Management
interviewing.com

This firm offers fee-based career management services to individuals who wish to change jobs or careers, as well as corporate outplacement services. The site outlines the company's approach, includes a map of its 16 U.S. offices, presents job search articles, and offers proprietary services to its clients.

Other firms offering similar or related career management and outplacement services include:

- CareerLab — careerlab.com
- Career Management International — cmi-imi.com
- Five O'Clock Club — fiveoclockclub.com
- Lee Hecht Harrison — lhh.com/us
- The Transition Team — transition-team.com
- WorkLife Solutions — worklife.com

Certified Career Counselors

Where can you quickly find a career counselor, especially one who has been trained and certified? Trained and certified career counselors have usually completed a two-year graduate training program in counseling from a recognized university. The following two websites focus on certified career counselors

National Board of Certified Counselors, Inc. nbcc.org	Career Counselors

This organization certifies counselors in several areas: career counseling, school counseling, clinical mental health counseling, and addictions counseling. Maintains a register of certified counselors.

National Career Development Association ncda.org	Career Counselors

The National Career Development Association (NCDA) is a division of the American Counseling Association. Its stated purpose is to promote everyone's career development. Made up of career professionals, NCDA sponsors professional development activities, publishes, conducts research, and promotes professional standards. It trains and certifies Career Development Facilitators. Includes a useful section entitled "Consumer Guidelines to Selecting a Career Counselor."

Commercial Career Coaching

Several other organizations are involved in certifying a variety of career professionals who are not necessarily career counselors. These range from career coaches to professional resume writers. Certification of these individuals may involve everything from taking a short $200 "training" course to completing a series of professional development courses. Most members of the following organizations have a passion for promoting career development.

Career Masters Institute **cminstitute.com**	**Career Coaching**

This relatively new organization focuses on certifying career specialists (CCM – Credentialed Career Master) as well as providing a professional network for exchanging information and advice relevant to its members who consist of many freelancers and small business owners. Includes online training programs, conference information, and tools for improving professional competence and business development. A complete listing of CMI members, by profession and specialization, can be found by searching the "Online Member Directory" or in the Appendix of the president's (Wendy S. Enelow) two new books, *Best Resumes for $100,000+ Jobs* and *Best Cover Letters for $100,000+ Jobs* (see order form at the end of this book). Users can search for a member by the following professional categories:

- Authors
- Business School
- Career Coaching
- Career Counseling
- College/University Placement
- Corporate - General
- Direct Mail Service
- Human Resources
- Internet Service and Sites
- Job Lead Report
- Military/Government Transition
- Outplacement
- Publishing
- Recruitment
- Reference Checking Service

- Resume Writing
- Secretarial Service
- Software and Information Technology
- Stationery Products
- Training and Development

Certified Career Coaches   **Career Coaches**
certifiedcareercoaches.com

This site pulls together a large number of career professionals who have been certified by a variety of organizations:

JCTC   Job and Career Transition Coach (certified by The Career Planning and Adult Development Network)

CCM   Credentialed Career Master (certified by the Career Masters Institute)

CEIP   Certified Employment Interview Professional (certified by the Professional Association of Resume Writers and Career Coaches)

The site functions as a gateway to these professional career certification organizations. A handy search engine lets users of this site find a certified career coach by city, state, country, company, specialty, and type of consultation. Career specialties include:

- Career Assessment
- Career Training and Development
- Career Transition
- International Interview Coaching/Salary Negotiation
- Interview Coaching/Salary Negotiation
- Job Performance Enhancement
- Military to Civilian Employment
- Other

Professional Association of Resume   Career Coaches
   Writers and Career Coaches
www.parw.com

This organization certifies individuals who want to become a Certified Employment Interview Professional (CEIP). Many members also are Certified Professional Resume Writers (CPRW). The site includes search engines to find members by name, city, country, state, province, or area code. Its members are listed by name, address, phone number, email, and home page. Most members are either freelance career specialists or operate small resume-writing businesses. If you need a professional resume writer to help you with your resume, this is a good place to start shopping for such career expertise.

International Association of   Career Coaches
   Career Management Professionals
iacmp.org

This is the professional association of career management professionals. Consisting of a network of hundreds of career experts, it draws most members from the United States (1103), Canada (211), United Kingdom (166), and Australia (72). You can search for an expert by country, state, and area of expertise. Areas of expertise include:

- Assessment
- Career Centers
- Career Management Educators
- Career Management Media
- Coaching
- Employee Retention
- Executive Recruitment
- Family/Spouse Relocation
- Financial Planning

- Internal Career Development
- Outplacement
- Organizational Development
- Personal Development

Career Planning and Adult Development Network careernetwork.org	Career Coaches

Operated by career development specialist Richard Knowdell, this website consists of a network of career professionals whose membership entitles them to a newsletter, journal, and access to other services, including certification workshops for job and career transition coaches and a very popular annual conference of career development professionals. The centerpiece for this site is its annual international career development conference which normally draws over 1,000 career professionals. Also certifies Job and Career Transition Coaches (JCTC).

13

Employer and Recruiter Sites

SINCE MANY EMPLOYMENT WEBSITES ARE DESIGNED for employers and recruiters, it's not surprising to find numerous sites sponsored by these online players. Indeed, the economics of online recruitment are such that both employers and recruiters have a lot to gain by using the Internet to screen candidates for job interviews. They basically want to scan through lots of resumes in order to locate the perfect candidates.

Executive Recruiters and Candidates

The Internet is a double-edged sword for headhunters or executive recruiters. On the one hand, the Internet is the executive recruiter's best friend because it is an efficient place to find resumes from which to screen candidates for corporate customers. On the other hand, the Internet can be the recruiter's worst nightmare because many employers are getting smart about online recruitment: they can bypass expensive recruiters and go directly to online recruitment sites that will screen candidates for a fraction of the cost involved in using a headhunter. As a result, many executive recruiters feel vulnerable to

Recruiters Online Network

A global community of
Recruiters, Headhunters, and Professional Staffing Firms.

Job Hunters Click Here!

Job Bank Search

Job Seekers - Recruiters Online Network is your gateway to the hidden job market

- Find 1,000s of current, open job listings posted by the top headhunters, recruiters, and search professionals in the world
- Post resumes for FREE

Recruiters Click Here!

Recruiting Tools

Recruiters - Make more job placements... Post jobs once, be everywhere! Our employment publishing network is the largest in the world with over 3,500 employment communities and access to hundreds of thousands of resumes

- Unlimited Job Posts

Net Temps

Tue Aug 07, 2001 → 90,122 + Jobs

Not Just Temp Jobs!
54,073 contract jobs
36,049 direct jobs

SEARCH JOBS   Area: [All Locations]   Keyword: [   ] [Go]

about us   post your resume   post jobs

to over 6,500 recruiters

- Job seekers
Free Desktop
Post Resume
Access Resume
Your Career
Weekly News

Recruiters

job search center

Accounting & Finance	Internet/New Media
Admin & Clerical	Light Industrial
Engineering	Management
Executive	Marketing
Health Care	Recruiting & HR
Legal	Sales
Information Technology	Other/Misc.

starting point
for newcomers

FREE **jobseekers desktop**

Login/Create Desktop

Net-Temps Canada

the new economics of Internet recruitment. In their quest for resumes, executive recruiters are frequent users of online resume databases. They also post numerous job listings as well as register to receive "free" resumes from the many resume-blasting firms outlined in Chapter 9 (pages 133-137).

The old days when candidates were told not to contact executive recruiters – they will contact you if interested – are largely gone. In this new era of online recruitment, it's incumbent upon you to get your resume into all the right hands, which means recruiters. If you make in excess of $50,000 a year, you may want to explore several of these websites. While some sites are designed for executive-level candidates, other sites focus on recruiting individuals with high-demand skill sets. Some of these sites, such as Netshare, ExecuNET, and ExecutiveOnly, reverse the revenue model by charging job seekers membership fees to use their sites but allowing employers and recruiters to use them free of charge. As you will quickly discover, executives earning $100,000+ a year tend to pay more for everything, from site memberships to resume-blasting, assessment, counseling, and coaching services.

The following sites are disproportionately operated by recruiters or designed for executive-level candidates and recruiters.

Oya's Directory of Recruiters   **Recruiters**
i-recruit.com

This is one of the Internet's best sites for locating recruiters. Free to both job seekers and recruiters, this site's database includes thousands of recruiters classified into 14 major categories:

- Agriculture
- Art and Media
- Computers & IT
- Construction
- Education
- Engineering & Science
- Executive
- Finance
- Hospitality
- Industrial
- International
- Medical
- Professional
- Transportation

If you want to target recruiters in a particular professional field, search for them by specialty and send them your resume. Most recruiters welcome resumes by indicating the types of skill sets they need and including their email addresses and telephone and fax numbers. You also can search for recruiters by location, including international recruiters. A great site for exploring the "hidden job market" of recruiters.

Chief Monster.com   Recruiter
my.chief.monster.com

A relatively new service of Monster.com, this senior executive site is free and confidential for job seekers who are seeking senior-level opportunities with major employers, executive search firms, and venture capitalists. Both job seekers and employers must join this site in order to use its many services. Job seekers must meet certain experience and salary qualifications in order to participate in the site. Includes a resume database, job listings, networking opportunities, and useful articles for job seekers. Before paying monthly membership fees to other executive recruiting sites, be sure to explore the free opportunities available through this Monster.com site. If it operates like the rest of Monster.com, it should offer some good opportunities for senior executives – and the price is right.

Recruiters Online Network   Recruiter
recruitersonline.com

Job seekers can view job postings online as well as post their resumes on this site for free. Includes a section for locating recruiters and headhunters by industry (67 specialty areas) and location. Over 8,000 registered recruiters, executive search firms, employment agencies, and headhunters use this site. Employers and recruiters pay monthly fees for using this site, which also includes broadcasting their job postings to over 1,500 other websites.

6 FigureJobs   Recruiter
sixfigurejobs.com

Designed for experienced professionals, this $100,000+ site
invites executive-level candidates to post their resumes online
as well as explore job postings of their client companies. You
must become a member in order to use this site. However,
unlike similar executive-level sites, membership for job seekers
is free. Includes several useful career resources, such as a salary
wizard (from Salary.com), bookstore (from Amazon.com),
expert advice (from Deltaroad.com), online learning (from
Thinq.com), resume services (from Career-resumes.com), an
executive newsletter, and recommended links. You also can
research companies (through Hoovers.com), explore relocation
issues, locate recruiters, and ask questions. Special features
include online seminars (from powerhiring.com), job-related
news, and success stories.

ExecutivesOnly   Recruiter
executivesonly.com

Focusing on executives with an annual earnings potential of
$70,000 to $750,000, this site includes numerous job postings
by employers and recruiters. Its revenue model is very different
from 99 percent of other employment-related websites. While
most sites are supported by employers and recruiters and free
to job seekers, this one is just the opposite – free to employers
and recruiters but costs job seekers membership fees to use it:
$145 for 14 weeks; $189 for 24 weeks; $259 for 36 weeks; and
$389 for 48 weeks. The site also offers a premium resume
service with a 14-week membership ($695) as well as several
other fee-based services (consulting, interview mentor, and
resume blasting at $1.95 per resume).

Netshare   Recruiter
netshare.com

This award-winning executive-level site is designed to connect executive job seekers ($100,000+) with companies and recruiters. Includes a resume database and nearly 2,000 executive job listings provided by executive recruiters and companies as well as special free services for job seekers (market intelligence, career coaching, resume critique, and Q&A). Individuals must register and pay monthly membership fees in order to use this site. These range from $125 for three months to $385 for 12 months, depending on the category of membership.

ExecuNet   Recruiter
execunet.com

Focusing on $100,000+ executive-level candidates, this popular site primarily offers job postings to potential candidates. This is a no-cost service to employers and recruiters who list positions. Job seekers pay membership fees to access the services of this site: 3 months for $135; 6 months for $199; and 12 months for $349. Members receive a free resume review, access to the job database and hundreds of recruiters and companies, job search tips, research tools, a newsletter, and local networking opportunities. However, you can access the networking opportunities, which are primarily listings of upcoming breakfast meetings and cocktail parties sponsored by ExecuNet and many other organizations, without being a member. Nonmembers also can access other free sections of this site that deal with career resources or what they call "Knowledge." Like a few other membership sites that charge job seekers for proprietary online services, we have no idea as to the relative effectiveness of this site compared to sites, such as Chief Monster.com, 6FigureJobs, and Recruiters Online Network, that are free to job seekers.

Management Recruiters International   Recruiter
brilliantpeople.com

Operated by one of the world's largest executive recruitment firms, this site includes three major sections:

- Search for Jobs
- Find a Recruiter
- Manage Your Career

All the listed jobs and recruiters are part of MRI's network, which includes more than 1,000 offices and 5,000 search professionals in North America, Europe, and Asia with total billings over $570 million – one of the largest and most active recruitment firms. It's also part of a large workplace solutions company with $1.7 billion in annual billings (cdicorp.com). This site also includes useful career tools for assessing skills (entrinskik.net), improving resumes, and acquiring salary (salary.com) and relocation information (homefair.com). Its career resources section includes tips on resumes, interviews, career counselors, and working with a recruiter.

ResumeZapper   Recruiter
resumezapper.com

This is one of the largest and most active resume-blasting firms that only works with third-party recruiters, headhunters, and search firms. Candidates who prefer using executive recruiters for locating employers pay this company $49.95 to blast their resume to thousands of top search, recruitment, and placement firms. Just go online with your credit card and resume and within a few hours your resume will be in the hands of key third-party recruiters who may contact you within 48 hours about possible job openings in your area of expertise. If you're lucky, you may soon be interviewing for a job you may not have found by other means. A quick and inexpensive way to get your resume into hands of individuals who may know how to market you to their clients.

Other useful websites with a decided emphasis on recruiters and executive-level candidates include:

- **Heidrick & Struggles**   heidrick.com
- **Korn/Ferry International**   ekornferry.com
                                   futurestep.com
- **Recruit USA**   recruitusa.com
- **Spencer Stuart**   spencerstuart.com

For additional resume-blasting services designed for reaching recruiters, see our listings of such firms in the resume distribution section of Chapter 9.

Staffing and Employment Firms

Thousands of staffing and employment firms provide placement services for part-time, full-time, and contract employees. In the Washington, DC area, for example, over 200 such firms compete for this lucrative staffing business. Employers normally contact these firms for identifying qualified candidates. The firms screen candidates as well as offer a variety of personnel services and hiring options to employers. If you're interested in getting your resume into the databases of these firms, you might start with the following companies, which have a large presence in the staffing industry. Many of these firms specialize in particular occupational fields and industries.

Staffing.com   **Staffing Firms**
staffing.com

This is a key gateway site to the staffing industry. Includes hundreds of staffing agencies by company category:

- Accounting
- Administration/Clerical
- Advertising
- Arts/Entertainment
- Biomedical
- Business Development
- Construction
- Domestic
- Education
- Engineering
- Food Service
- Law/Legal Services
- Manufacturing
- Marketing
- Pharmaceutical
- Printing
- Recruiting
- Talent Agents
- Technical
- Temporary

Use this site to identify a staffing agency appropriate to your interests and skills. The site also includes useful articles as well as links to other sites.

Net-Temps   **Staffing Firms**
net-temps.com

This is one of the Internet's top employment sites designed for three groups: job seekers, recruiters, and employers. The site is organized into three major sections – Job Search Center (for job seekers), Recruiting Center (for recruiters), and Talent Center (for employers). Job seekers can post their resume as well as search for job openings. The relatively new Talent Center, which is designed for connecting job seekers to employers, includes profiles of individuals who are interested in contract or full-time employment.

Robert Half International   **Staffing Firms**
www.rhii.com

This is one of the world's largest staffing agencies specializing in the fields of accounting and finance, administrative support, information technology, law, advertising, marketing, and web design. See Chapter 11 (pages 156-157) for more information on this firm.

Manpower   Staffing Firms
www.manpower.com

This is the world's largest staffing firm with 3,700 offices and franchises in 59 countries around the world. Manpower has over 1,200 offices in North America. It literally places over 2 million candidates each year for part-time and full-time positions. Since individuals become employees of Manpower, which sends them on job assignments, they acquire a certain level of job stability normally associated with large well established and growing firms. Using an online upload form, job seekers can apply to Manpower by submitting their resume to 10 different Manpower offices. The firm's innovative Global Learning Center is designed to help its employees upgrade their skills online by offering more than 100 business skills courses and over 1,000 software and IT courses.

Olsten Staffing Services   Staffing Firms
olsten.com

This is another large player in the staffing industry. Offers temporary, temp-to-hire, and full-time job opportunities with their many corporate and government clients. Job seekers interested in joining the Olsten team need to go to a separate recruitment site – www.worknow.com.

Kelly Services   Staffing Firms
kellyservices.com

This well established staffing services firm operates offices in 26 countries around the world. It places over 800,000 employees with more than 200,000 employers each year. Individuals can register online by uploading their resume or "Profile" (site also include tips on composing and sending such a resume).

Model Employer Sites

One of the most important employment trends today is the continuing development of sophisticated employer websites, which include special employment sections with job boards, resume databases, and job tips. As noted in Chapter 9, more and more employers encourage applicants to visit their website in order to become better acquainted with the company, explore employment opportunities, and apply for jobs online. Such websites save both the company and applicants a great deal of time and money by improving the speed and quality of the whole screening process. As more and more companies develop such functional websites, fewer employers will use the many mega employment websites outlined in Chapter 5. Indeed, smaller companies, which do not have a great deal of visibility with job seekers, are most likely to use the online recruitment services of these mega sites.

Most employers maintain an employment section on their website, which usually appears on the homepage. Depending on the size and employment needs of an company, this section may include the latest job openings as well as a resume database into which a visitor can enter his or her resume. Some company websites also include profiles of current employees, insights into the company culture, and relatively frank tips on how to best write a resume and interview for jobs with the company. Many sites now include self-tests for determining whether or not a candidate would fit well into the company culture.

There are literally hundreds of thousands of such employer websites on the Internet. If you are interested in targeting particular employers, you are well advised to identify employers for which you would like to work, explore their website for employment information, and respond to relevant online job listings and/or enter your resume into their resume database. Here are two excellent examples of employer websites which include a wealth of employment information.

Boston Consulting Group	Employer
bcg.com/careers/careers_splash.asp	

The Boston Consulting Group is one of the world's major consulting groups and one of the best places to work. It attracts the top talent from America's top universities. If you're interested in working for BCG, be sure to explore their "Careers @ BCG" section. More than most other company websites, BCG's includes a wealth of job search information, from career tracks (there is basically one), profiles of personnel (very informative), and information on virtual project teams, to interview preparation and online applications. It also includes information on life after BCG, including associates, consultants, and alumni. The interview section is useful for any job seeker, since it deals with case interviews, interactive cases, brain teasers, and questions likely to be asked in a BCG interview. This site also includes a link to <u>Wetfeet.com</u> for a special report on BCG. For an employer website, it simply does not get much better than BCG. Indeed, this may be a model for other employer websites in the future.

Microsoft	**Employer**
<u>**microsoft.com/jobs/**</u>	

Microsoft literally receives hundreds, and sometimes thousands, of unsolicited resumes each day. In order to best manage the resume intake and screening processes, Microsoft maintains a separate "Jobs" section on its website. This section provides a good overview of life at Microsoft (campus, culture, diversity, benefits), information on its locations in the United States and abroad, career paths, and related job information. Job seekers can submit their resume online as well as search online job listings and apply for specific jobs. The site also includes feature articles and a "Hot Jobs" button. In many respects, this is a model recruitment site for a large corporation that has an excellent word-of-mouth reputation as being a great place to work. Since Microsoft is able to meet many of its personnel needs just through the operation of this section on their website, you may not find many Microsoft positions listed in the many websites outlined in this book. In other words, if you want to work for Microsoft, go directly to the "Jobs" section on their site and follow the application and database instructions.

14

Specialty Occupational and Job Sites

WHILE MANY OF THE MEGA EMPLOYMENT SITES identified in Chapter 5 may include job postings and resume databases related to your occupational interests, numerous other sites specialize in particular occupational fields. Often referred to as "niche" or "boutique" employment sites, these are very focused websites. Employers and recruiters increasingly use these sites because they are more likely to attract the types of candidates they are looking for than the more general mega employment sites. Best of all for job seekers, these niche sites include lots of useful information on their profession, from special news features to networking opportunities with fellow professionals.

Finding Your Specialty

The sites featured in this chapter represent a few of many employment websites that primarily focus on specific occupational fields. If your field is not represented here, we recommend using the search engines identified in Chapter 2, such as google.com or the meta search engine 1-Page Multi Search (bjorgul.com), to find additional sites related to

your occupational interests. At the same time, you should visit several of the mega employment websites outlined in Chapter 5. Monster.com and Headhunter.net, as well as a few other sites, operate specialty occupational sites. You also should review the websites of professional associations related to your occupational interests. Many of these associations operate placement services and online databases for linking job seekers with employers. For quick online access to these groups, check out these two sites for identifying your relevant professional associations:

- **Associations on the Net**   ipl.org/ref/AON
- **Association Center**   associationcentral.com

Academia and Education

Numerous websites focus on job opportunities for educators. Over 80 percent of these sites are found within professional academic associations or focus on particular disciplines, such as library science, physics, and mathematics. You may want to first explore the career or employment sections of your professional association and then check out several education employment sites found here. Ironically, the Internet has not significantly altered the way many educational institutions hire (lengthy job descriptions with lots of formal duties and responsibilities and application requirements involving a curriculum vitae, three letters of recommendation, and perhaps samples of articles written or copies of teaching evaluations). With a few exceptions, this employment sector is still primarily wedded to the traditional print job announcement that usually goes into the placement section of their professional association's magazine or newspaper. The following websites are well worth visiting for uncovering employment opportunities in education at all levels, from teaching to administration.

Academic360.com	Academia
academic360.com	

This site represents a meta-collection of websites for the academic hunter. It includes links to HR announcements at nearly 1,800 colleges and universities in the U.S., Canada, Australia, and the United Kingdom. It also links to faculty and administrative listings at various institutions as well as faculty and administrative position announcements by discipline found with professional associations.

Chronicle of Higher Education	**Academia**
chronicle.com/jobs	

If you are in academia – faculty, administrative, executive, or nonacademic position – you'll want to make this one of your first Internet stops. After all, most major colleges and universities routinely post their job announcements with *The Chronicle of Higher Education*. This site includes hundreds of traditional job listings which also appear in the print edition of *The Chronicle of Higher Education*. While the site does not offer a resume database, it does include a keyword search function, an email alert option, career news, salary surveys (averages by institution and rank), articles, advice, and much more. A recent article showed readers how to transform their traditional academic C.V. into a resume. Great site for career information but not very inspired use of Internet technology, especially given the absence of a resume database.

Higher Education Jobs	**Academia**
higheredjobs.com	

One of the fastest growing and most popular academic employment sites, Higher Education Jobs claims to have over 3,300 faculty and staff positions at more than 550 colleges and universities in its database. Job seekers can search positions by academic category (administrative/staff, executive, faculty, part-time/adjunct) and location (state/province or institution). The site also allows individuals to post their resumes online, receive job announcements by email, and track their applications.

Education America Network   Academia
educationamerica.net

This is a very user-friendly site that allows job seekers to post resumes online and search for positions by category and location. Covers all types of educational institutions. Allows users to browse for employers. Includes a useful resource section (state certification and salary information and job search tips on resumes, cover letters, and interviews) and an international education section.

K-12Jobs   Education
k12jobs.com

This no-frills site does exactly what you might expect – includes a large job posting section where job seekers can view available opportunities at kindergarten, elementary schools, junior high schools, high schools, and vocational schools. Job seekers also can post their resumes online. The site includes sections on job fairs, state certifications, education resources, resumes, salaries, news groups, and Q&A.

Academic Employment Network   Academia
academploy.com

This site covers academic positions at all levels – from primary to higher education. Allows job seekers to post their resumes online, search job listings, and review useful professional development resources. Job seekers can use the locator database, which includes 675 school districts and universities, by paying a user fee of $19.95 for six months. They also can post their resume for a fee of $9.95 for six months. Employers pay to post positions online. Compared to most employment websites that have worked out a more user-friendly revenue model, this one seems to be a nickel-dime operation by charging fees at both ends – job seeker and employer.

Several additional websites also focus on teaching and other academic jobs:

- Academic Careers Online   academiccareers.com
- Academic Position Network   apnjobs.com
- American Association of   aacc.nche.edu/career/
  Community Colleges   careerline.asp
- Carney Sandoe & Associates   csa-teach.com
- C-collegeJobs.com   ccollegejobs.com
- Ed-U-Link   edulink.com
- Education Jobs   nationjob.com/education
- Education-Jobs.net   education-jobs.net
- EducationJobs.com   educationjobs.com
- Education World   educationworld.com/jobs
- ESLworldwide.com   eslworldwide.com
- iTeachNet (international)   iteachnet.com
- Jobsinschools.com   jobsinschools.com
- National Teacher
  Recruitment Clearinghouse   recruitingteachers.org
- Private School Jobs   privateschooljobs.com
- School Staff   schoolstaff.com
- Teacher Job Links   geocities.com/athens/forum/
                                     2080
- Teacherjobsite.com   teacherjobsite.com
- Teachers Employment
  Network   teachingjobs.com
- TeachersNet   teachers.net/jobs
- Teacher's Planet.com   teachersplanet.com
- Teachers @ Work   teachersatwork.com
- Teachers-Teachers.com   teachers-teachers.com
- Teaching Jobs Overseas   joyjobs.com
- TeachWave   teachwave.com
- TEFLnetJobs   tefl.net/jobs
- TESOL JobFinder   tesol.org/careers
- The International Educator   tieonline.com

- USTeach.com   usteach.com
- WantToTeach.com   wanttoteach.com
- Women in Higher Education   wihe.com/jobs

Airline Industry

While most airlines maintain an employment section on their websites, check out these websites for job information related to the airline industry.

AirlineCareer.com   **Airlines**
airlinecareer.com

If you are interested in becoming a flight attendant, this site will help focus your job search and give you a competitive advantage in what remains a highly competitive career field. It includes an online pre-qualification test and feature articles about flight attendants. It includes numerous services to help individuals become flight attendants – a career Evaluation Center, a comprehensive Application Center, an interactive Testing Center, 60 sample interview questions, pay rates for the 10 major airlines, sample resumes, cover and thank-you letters, employment data on the 10 major airlines, an interactive message board, numerous links to other sites, and much more. The membership fee for this site is $39.95 for one year or $59.95 for two years.

Aviation Jobs Online   **Airlines**
www.aviationjobsonline.com

Individuals can become members of this site by paying $9.95 a month to access its job listings, post resumes online, and receive job search tips, including sample interview questions. This site also offers special six-month ($59.98) and one-year ($79.98) rates and an occasional special. Membership entitles user access to one of the following job areas: pilots and flight instructors; mechanics and avionics (maintenance); and flight attendants. Includes an extensive free section with links to numerous aviation-related employers.

Airline Employment Assistance Corps   Airlines
   and AV Jobs Worldwide
   avjobs.com

This is a very rich site for anyone seeking a job in aviation. Includes hundreds of job postings drawn from classified ads and a resume database. The site also includes job search tips, news, statistics, chat, links, education opportunities, and much more. Individuals must become members in order to use the job search and resume services. The monthly cost is $19.95 for basic membership (job search only) or $24.95 for extended membership (job search plus resume services).

Other useful airline employment sites, which cover everyone from ground crew to flight crew, include:

- Airline Employee
  Placement Service   aeps.com
- Airline Job Site   airlinejobsite.com
- Airport Job Hub   airportjobhub.com
- Airport Job Kiosk   airportjobkiosk.com
- AviationNet   aviationnet.com
- Aviation Job Search   aviationjobsearch.com
- Find a Pilot   findapilot.com
- Flight Deck Recruitment   flightdeckrecruitment.com
- Flying Talent   flyingtalent.com
- Helicopter Employment   avemployment.com
- Jet Careers   jetcareers.com
- Jobs in Aviation   jobsinaviation.com
- Pilots Wanted   pilotswanted.com
- Traveljobz.net   traveljobz.net

Architecture

Architects have numerous job search sites from which to locate job opportunities. Two popular such sites include the following:

Architect Jobs	**Architects**
architectjobs.com	

This site is one of the largest online sources for architect jobs. Job seekers can review online job listings as well as post their resume into the site's resume database. Includes architect salary information, an email service to automatically receive new job postings, a resume writing service, and a searchable database of recruiters specializing in architect placements.

Architect Search	**Architects**
archsearch.com	
architect-placement.com	

This is an online headhunter site. Offers job seekers job listings and asks them to submit their resume online. The job listings are very brief and can only be pulled down by state location. Includes three online downloadable resume templates for creating a resume – really dreadful templates that will most likely result in creating a resume appropriate for the 1970s but is used in-house to market candidates to employers! Includes a useful section on job interview tips. Testimonials from satisfied job seekers indicate there may be more to this site than what is initially apparent.

Several sites specializing in construction jobs also includes jobs for architects. Other useful employment websites for architects include the following:

- A/E/C JobBank   aecjobbank.com
- Computer Architect Jobs   computerarchitectjobs.com

Welcome to
bankjobs.com!
Wednesday, August
08, 2001 12:52:39

bankjobs.com
turning jobs into careers

financial
services
careers
online

about + contact + advertising/partnerships

▼ Quick Searches ▼

job seekers

For Jobs

All States
Alabama
Alaska
Arizona

search NOW!

- ▸ post your resume
- ▸ view your resume
- ▸ search jobs
- ▸ bank profiles/links

choose your own path

employers

- post jobs ◂
- search resumes ◂
- preview resumes ◂
- buy resume password ◂

Click Below to Visit

WACHOVIA

IJL ● Wachovia

Regions Bank

AMERICAN BANKER.com

For Resumes

All States
Alabama
Alaska
Arizona

search NOW!

For a detailed
search:
Search Jobs or
Preview Resumes

Client Services, Banking Operations
& IT Positions Available

BISYS

Employers / Recruiters

View my Jobs

Click here to view your
posted positions...*fast!*

AMERICAN BANKER NEWS

After Wachovia, Don't Expect a Slew of Hostile Deals: "Banks have not
frequently attempted hostile bids and most have failed. In the past 15 years
bankers have attempted fewer than a dozen hostile bids " *go to story*

**M & A Midyear Review- Cheaper, Lower Profile than Whole-Bank
Deals, Branch Buys on the Rise :** "Industry insiders say that an important
difference between buying branches and a whole institution is that branches
are revenue-producing and functional only after they have been
converted " *go to story*

- Craig's List   craigslist.org
- Just Architect Jobs   justarchitectjobs.com
- Landscape Architects   landscapearchitects.org

Arts, Entertainment, and Media

If you are in the arts, entertainment, and/or media business, you're in luck. Numerous sites focus on the diverse employment needs of several occupational groups subsumed under arts and entertainment.

Entertainment Careers   **Entertainment**
entertainmentcareers.net

Primarily a job bulletin board, this site allows job seekers to browse listings by position, including internships. Maintains regional sites for New York, Northern California, Southern California, and Chicago. Includes the names and telephone numbers of the major studios (under "Job Lines") as well as hotlinks to 34 studios (under "Studios").

ShowBizJobs.com   **Entertainment**
showbizjobs.com

This is a highly functional site for job seekers in the entertainment business. Job seekers can browse job listings by region, job category, minimum salary, company, and date. They also can search by keyword for full-time, part-time, and contract jobs. A career resource section, which includes free and fee-based (Premium Service at $35.00 for six months) services, offers chat and message boards, networking opportunities, email, industry news, bookstore, salary comparables, lists of headhunters, company research, and job placement agency recommendations.

Hollywood Web   Entertainment
hollywoodweb.com

This is a casting search center for directors, actors, actresses, writers, technicians, models, extras, and other professionals involved in the entertainment industry. It's primarily an online job bulletin board consisting of hundreds of job postings. Not particularly user-friendly, it only has one large page that starts with "Actors" and proceeds to "Male Models." Everything in between is a job summary. Many positions are probably no longer open since they were initially posted one to two years ago. The site also provides links to other sites.

Art Job Online   Arts
artjob.org

This site allows job seekers in the visual arts to search for full- and part-time employment, internships, grants, public art projects, and residencies by region, art discipline, and type of organization. The site also includes featured articles and links to other sites that provide job search assistance on everything from assessing skills and writing resumes to interviewing and negotiating salary. Job seekers must register and pay fees for accessing the job postings – $25 for three months, $40 for six months, and $75 for one year.

Other useful websites focusing on jobs in arts and entertainment include:

- 440 International (Radio)   440int.com
- AM/FM Jobs   amfmjobs.com
- Aquent   portfolio.skill.com
- ArtHire   arthire.com
- Artist Resource   www.artistresource.org/jobs.htm

- Arts Resume Resources — wwar.com/employment-resume
- ArtSource — artsource.com
- Entertainment Job Search — dnaproductions.com/jobs.htm
- HollywoodWeb — hollywoodweb.com
- Medialine — medialine.com
- Media Jobz — mediajobz.com
- MediaRecruiter — mediarecruiter.com
- National Association of Broadcasters Career Center — nab.org/bcc
- Playbill Online — playbill.com/cgi-bin/plb/jobs?cmd=search
- Radio Online — radioonline.com
- Talent Works — talentworks.com
- Temp Art — tempart.com
- TVandRadioJobs.com — tvandradiojobs.com
- TVJobs.com — tvjobs.com

Business

In many respects, most of the mega employment sites outlined in Chapter 5 focus on business. However, many segments of the business community operate their own specialized sites. Some of them are connected to professional business associations while others are operated by entrepreneurs and headhunters. Here is a sampling of some of the best business sites.

Careers in Business   **Business**
careers-in-business.com

This site functions as a gateway to jobs in various business-related fields: accounting, consulting, finance, marketing, and nonprofit. Includes summaries of fields, recommended readings, links to online resources, and websites specializing in the particular career field. It's especially appropriate for someone interested in exploring different business fields or just embarking on a career in business.

Bank Jobs   Banking
bankjobs.com

During the past 10 years, banking has become one of the most volatile career fields with numerous institutions closing, cutting back, or merging with other banks. This site provides job search services to bank specialists. Individual job seekers can post their resume online as well as search a database of job listings (currently 15,000 postings). The site includes banking news features, bank profiles, and links to other sites.

Benefitslink.com   Business
benefitslink.com/jobs/index.shtml

If you are in the benefits field, this is the site for you. It's very small and narrowly focused. And there's nothing fancy about this rather simple-minded but very focused site – employers post "help wanted" ads and candidates post their resumes. The goal is simple – connect the two! The jobs can be searched by date, title, location, and employer; candidates can be searched by date, title, and state. You also can sign up for the free, confidential benefits-jobs mailing list. Includes a database of nearly 1,000 candidates and 300 jobs.

Telecom Careers   Telecom
telecomcareers.net

If you are in the telecommunications field, this site may be able to put you in contact with your next employer. Includes the standard online resume database and job postings. Job seekers can search for jobs by keyword, industry category, and location. The site also allows job seekers to set up a Telecom Search Agent, create an "in box" to store interesting jobs, and use several online career resources. The site includes a career center, training center, news, dictionary (to look up telecommunications terminology and abbreviations), bookstore, and a stock market center.

Accountant Jobs   Accounting
accountantjobs.com

Includes numerous job postings for job seekers as well as an online resume database for employers. Job seekers can elect to have new job postings automatically emailed to them. Offers online resume writing/revising assistance (fee-based) and links to its more than 225 other eJobstore sites (organized by occupational field).

Financial Jobs   Finance
www.financialjobs.com

This award-winning site includes a wealth of job search information for individuals seeking jobs in accounting and finance. In addition to its numerous job postings and resume database, the site includes expert advice, articles, and resources for improving one's job search and resume. Includes links to several other sites that provide career and relocation assistance, such as distinctiveweb.com and homefair.com.

Jobs4Sales   Sales
jobs4sales.com

This is one of the best online sites for sales and marketing jobs which also is part of the LocalCareers.com network. Job seekers can post their resume online as well as search for job listings. They can search for jobs by keywords, location, categories, and job class (from contract to full time). Includes numerous job search tips by career experts on resumes, interviews, and career fairs as well as links to other online job resources and sites with classified ads.

For additional examples of business-related employment websites, we recommend using google.com or the following meta search engine:

1-Page Multi Search   bjorgul.com

Alternatively, examine the directory listings available through these two gateway career sites:

- **AIRS Job Board Directory**   airsdirectory.com/jobboards
- **Quintessential Careers**   quintcareers.com

Computers and Information Technology

This is one of the largest categories of employment websites with literally hundreds of specialized sites focusing on high-tech jobs. Many of the sites are very narrowly focused around specific applications, such as Oracle and UNIX, new media, web design, telecom, and specific hardware and software. These also are some of the best designed sites since they showcase the talents of computer and IT professionals. The following sites are just a small sampling of more than 1,000 specialized computer and IT employment websites:

DICE	**Computers/IT**
dice.com	

This is one of the most popular websites for IT professionals interested in permanent, contract, and consulting jobs. It's also a popular site for both employers and recruiters in search of talent. The site includes over 50,000 high-tech jobs which users can search by keywords, skills, job titles, locations, and zip codes. While this is primarily a job posting site, it does allow job seekers to store their resume online, automatically receive new job postings by email, subscribe to a free career newsletter, and use several online job search tools and career resources. DICE's annual salary survey should be of special interest to job seekers.

Computer Jobs   Computers
computerjobs.com

This is one of the largest and most popular websites for job seekers in the computer field. Includes a database of over 16,000 jobs in 18 specialty areas. Job seekers can post their resumes on this site as well as search for jobs by location and keywords. Includes numerous useful career resources, such as career assessment, resume services, publications, user groups, and training events. Its annual salary survey is of special interest to anyone attempting to keep abreast of salary comparables in this fast-paced field.

IT Careers.com   Computers/IT
itcareers.com

This site is part of a larger publishing empire which includes several major IT magazines. Includes numerous job postings searchable by keyword and state location. Job seekers can create their own customized "Job Alert" profile that will result in having new job listings automatically sent to them by email. The site also includes informative articles, featured employers, and a link to its sister international IT site – jobuniverse.com.

Computer Work   Computers/IT
computerwork.com

Job seekers can enter their resume in the site's database and search for job postings by keywords, skills, job titles, or locations. Includes a "Family of Sites" for 47 different locations (cities and states) and skills sets (Unix, Networking, C++, Java, Windows, Oracle, and 10 other applications). The site usually has more than 10,000 active job postings and over 100,000 resumes in its database. Also operates two other related sites – www.resourcecenter.com and jobboard.net – which include links to numerous other employment websites.

American Jobs americanjobs.com	Computers/IT

This popular, award-winning site is designed to link high-tech computer and engineering job seekers with employers. Individuals can post resumes and search for jobs posted on the site by keywords, location, and job category. The site also includes separate newsletter and resource sections for both job seekers and employers as well as offers job seekers employer profiles.

Many other websites also focus on job opportunities in computers and information technology:

- AwesomeTechs.com   awesometechs.com
- Brainbench   brainbench.com
- Brainpower   brainpower.com
- Brainbuzz   brainbuzz.com
- Brassring (see Chapter 5)   brassring.com
- CareerShopIT   it.careershop.com
- CareerWeb (see Chapter 5)   careerweb.com
- ComputerScience Jobs   computersciencejobs.com
- Craig's List   craigslist.org
- DatabaseJobs.com   databasejobs.com
- Hire Strategy   hirestrategy.com
- Hot Tech Careers   www.hottechcareers.com
- IT Net   itnet.com
- IT Talent   ittalent.com
- Jobs4IT   jobs4it.com
- JustASPJobs   justaspjobs.com
- Operation IT   operationit.com
- Search Database   searchdatabase.com
- Techies.com   techies.com

Construction

The construction industry includes a wide range of jobs, from construction manager and carpenter to plumber and welder. The following sites include a wide variety of construction positions for numerous types of construction industries. Many of the sites focusing on architects, engineers, and real estate also deal with construction.

Construction Jobs   **Construction**
constructionjobs.com

Allows job seekers to post their resumes online and search for job listings relevant to more than 100 construction-related positions. Individuals can post their resumes free of charge to multiple construction industries and job titles. Employers pay subscription fees to post jobs and access the resume database.

Construction Job Store   **Construction**
constructionjobstore.com

This site allows users to post their resumes and review current job openings in construction search jobs by job title, company, and keyword. Includes employer profiles, an automatic email option, salary information, and links to related families of websites. Primarily functions as a job bank.

Other construction-related sites worth visiting include the following:

- Architect Jobs — architectjobs.com
- Careers in Construction — careersinconstruction.com
- Carpenter Jobs — carpenterjobs.com
- Construction Gigs — constructiongigs.com
- Construction Managers Job — constructionmanagerjob.com
- Construction Work Jobs — constructionworkjobs.com
- Contract Professionals — contractprofessionals.net
- Craft Hotline — crafthotline.com
- Electrician Jobs — electricianjobs.com
- Engineer Employment — engineeremployment.com

- Estimator Jobs   estimatorjobs.com
- Find a Sub   findasub.com
- iHire Construction   ihireconstruction.com
- Jobsite   jobsite.com
- Newhome Sales Jobs   newhomesalesjobs.com
- Plumber Jobs   plumberjobs.com
- Project Manager Jobs   projectmanagerjobs.com
- Trade Jobs Online   www.tradejobsonline.com

Engineering

Engineering is a very broad and diverse field encompassing a large variety of engineers. The following websites connect the employment world of engineers.

EngineeringJobs   **Engineering**
www.engineeringjobs.com

This is a rich site for job seekers who can post their resumes online and explore numerous employment resources. Includes alphabetical listings, along with contact information and links, of engineering firms, recruiters, and headhunters. Its sister site, contractengineering.com, is designed for individuals seeking contract, rather than permanent, work. Offers a fee-based ($35) resume distribution service that will blast your resume to 500 engineering recruitment agencies or headhunters. Includes links to several professional associations of engineers, many of which have their own job banks.

EngineerEmployment   **Engineering**
www.engineeremployment.com

Another site which is part of the ejobstores.com family of employment websites. Includes a resume database and job postings along with employer profiles and an automatic email notification option.

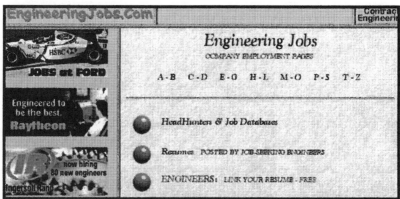

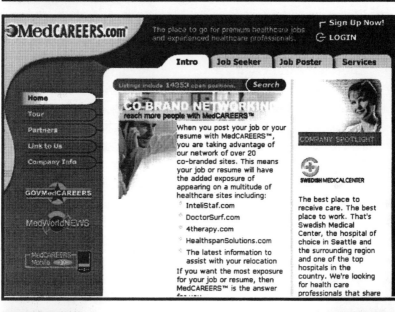

Other engineering sites, which tend to specialize in particular types of engineers, include:

■ Application-engineer-jobs	application-engineer-jobs.com
■ Biomedical Engineer	biomedicalengineer.com
■ Chemical Engineer	chemicalengineer.com
■ Chemical Engineer Jobs	chemicalengineerjobs.com
■ Civil Engineer Jobs	civilengineerjobs.com
■ Contract Engineering	contractengineering.com
■ Craig's List	craigslist.com
■ Electronic Engineer Jobs	electronicengineerjobs.com
■ Electronic Engineer	electronicengineer.com
■ Engineering-jobs-here	engineering-jobs-here.com
■ Environmental Engineer	environmentalengineer.com
■ Industrial Engineer	industrialengineer.com
■ Manufacturing Engineer	manufacturingengineer.com
■ Mechanical Engineer	mechanicalengineer.com
■ Network Engineer	networkengineer.com
■ Petroleum Engineer	petroleumengineer.com
■ Process Engineer Jobs	processengineerjobs.com
■ Sales Engineer	salesengineer.com
■ Semiconductor Engineer	semiconductorengineer.com
■ Software Engineer	softwareengineer.com

Health Care

Health care is one of today's fastest growing employment arenas. As hospitals and other health care providers scramble to meet continuing demand for talented employees, more and more health care-related websites have evolved to meet their needs. Several sites specialize in particular health care occupations, such as physician, nurse, hospital, radiology, dental, allied health, and emergency medicine.

Absolutely Health Care   **Healthcare**
healthcarejobsusa.com

This award-winning health care employment site includes a searchable resume database, job postings for 100 health care recruitment categories, and links to numerous employers. Includes corporate sponsor and nonprofit sections.

Monster Healthcare   **Healthcare**
healthcare.monster.com

Another well organized site operated by Monster.com. In addition to job postings and a resume database, this site includes informative articles, career resources, a message board, and a chat schedule.

MedHunters.com   **Healthcare**
medhunters.com

This site allows job seekers to post resumes and search job listings in all health care specialties. Its database includes over 9,000 job postings and more than 300 hospitals and employers. Special features include featured employers and location, career resources, employer events, testimonials, and tips. The "Professions" section includes valuable information on job postings, licensing requirements, professional organizations, education, contact information, and visa and immigration assistance for 20 health care professions.

MedCAREERS   **Healthcare**
www.medcareers.com

Job seekers can post resumes and search online job listings, which number nearly 15,000. This also profiles companies and includes several useful job search resources such as articles, salary calculator, and newsletter. Its "Networking" section includes links to several professional associations.

Numerous other health-related websites offer job opportunities for a large range of occupational specialties:

- 4 MD Jobs.com   4mdjobs.com
- 4 Nursing Jobs.Com   4nursingjobs.com
- Allied Health Employment   gvpub.com
- CompHealth   comphealth.com
- Dentist Jobs   dentistjobs.com
- DentSearch   dentsearch.com
- DocJob.com   docjob.com
- Echo-Web   echocareers.com
- e-Dental   e-dental.com
- EmployMED   employmed.com
- Future Med   futuremedical.com
- GovMedCareers   govmedcareers.com
- Health Care Jobs Online   hcjobsonline.com
- Health Care Recruiters   hcrecruiters.com
- Healthcare Careers Online   healthcareers.com
- Health Care Jobs (book)   healthcarejobs.org
- Health Care Job Store   healthcarejobstore.com
- Health Care Recruitment   healthcareers-online.com
- Health Care Source   healthcaresource.com
- Health Care Talents   healthcaretalents.com
- Health Care Works   healthcareworks.org
- Health CareerWeb   healthcareerweb.com
- Health Jobsite.com   healthjobsite.com
- Healthlinks.net   healthlinks.net
- HealthMedJobs.com   healthmedjobs.com
- Health Network USA   www.hnusa.com
- Health Opps   healthopps.com
- HIPjobs.net   HIPjobs.net
- Hospitalhub.com   hospitalhub.com
- Hospital Jobs Online   hospitaljobsonline.com
- Hospital Jobs USA   hospitaljobsusa.com
- iHireNursing   ihirenursing.com
- iHirePhysicians.com   ihirephysicians.com
- Job Health   jobhealth.net
- Job Health Careers   jobhealthcareers.net
- Jobscience   jobscience.com
- MD Direct.com   mddirect.com
- MDJobSite.com   mdjobsite.com

- Med Bulletin   mdbulletin.com
- Med Options   medoptions.com
- Medical Office Resources   mor-online.com
- Medical-Posts.com   medical-posts.com
- Medical Sales Jobs   medicalsalesjobs.com
- Medimorphus.com   medimorphus.com
- MedJobs2000   medjobs2000.com
- Medjump   medjump.com
- MedSearch   medsearch.com
- MedZilla   medzilla.com
- Nursejobz   nursejobz.com
- Nurse-Recruiter.com   nurse-recruiter.com
- Nursing Spectrum   nursingspectrum.com
- Pharmaceutical Rep Jobs   pharmaceuticalrepjobs.com
- PhysicianBoard   physicianboard.com
- Physician Employment   phyemp.com
- Practice Choice   practicechoice.com
- RTJobs.com   rtjobs.com
- Ultrasoundjobs.com   ultrasoundjobs.com
- Vital Careers   vitalcareers.com

Hospitality and Travel

The hospitality and travel industry is one of the largest and fastest growing industries in the world. It's also a truly global industry with millions of jobs available at home and abroad. Compared to most industries, this one tends to offer a very high level of job satisfaction. As long as economies grow, this sector of the job market should experience continuing growth.

While most major hospitality providers (hotels, resorts, restaurants, chefs, caterers, amusement parks, bars, convention centers, spas, travel agencies and operators, rail services, corporate travel managers, convention and meeting planners, tourist promotion offices, car rental companies, cruise lines, clubs, casinos) maintain their own websites with employment information, numerous other websites focus on supplying a fascinating range of talent to various sectors of this industry, from chefs (chefjob.com and chefnet.com) to gentlemen hosts (theworkingvacation.com).

Hospitality Adventures   Hospitality
hospitalityadventures.com

This is a major meeting place where employers and candidates in the hospitality industry meet, especially for hotel, restaurant, club, and cruise ship positions. Includes an online resume database and job listings that enable candidates to apply online for jobs. Include featured employers and links to numerous related clubs and organizations, colleges and universities, employment resources, publications, and state associations.

Hospitality Careers Online   Hospitality
hcareers.com

This very focused site basically does two things – allows job seekers to post their resumes online and search job postings and offers employers and recruiters the opportunity to access the resume database and advertise their opportunities online. Job seekers can search jobs by industry, position, management level, domestic and international locations, and keywords. Also includes employer profiles, links to professional organizations and services, career resources, hospitality programs at universities and colleges, and linkages to their separate sites for Canada and the United Kingdom/Ireland. Just for fun, check out the hilarious observations found under the "Unique Sites" section.

Job Monkey.com   Hospitality
jobmonkey.com

This friendly and colorful site allows job seekers to upload their resume or profile online as well as search and apply for jobs online. An especially appealing site for young people just starting a career or those looking for seasonal or part-time work in "cool" hospitality and travel jobs. Includes special coverage of jobs with Alaska fisheries, cruise lines, outdoors, airlines and airports, land tours, casinos and gaming, resorts, ski industry, and teaching abroad. The site is rich with resources, linkages, and special features. It also includes a travel center and a message board.

Numerous other websites focus on jobs and careers in the hospitality and travel industry. Some of the most interesting include:

- **Action Jobs**   actionjobs.com
- **Casino Careers Online**   casinocareers.com
- **Chef Job**   chefjob.com
- **Chef Jobs Network**   chefjobsnetwork.com
- **Chefs on the Net**   chefnet.com
- **Cool Works**   coolworks.com
- **e-Hospitality.com**   e-hospitality.com
- **Entree Job Bank**   entreejobbank.com
- **Escoffier.com**   escoffier.com
- **Food Industry Jobs.com**   foodindustryjobs.com
- **Food Management Search**   foodmanagementsearch.com
- **Foodservice Central**   foodservicecentral.com
- **Food Service.com**   foodservice.com
- **Food Smack**   foodsmack.com
- **Harrison Business Group**   harrisonbusinessgroup.com
- **Hospitality Careers**   www.hospitalitycareers.net
- **Hospitality Financial and Technology Professionals**   iaha.org
- **Hospitality Jobs Online**   hotel-jobs.com
- **Hospitality Link**   hospitalitylink.com
- **Hospitality Net**   hospitalitynet.org
- **Hospitality Online**   hospitalityonline.com
- **Hotel Job Resource**   hoteljobresource.com
- **Hoteljobs.com**   hoteljobs.com
- **Hotel Jobs Network**   hoteljobsnetwork.com
- **Hotel Online Classifieds**   hotel-online.com
- **Hotel Resource**   hotelresource.com
- **Hotels Hiring Online**   hotels.hiringonline.com
- **iHire Hospitality**   ihirehospitality.com
- **iHire Hospitality Services**   ihirehospitalityservices.com

- International Seafarers   jobxchange.com
- Jobs in Paradise   jobsinparadise.com
- Jobspot   jobspotwildnetafrica.com
- Meeting Jobs   meetingjobs.com
- Meeting Professionals
  International   mpiweb.org/resources/jobs
- Outdoor Network   outdoornetwork.com
- Resort Jobs   resortjobs.com
- Resort Recruitment   resortrecruitment.com
- Restaurant Manager.net   restaurantmanager.net
- Restaurant Managers.Com   restaurantmanagers.com
- SE Hospitality   sehospitality.net
- Ship Center.com   shipcenter.com
- SkiingtheNet.com   skiingthenet.com
- Ski Resort Jobs   skiresortjobs.com
- Spa Jobs   spajobs.com
- Travel Jobs   traveljobs.com
- Traveljobz.net   traveljobz.net
- Workamper.com   workamper.com
- Working Vacation   theworkingvacation.com

Law

Whether you're looking for a job in law or changing careers within the legal field, you'll find several websites to assist you with your job search. The following sites showcase thousands of job postings and resumes of individuals in the legal field.

Legalstaff   **Law**
legalstaff.com

Attorneys, paralegals, and other legal support staff professionals can enter their resume into the online database as well as search for jobs posted in the employer database. The site also includes tips on setting goals, writing resumes and letters, handling references, and interviewing; a salary wizard; relocation tools; and a directory of legal schools and associations.

Attorney Jobs Online   Law
attorneyjobsonline.com

Attorneys turn to this site for exploring legal and law-related jobs. Attorneys can post their resume online as well as review online job listings of employers. Individuals must subscribe to this online service – $15.00 for 30 days, $25.00 for 60 days, $37.50 for 90 days, and $75.00 for six months. Institutions can subscribe at the rate of $500.00 a year for up to two computers. The site also includes frequently asked questions, a legal search center, and online career counseling. A Legal Career Center includes information on publications, advisories, trends, and questions as well as offers numerous suggestions for directions where attorneys might steer their careers other than the practice of law.

Law.com CareerCenter   Law
lawjobs.com

This is primarily a job board for lawyers, paralegals, and support staff. Includes job listings for five occupational groups: attorneys, paralegals, secretaries, administrative/support staff, and management and technical personnel. The site also includes news articles, a directory of search firms, links to recruiting pages of top law firms, links to temporary legal staffing services, salary surveys, and special lists, such as "The Global 50" law firms and "The 100 Most Influential Lawyers." Users also can search for legal recruiters by state. Does not include a resume database.

Other useful websites for individuals in the legal fields include the following:

- **411 Legal Info**   411legalinfo.com/JOBS
- **Attorney Job Store**   attorneyjobstore.com

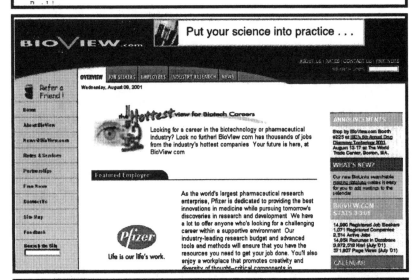

- AttorneyJobs.com   www.attorneyjobs.com
- Corporate Attorney Jobs   corporateattorneyjobs.com
- CounselHounds.com   counselhounds.com
- Counsel.net   counsel.net
- Craig's List   craigslist.com
- eAttorney   eattorney.com
- Emplawyer.net   emplawyernet.com
- Environmentalattorneyjobs   environmentalattorney
                                      jobs.com

- FindLaw Career Center   careers.findlaw.com
- Find Law Job.com   findlawjob.com
- Global Law Jobs   paralegal.il2.com
- iHire Legal   ihirelegal.com
- Jobs.LawInfo.com   jobs.lawinfo.com
- Juris Resources.com   jurisresources.com
- LawGuru.com   lawguru.com
- LawListings.com   lawlistings.com
- Law Match   lawmatch.com
- LawyersweeklyJobs.com   lawyersweeklyjobs.com
- LegalCV.com (UK)   legalcv.com
- Legal Employment   legalemploy.com
- LegalHire.com   legalhire.com
- Legal Job Store   legaljobstore.com
- Litigation Attorney Jobs   litigationattorneyjobs.com
- NationJob Network   nationjob.com/legal
- Paralegal.com   paralegal.com
- Paralegal-Jobs.com   paralegal-jobs.com
                                      paralegalclassifieds.com

- Paralegals.org   paralegals.org
- US Legal Jobs   uslegaljobs.com

Science

Science consists of numerous fields and specialties. Depending on your area of expertise, you should be able to find employment websites focusing on your occupational specialty. Some of the most popular science websites include the following:

BioView   Science
bioview.com

This well organized site is where top talent and employers in the biotechnology and pharmaceutical industries meet. Includes job postings and a capability to search private and public resume databases as well as search for resumes found on personal home pages and websites of professional associations and colleges. Job seekers can search jobs by discipline, location, and company. A special email feature will automatically send job postings to users who indicate a preference for receiving listings that match their profiles. Includes company profiles, company links, education resources, career resources (salary and relocation information, resume writing tips, and career links), meeting calendar, internships, and contract positions.

Science Careers   Science
recruit.sciencemag.org

This is the employment website of the American Association for the Advancement of Science and *Science Magazine*. It includes over 8,000 searchable job postings as well as a searchable resume database for employers. Its "Job Alerts" section automatically sends email notifications of jobs. The site also includes employer profiles, employer links, career fairs, advice and perspectives, meetings and announcements, career news, a salary survey, grants network, postdoc network, forums, articles, and academic programs. Be sure to check out the "Next Wave" section, which includes numerous job search tips and advice for scientists. A very well organized, intuitive, and informative website for job seekers. Indeed, many other employment websites could learn a lot by exploring the structure and content of this fine site.

JobSpectrum.org	Science
jobspectrum.org	

This is the official employment website of one of the world's largest professional associations of scientists, the American Chemical Society (ACS). Designed by chemists for chemists, the site includes hundreds of job postings as well as a searchable resume database for employers. The "New Jobs Alert" automatically emails job seekers the latest job listings relevant to their career interests. Includes salary information, employment trends, international opportunities, job search tips, career events, and company database links. Its many career development and job search tips come from the ACS Department of Career Services. A terrific site designed to provide first-class assistance to chemists but also very useful to anyone involved in job hunting.

Other websites targeted at different groups of scientists include the following:

- **Air Weather Association**   airweaassn.org/jobs.htm
- **Bio Online**   career.bio.com
- **ChemCenter**   acs.org/careers/employer/index.html
- **Chemical Online**   chemicalonline.com
- **ChemistryJobs.com**   chemistryjobs.com
- **ChemJobs.net**   chemjobs.net
- **DiscoverJobs**   discoverjobs.com
- **Earthworks**   earthworks-jobs.com
- **GeoJobs International**   geojobs.com
- **GeoSearch**   geosearch.com
- **GeoTechJobs**   geotechjobs.com
- **JobScience.com**   jobscience.com
- **Jobs4Scientists**   ajobs4scientists.com
- **NatureJobs**   nature.com/naturejobs
- **ScienceOnline**   recruit.sciencemag.org

- SciJobs.org   scijobs.org
- WeatherJobs.com   weatherjobs.com

Sports and Recreation

If sports and recreation are your passions, you're in luck with the Internet. Numerous sports- and recreation-related websites offer employment opportunities relating to golf, tennis, mountain climbing, skiing, racing, sports medicine, coaching, sports broadcasting, summer camps, clubs, resorts, stadiums, arenas, high schools, colleges, women, and the outdoors. While most of the positions are full-time, many jobs, especially in resorts and summer camps, are seasonal and part-time.

JobsinSports.com	Sports
jobsinsports.com	

This is a subscription-based online employment service. Individuals pay $29.95 per month to access the site's sports job and internship listings. Individuals also can post their resume to the site's database. Covers sports marketing, media, administration/management, sales, and computer/hi-tech positions.

CoolWorks.com	Recreation
coolworks.com	

This site includes over 75,000 jobs in its database. Job seekers can search the database as well as post their resume to the online searchable (employers) resume bank. Includes jobs with national parks, camps, resorts and lodges, amusement parks, ski resorts, guest ranches, boats and ships, state parks, internships, and volunteering. Especially appeals to students in search of seasonal recreational employment but also includes career professional employment.

GolfingCareers   **Sports**
golfingcareers.com

If you want to work in the golf industry, this may be the perfect site for locating job vacancies and posting your resume online. Includes several online job search tools for posting, editing, sending, and deleting a resume; searching for employers; accessing job postings; and reviewing upcoming golf events. The site also includes a list of golf associations in each state, including their telephone numbers and email addresses.

Other sports- and recreation-related employment sites worth exploring include the following:

- ActionJobs.com   actionjobs.com
- Camp Channel   campchannel.com/campjobs
- Camp Jobs   campjobs.com
- Camp Staff   campstaff.com
- C.O.A.C.H.   coachhelp.com/exe-bin/
                                    jsearch.cfm

- Coaching Jobs   coachingjobs.com
- Executive Sports Placement   prosportsjobs.com
- Gameops.com   gameops.com/tools/jobs/htm
- GolfSurfin   golfsurfin.com
- Great Summer Jobs   gsj.petersons.com
- JobMonkey   jobmonkey.com
- Monster Sports Jobs/ESPN   espn.monster.com
- Mountain Jobs   mountainjobs.com
- My Summers   mysummers.com
- NCAA Online   ncaa.org/employment.html
- OnlineSports.com   onlinesports.com
- Outdoor JobNet   outdoornetwork.com/
                                    jobnetdb/index.html

- Racing Jobs   racingjobs.com
- SkiingtheNet.com   skiingthenet.com
- Ski Resort Jobs   skiresortjobs.com

- Sports Business   sportsbusiness.about.com/
                            cs/employment
- Sports Careers   1andall-sportsjobs.com
- Sports Employment   sportsemployment.com
- Sports Jobs For Women   sportsjobsforwomen.com
- Sports Medicine   sportsmedicinejobs.com
- Sports Work   sportswork.com
- Sports Workers   sportsworkers.com
- TeamJobs.com   teamjobs.com
- Tennis Jobs   tennisjobs.com
- Title 9 Sports   title9sports.com/jobs/html
- Women's Sports Careers   womensportsjobs.com
- Work in Sports   workinsports.com

15

Niche Sites For
Special Job Seekers

OST OF THE JOB SITES FEATURED OR LISTED IN
Chapter 14 are relevant to specific communities of job
seekers who pursue certain occupations, such as education, law, chemistry, banking, nursing, medicine, engineering, information technology, art, entertainment, travel and hospitality, accounting, architecture, construction, and sports. Individuals
using these sites tend to identify with large and competitive occupational groups defined by their special skill sets.

At the same time, several communities of job seekers cut across
these standard occupational groups. They have special employment
needs because of their education, age, occupational status, gender, or
orientation toward particular types of employment. In this chapter we
feature numerous websites for these special groups.

College Students and Recent Grads

It's one of the largest and most targeted number of job seekers –
college students and recent graduates. Indeed, numerous employment
websites are designed to service the more than 5 million students who

graduate from college each year. These also can be some very volatile websites, as many open with high expectations but soon close because of the special challenges involved in working with this unique audience. For example, one of the best internship sites for college students, futurecollegegrads.com, closed on August 11, 2001. What remains are some very well organized and informative sites that can help college students, who are notoriously noted for putting off career planning and job search decisions until the very last minute – about one or two months before graduation! The following websites should be of special interest to college students and recent grads who need to get their act together to find a job and start a new, and hopefully rewarding, career.

CampusCareerCenter   **College Students**
campuscareercenter.com

This popular and informative site allows students to browse online job listings, apply for jobs, research companies, and acquire resume and interview tips. Includes numerous articles and featured employers as well as several unique elements – Career Corner, Foreign Exchange, Honor Roll, Inside Career Info, CCC Café, Diversity Center, and Visa Center. One of the few student sites with an international orientation by including visiting foreign national students in its scope of services. Oriented toward three audiences: students, employers, and university administrators. Students must register in order to use this site for free. Offers employers different recruitment options. A very well organized and focused site.

Job Web   **College Students**
www.jobweb.com

This is the student-oriented website of the National Association of Colleges and Employers. Since almost every college career services center belongs to this professional organization, the site reflects many of the information needs of its members. Indeed, it's one of the richest sites for career and job search information (see description on page 74). While it does not include job postings or a resume database, it does include articles, tips, advice, salary information, online career fairs, job market news, employer profiles, career library, and links to alumni groups, career centers, graduate schools, relocation resources, and much more. Students and employers will be especially interested in NACE's authoritative annual *Salary Survey* information on starting salaries for college graduates.

JobTrak   **College Students**
jobtrak.com

Operated by Monster.com, this site targets college students and recent graduates with all the resources and tools available in the Monster.com job search arsenal (see pages 74-75). It includes thousands of job listings and internships through both Monster and affiliate college and university career centers (most are password protected), career advice and tips, a college major to career converter, a salary center (online calculator powered by Robert Half International), chat center, and numerous archived articles. Includes featured resources, an online poll, alumni contacts, online car center, scholarship assistance, a tutoring service, and relocation information. A useful site for college students who need to start planning their job search by accessing many career-relevant resources.

CollegeJobs.com   **College Students**
www.collegejobs.com

This rather dark and foreboding college site allows job seekers to post resumes to the site's database as well as search for job listings online. Employers can post jobs online for free. Students can store multiple resumes online, just in case they're not sure what they want to do! The site features a few employers, highlights jobs, and includes a start-up center for targeting start-up companies (maybe not a good idea after the post-2000 crash of many such companies). Also includes a message board. Individuals must register in order to use this site.

Other college-oriented employment sites worth examining include the following:

- 123Intern.com — 123intern.com
- AboutJobs.com — aboutjobs.com
- AfterCollege.com — aftercollege.com
- Black Collegian — blackcollegian.com
- BrassRing Campus — brassringcampus.com
- CareerBuilder — college.careerbuilder.com
- CcollegeJobs.com — ccollegejobs.com
- College Central Network — collegecentral.com
- College Grad Job Hunter — collegegrad.com
- Collegejournal.com — collegejournal.com
- College News — collegenews.com/jobs.htm
- College Recruiter — collegerecruiter.com
- EmployU.com — employu.com
- Entryleveljobstore.com — entryleveljobstore.com
- eProNet — epronet.com
- EnviroLink Network — envirolink.netforchange.com
- Experience.com — experience.com
- Graduating Engineer Online — graduatingengineer.com
- InternJobs.com — internjobs.com
- InternshipPrograms.com — internshipprograms.com
- Internweb.com — www.internweb.com
- JobDirect.com — jobdirect.com
- JobMonkey.com — jobmonkey.com
- Kaplan, Inc. — kaplan.com
- NAGPS Internet Job Bank — nagps.org/Mailing-List.asp?target=job-bank

Military in Transition

Each year 260,000 members of the U.S. military service transition to the civilian world. While some of these transitioning service members go into full-time retirement, the majority look for civilian jobs in

government, business, or the nonprofit sector. Many enlisted personnel look for jobs in law enforcement, information technology, and
related security and technical fields. Junior and senior officers often
look for leadership and management jobs in a variety of occupational
areas.

Given the special employment needs of this talented group of
transitioning job seekers, several websites have been created to help
them connect with employers who especially wish to recruit individuals with military experience. While many employers are defense
contractors in need of military expertise and connections, other
employers understand the value of recruiting individuals with special
skills and work discipline normally associated with a military background. The following sites, as well as several websites featured in the
government, nonprofit, international, and spooks/spies/intel sections
of this chapter, also are relevant to this special group of job seekers.

Corporate Gray Online   **Military Transition**
www.greentogray.com or **www.bluetogray.com**

This unique site combines key online and offline job search
products and services to help transitioning military members
find employment: books, job fairs, and online job postings,
resume database, and other services. Unlike most websites that
use a strictly digital approach to employment, Corporate Gray
Online publishes with Impact Publications annual editions of
three self-directed career transition books that are given free of
charge to 260,000 transitioning military members: *From Army
Green to Corporate Gray*, *From Navy Blue to Corporate Gray*,
and *From Air Force Blue to Corporate Gray*. Sponsored by
employers interested in recruiting service members, the books
literally provide hands-on career guidance which, in turn, are
linked to a series of eight real-live job fairs held in six U.S. and
two European locations. Members of the military community
also can use this site to post their resumes online, browse job
listings, check on up-coming job fairs, and acquire additional
resources – from training and education to relocation assistance
– to help with their transition. In the interests of full disclosure,

we are closely associated with the writing, production, and distribution of the three books as well as providing content for this site. We believe combining both online and offline products and services – offline books and job fairs with an online database – provides one of the most powerful employment and recruitment approaches. Indeed, this is the only such employment site on the Internet that uses this unique approach to finding jobs and recruiting candidates. All products and services – books, job fairs, and website – are free to job seekers. The site also includes links to the homepages of sponsoring employers who are interested in recruiting individuals with military experience.

VetJobs.com	**Military Transition**
vetjobs.com	

This well designed site enables service members to post their resumes online, search for job postings, and explore numerous resources relevant to veterans. Special features include veteran service organizations, job search tips, veteran's and employer's newsletters, success stories, a military spouse section, forums, and links to exchanges, communities, and education services. Operated by Navy veterans dedicated to assisting fellow veterans in making job and career transitions as well as connecting to fellow members of the military community.

The Destiny Group	**Military Transition**
destinygroup.com	

This site enables job seekers to search for job postings by profession and location as well as post their resumes online. Includes additional services for employers and applicants, such as hiring forums, resume tools, and transition and interview advice. The Destiny Group also powers the employment sections of some other military-relevant websites, including alumni groups. Individuals must register to use this site.

TAOnline	Military Transition
taonline.com	

Now part of the Lucas Group, TAOnline offers a large range of online employment services to transitioning service members and veterans. Includes a resume database, job postings, and links to military job fairs and hiring conferences. Special sections provide useful information for spouses and dependents as well as relocation. The site markets its proprietary software products, First-Step (for students), JobMaker (for everyone), and Transition Assistance Software (for military).

Other websites focusing on transitioning military personnel include the following:

- Army Times   armytimes.com
- Armed Forces.com   armedforces.com
- Bradley-Morris.com   bradley-morris.com
- Cameron-Brooks   cameron-brooks.com
- IntelligenceCareers.com   intelligencecareers.com
- JMO Jobs   jmojobs.com
- Lucas Group   lucascareers.com/general/
                                      military
- Mil2Civ.com   mil2civ.com
- MilitaryCity.com   militarycity.com
- Military.com   military.com
- MilitaryHire.com   militaryhire.com
- Military Outplacement Post   midwestmilitary.com
- Military Partners   militarypartners.com
- Military Transition   militarytransition.com
- Military Transition Group   careercommandpost.com
- Monster.com   content.monster.com/military
- Military Overseas
  Recruiting Events, Inc.   morejobfairs.net
- Non Commission Officers
  Association (NCOA)   ncoausa.org

- Orion International   orion-careernetwork.com
- TekSystems.com   teksystems.com
- The Retired Officers
  Association (TROA)   troa.org/tops
- Veteran Net   veteran.net
- VeteransWorld.com   veteransworld.com
- Vets4Hire   vets4hire.com

Executive-Level Candidates

If you expect to be making $100,000+ a year, chances are you will find over 90 percent of the Internet employment sites irrelevant to your job search. You have very special employment needs that are best met by connecting with headhunters and CEOs rather than surveying job listings and entering your resume in a mega resume database that is primarily accessed by human resources personnel for lower level positions. Numerous websites now specialize on executive-level positions and candidates. We outlined several of these sites in Chapter 13 (pages 177-182) when we discussed recruiter sites. You should start with the following gateway site to executive recruiters: i-recruit.com.

Individuals interested in executive-level positions are well advised to visit the following sites. Several of them charge a monthly or quarterly "membership" fee to access their site while others are free. We recommend starting with the free sites since they may prove to be just as effective as the fee-based sites (we've seen no evidence to the contrary, but you'll have to be the judge). The free sites include:

- 6 Figure Jobs   sixfigurejobs.com
- Chief Monster.com   my.chief.monster.com
- Management Recruiters
  International   brilliantpeople.com
- Recruiters Online Network recruitersonline.com

Major fee-based sites for executive-level job seekers include:

- ExecuNet   execunet.com
- ExecutivesOnly   executivesonly.com
- Netshare   netshare.com

Women

If you are female, you'll find numerous websites devoted to women's employment and networking issues. As outlined in Chapter 10 (page 142), the web has become a very popular place for women's networks. From an employment perspective, many women's sites are organized by professions, such as women in accountancy, journalism, communication, real estate, higher education, technology, mathematics, sports, engineering, construction, and new media. Most of these sites include a career or employment section to assist their members in finding jobs through networking and job listings. The following associations are only a few of the many professional associations of women:

- **American Society of Women Accountants**   aswa.org
- **Association of Women in Mathematics**   awm-math.org
- **Association for Women in Sports Media**   awsmonline.org
- **Society of Women Engineers**   swe.org
- **Women in Communication**   womcom.org
- **Women in Higher Education**   wihe.com
- **Women in Technology International**   www.witi.com

The following websites represent communities of women who have common professional and personal interests, with special emphasis on jobs, careers, and work issues. Most of these sites include informative job or employment sections.

iVillage	Women
ivillage.com	

This is the mega website for women – the largest on the Internet. Includes numerous channels that focus on a wide range of issues of interest to women – from babies to work. The "Work" section includes tips on resumes, interviews, salaries, motivation, balancing work and family, networking, getting ahead, and working from home. It also includes quizzes, news, expert advice, articles, message boards, chats, and an entrepreneur institute. Its resume database and job postings are courtesy of a link with <u>careerbuilder.com</u>. It even includes a "Career Astrology" link to <u>career.astrology.com</u> – just for fun or perhaps a serious approach for some job seekers who feel powerless in today's job market! A very useful site that focuses on many employment issues of special interest to women.

Career-Intelligence.com <u>career-intelligence.com</u>	**Women**

Dubbed "The smart woman's online career resource," this site focuses on providing career tips and advice for women. It includes separate channels on assessment, job search, career management, and tools for success. The assessment section includes information on and examples of the Myers-Briggs Type Indicator®, Strong Interest Inventory®, and other assessment instruments. Includes a free newsletter, expert advice, and a separate section for freelancers and consultants.

CareerWomen <u>careerwomen.com</u>	**Women**

This is a full-service career site for women. Includes a resume database and job postings as well as several additional career services: corporate profiles, job search resources, career news, and expert advice. Its "Career Women Resources" sections include links to several professional associations for women in business. The "CW Living" section includes many links to websites of interest to women that deal with everything from education, relationships, and entertainment to health, fashion, lifestyle, parenting, travel, and diversity.

Womans-Work **womans-work.com**	**Women**

This site is rich with employment content for women. Includes a job board, resume database, and job search resources. Special sections include freelance jobs, family friendly employers, job share, salary comparisons, home businesses, and tips on balancing career and life. Offers featured articles and links to online education and training.

Other employment websites of special interest to women include the following:

- CareerWoman2000 — careerwoman2000.com
- ClassifiedsForWomen — classifiedsforwomen.com
- Digital Women — digital-women.com/work.htm
- Feminist Majority Foundation Online — feminist.org
- Girlgeeks — girlgeeks.com
- Herwebbiz.com — herwebgbiz.com
- Jobs4Women — jobs4women.com
- Msmoney.com — msmoney.com
- Women.com — ivillage.com
- WomenInfoline.com — www.womeninfoline.com/careers
- Womensforum.com — womensforum.com
- WomensJobSite.com — www.womensjobsite.com
- Women Sports Careers — womensportscareers.com / womensportsjobs.com
- WomenWork.com — womenwork.com

Minorities and Diversity

Minorities and diversity come in many different forms, from racial and ethnic minorities to immigrants, religious groups, gays and lesbians, women, disabled, and mature workers. The following websites provide a sampling of the many sites that are designed to service a wide range of minorities. Most of these sites include information on employment opportunities.

LatPro	Minorities
latpro.com	

This international job site is designed for Spanish and Portuguese Speakers. Offers a wide range of job listings from many top employers. Job seekers can search for jobs by region, country, and function. Includes numerous job search resources, such as job mailing lists, relocation center, newsletters, salary expert, online English, legal advice, resume writers, articles, and links to resources in seven Latin American countries, including international search firms. An excellent resource for bilingual job seekers.

Hire Diversity.com	Minorities
hirediversity.com	

Offers special diversity channels for African Americans, Asian Americans, disabled, gays and lesbians, Hispanics, mature workers, Native Americans, veterans, and women. Includes job postings and a resume database. Job seekers can search the job database by area of expertise and location. This site also includes separate sections on career resources, employers, government, and entrepreneurship.

DiversityLink.com	Minorities
diversitylink.com	

Targets female, minority, and other diversity professionals. Includes a resume database, job postings, profiles of candidates, featured employers, and a list of supporting organizations.

Other useful minority and diversity sites, many of which tend to specialize on a particular minority or diversity issue, include:

- Africareers.com   africareers.com
- Asia-Net.com   asia-net.com
- Asia-Jobs.com   asia-jobs.com
- Asian Careers.com   asiancareers.com
- Best Diversity Employers   bestdiversityemployers.com
- Bilingual-Jobs   bilingual-jobs.com
- Black Collegian   blackcollegian.com
- Blackenterprise.com   blackenterprise.com
- Black Voices   blackvoices.com/classified/
                                          jobs
- CareerMoves (Jewish)   www.jvsjobs.org
- ChristiaNet (Religious)   christianet.com/christianjobs
- ChristianJobs (Religious)   christianjobs.com
- CVLatino (Hispanic)   cvlatino.com
- Diversity Job Network   diversityjobnetwork.com
- Diversity Recruiting   diversityrecruiting.com
- Diversity Search.com   diversitysearch.com
- DiversiLink (Hispanic)   diversilink.com
- Diversity Employment   diversityemployment.com
- EOP Online   eop.com
- Gaywork.com (Gays)   gaywork.com
- Global Mission (Religious)   globalmission.org
- HireDiversity   hirediversity.com
- HispaniaNet.com (Hispanic)   www.rapsystem.com/
                                          gateway/has
- Hispanic Online Cyber
  Career Center   hispaniconline.com
- IMdiversity.com   imdiversity.com
- Jewishcampstaff.com (Jewish)   jewishcampstaff.com
- JobCentro (Hispanic)   jobcentro.com
- JobLatino (Hispanic)   jobslatino.com
- LatinoWeb.com (Hispanic)   latinoweb.com
- MBXonline   mbxonline.com
- Ministry Connect (Religious)   ministryconnect.org
- MinistryJobs (Religious)   ministryjobs.com

- MinistrySearch.com   ministrysearch.com
- MinorityCareer.Com   www.minoritycareer.com
- MinorityNurse.com   minoritynurse.com
- Multicultural Advantage   tmaonline.net
- NativeAmericanJobs.com   nativeamericanjobs.com
- ProGayJobs.com (Gays)   progayjobs.com
- Saludos Hispanos (Hispanic)   saludoshispanos.com
- TodoLatino (Hispanic)   todolatino.com
- NativeJobs (Native-Americans) nativejobs.com
- VisaJobs (Immigrants)   visajobs.com
- Youth Specialities (Religious) youthspecialties.com
- WorkplaceDiversity.com   www.workplacediversity.com

People With Disabilities

Over 50 million people in the United States have some form of disability that may affect their work as well as their occupational choices. According to studies, everyone joins the disabled for several years during their lives, with 13 years often given as the average period for disabilities.

People with disabilities can turn to several websites for assistance. However, very few sites include resume databases and job listings for the disabled. Unfortunately, most such websites primarily dispense information about disabilities and focus on training. But more and more websites focus on linking disabled job seekers with employers who actively seek to recruit such candidates.

> **State Vocational and   Disabled Rehabilitation Agencies**
> **http://trfn.clpgh.org/srac/state-vr.html**

This is a gateway site to state vocational and rehabilitation agencies that provide important services for disabled persons – counseling, evaluation, training, and job placement. These agencies also provide services for the sight and hearing impaired. Includes names, addresses, phone and fax numbers, and email addresses of key agencies.

Job Accommodation Network   Disabled
www.jan.wvu.edu

This is another useful gateway site for accessing numerous resources relevant to disabled people. Includes linkages to websites that specialize in particular types of disabilities, such as addictions, cardiovascular and pulmonary, musculoskeletal, psychiatric, and sensory.

Job Access   Disabled
jobaccess.org

This site is designed to assist job seekers in finding employment with businesses, government agencies, and nonprofit organizations. It includes a resume database, job postings, and online career fairs through its relationship with headhunter.net. Most of the job services are generic to all job seekers, regardless of disabilities.

Disabled Person   Disabled
disabledperson.com

Includes a "Recruitability" section designed to assist disabled people in finding a job. Includes job postings and a resume database for employers and placement agencies. Other sections on this site deal with a variety of issues relevant to disabled people.

Several other websites also focus on the employment needs of disabled people:

- Able to Work   abletowork.org
- Act-Together   geocities.com/CapitolHill/
                             5975

- American Association of
  People With Disabilities   www.aapd-dc.org
- Careers On-Line   disserv3.stu.umn.edu/COL/
                                    index.html
- Challenge 2000   www2.interaccess.c om/
                                    netown/eeo/eeoempl.htm
- Choice Employment   choiceemployment.com
- Davjobs.com   davjobs.com
- Department of Labor   www.dol.gov/dol/odep/
                                    public/joblinks.htm
- EOP.com   eop.com/mag-cd.html
- Federal Jobs   federaljobs.net/disabled.htm
- Handiwork Online   handiworkonline.com
- New Mobility   newmobility.com
- The Work Site (SSA)   ssa.gov/work/index2.html
- Training Resource Network   trninc.com
- WorkSupport   worksupport.com

Government and Law Enforcement

If you're interested in working with government – over 20 million U.S. citizens do – you will find numerous websites focused on federal, state, and local government. While most U.S. federal, state, and local government agencies maintain their own websites, similar to the company websites of businesses, other websites bring together all of government. Several websites also focus on specialty areas, such as law enforcement, within government at all levels.

USA Jobs	Government
www.usajobs.opm.gov	

This is the federal government's (Office of Personnel Management) gateway site to federal employment. Functions as a job board for vacancies with various federal agencies. Includes information on the application process, Senior Executive Service, student employment, veterans preference, and online applications.

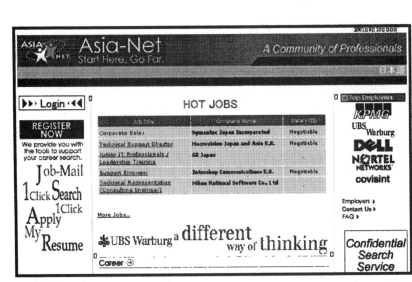

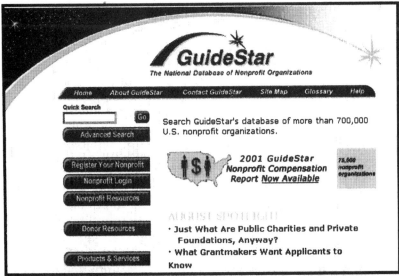

Federal Jobs Central   Government
fedjobs.com

Publishers of the popular *Federal Jobs Digest*, which lists vacancies with most federal agencies, this site includes one of the most comprehensive databases of current federal job openings. Includes featured agencies, pay scales, application tools, tips, and links to other resources.

Federal Jobs Digest   Government
jobsfed.com

Publishers of the long-running Federal Jobs Digest, this site includes a huge database of agency vacancies along with a job matching service, federal benefits, hiring news, federal resume advice, and a bookstore (includes only two of their own titles).

Lawenforcementjob.com   Law Enforcement
lawenforcementjob.com

Offices a wealth of information on law enforcement careers. Includes job postings, message boards, online tests, linkages to other relevant sites, and bookstore.

Numerous other websites also focus on government and law enforcement jobs:

- **Careers in Government**   careersingovernment.com
- **Careers in Law Enforcement**   lejobs.com
- **Classified Employment**
  Web Site   yourinfosource.com/CLEWS
- **Cop Career.com**   copcareer.com
- **Corrections.com**   database.corrections.com/
                                     career

- Federal Jobs Digest   jobsfed.com
- Federal Jobs Net   federaljobs.net
- FederalJobSearch   federaljobsearch.com
- Federal Times   federaltimes.com
- FedGate   fedgate.org
- FedWorld.gov   www.fedworld.gov
- FirstGov   firstgov.gov
- GovernmentJobs.com   governmentjobs.com
- Govjobs.com   govjobs.com
                             govtjob.net
- Jobs4PublicSector (Europe) jobs4publicsector.com
- Law Enforcement Job   lawenforcementjob.com
- Law Enforcement Jobs   lawenforcementjobs.com
- Officer.com   officer.com
- PoliceCareer.com   policecareer.com
- PSE-NET.com   PSE-NET.com
- StateJobs.com   statejobs.com
- United Nations   unsystem.org
- US Government Jobs.com   usgovernmentjobs.com
- Whitehouse   whitehouse.gov

If you're interested in working for the federal government, you may want to explore employment opportunities with these major federal agencies:

- African Development
  Foundation   www.adj.gov
- Agency for International
  Development (USAID)   www.usaid.gov
- Central Intelligence Agency www.cia.gov
- Consumer Product Safety
  Commission   www.cpsc.gov
- Department of Agriculture   www.usda.gov
- Department of Commerce   www.doc.gov
- Department of Defense   www.dtic.mil
- Department of Energy   www.doe.gov
- Department of Health
  and Human Services   www.os.dhhs.gov

- Department of Justice   www.usdoj.gov
- Department of State   www.state.gov
- Department of
  Transportation   www.dot.gov
- Environmental Protection
  Agency   www.epa.gov
- Export-Import Bank   www.exim.gov
- Federal Communications
  Commission   www.fcc.gov
- Federal Emergency
  Management Agency   www.fema.gov
- General Services
  Administration   www.gsa.gov
- Immigration and
  Naturalization Service   www.ins.usdoj.gov
- Inter-American Foundation   www.iaf.gov
- Internal Revenue Service   www.irs.ustreas.gov
- Peace Corps   www.peacecorps.com
- Smithsonian Institution   www.si.edu
- U.S. Postal Service   www.usps.gov

Nonprofit Sector

The U.S. nonprofit sector employs over 10 million people in the United States and abroad. It offers numerous opportunities for people interested in pursuing a cause and helping people. Initially slow to use the Internet, the nonprofit sector has increasingly become active in recruiting online. The following sites function as gateways to the employment world of the nonprofit sector.

GuideStar	Nonprofits
guidestar.org	

This is the ultimate gateway site for researching the nonprofit sector. Includes a database of more the 700,000 U.S. nonprofit organizations. Use the search engine to find a nonprofit that fits your particular interests. The site also includes an annual nonprofit compensation report, articles, news, conferences, and links to other related sites.

Action Without Borders idealist.org	Nonprofits

If you are interested in international nonprofit organizations, it doesn't get any better than this gateway site to jobs with international nonprofits. Includes links to thousands of job resources in 153countries. Offers job postings, a "push" email service, and newsletter. Resources cover organizations, jobs, volunteering, services, campaigns, events, internships, career affairs, career information, and tools for organizations.

Access www.accessjobs.org	Nonprofits

Access operates as an employment clearinghouse for the non-profit sector. Includes a database of jobs with the nonprofit sector. Job seekers can post their resumes online. Regularly sponsors job fairs for nonprofit organizations. Includes an internship and volunteer section, career counseling services, links to partner sites, and a bookstore.

Several of the following websites function as gateways to thousands of nonprofit organizations:

- **Charity Village**   charityvillage.com
- **Council on Foundations**   cof.org
- **Foundation Center**   fdncenter.org
- **Impact Online**   impactonline.org
- **Independent Sector**   indepsec.org
- **Internet Nonprofit Center**   nonprofits.org

If you are interested in working with international nonprofit organizations, begin by exploring the gateway website, Action Without

Borders site (idealist.org). Also, include in your research the following websites:

- AIESEC   aiesec.org
- Global Health Council   www.globalhealth.org
- IAESTE   iaeste.org
- InterAction   interaction.org
- Intercristo   jobleads.org
- International Service
  Agencies   charity.org
- JustAct (Youth Action
  for Global Justice)   justact.org
- PACT   pactworld.com
- Volunteers for Peace   www.vfp.org
- World Learning   worldlearning.org

Some of the major nonprofit organizations that also maintain informative websites include:

- Academy For Educational
  Development   aed.org
- ACCION International   accion.org
- Adventist Development and
  Relief Agency International   www.adra.org
- Africare, Inc.   africare.org
- Agricultural Co-op
  Development International   www.acdivoca.org
- Air Serv International   airserv.org
- American Friends
  Service Committee   www.afsc.org
- American Jewish Joint
  Distribution Committee   www.ajc.org
- American Red Cross
  International Services   redcross.org/services/intl
- AmeriCares Foundation   www.americares.org
- Amnesty International (USA)   amnesty-usa.org
- Asia Foundation   www.asiafoundation.org
- Battelle Memorial Institute   www.battelle.org

- Bread for the World   www.bread.org
- Brother's Brother Foundation   www.brothersbrother.org
- CARE   www.care.org
- Catholic Relief Services   www.catholicrelief.org
- Centre For Development
  and Population Activities   www.cedpa.org
- Childreach   www.childreach.org
- Christian Children's Fund   christianchildrensfund.org
- Church World Service   churchworldservice.org
- Compassion International   www.ci.org
- Direct Relief International   directrelief.org
- Doctors Without Borders   dwb.org
- Educational Development
  Center   www.edc.org
- Family Health International   www.fhi.org
- Food For the Hungry, Inc.   fh.org
- Global Health Council   www.globalhealth.org
- Greenpeace   greenpeaceusa.org
- Habitat For Humanity
  International   habitat.org
- Heifer Project International   heifer.org
- Helen Keller International   hki.org
- The Hunger Project   www.thp.org
- Institute of International
  Education   www.iie.org
- InterExchange   interexchange.org
- International Aid, Inc.   internationalaid.org
- International Catholic
  Migration Commission   www.icmc.net
- International Development
  Enterprises   ideorg.org
- International Executive
  Service Corps   www.iesc.org
- International Eye Foundation   iefusa.org
- International Institute of
  Rural Reconstruction   panasia.org.sg/iirr
- International Rescue
  Committee   www.intrescom.org

- LASPAU – Academic and
  Professional Programs
  for the Americas   www.laspau.harvard.edu
- Laubach Literacy
  International   laubach.org
- Lutheran Immigration
  and Refugee Service   www.lirs.org
- Lutheran World Relief   www.lwr.org
- MAP International   www.map.org
- Mennonite Central
  Committee   www.mcc.org
- Mercy Corps International   mercycorps.org
- MidAmerica International
  Agricultural Consortium   miac.org
- National Cooperative
  Business Association   www.cooperative.org
- National Widelife Federation   nwf.org
- The Nature Conservancy   tnc.org
- OIC (Opportunities Industrial
  Centers) International   www.oicinternational.org
- Operation USA   opusa.org
- Opportunity International   www.opportunity.org
- Oxfam America   www.oxfamamerica.org
- PACT (Private Agencies
  Collaborating Together)   pactworld.org
- Partners of the Americas   www.partners.net
- Pathfinder International   www.pathfind.org
- People to People Health
  Foundation (Project HOPE)   projhope.org
- PLAN International   www.plan-international.org
- Planned Parenthood
  Federation   plannedparenthood.org
- Population Action
  International   populationaction.org
- Population Council   www.popcouncil.org
- Population Reference Bureau   www.prb.org
- Population Services
  International   www.psi.org

- Program for Appropriate
  Technology in Health   path.org
- Project Concern International projectconcern.org
- Research Triangle Institute www.rti.org
- Salvation Army World
  Service Office   www.salvationarmy.org
- Save the Children
  Foundation, Inc.   savethechildren.org
- The Sierra Club   sierraclub.org
- TechnoServe   technoserve.org
- U.S. Catholic Conference
  Office of Migration
  and Refugee Services   www.nccbuscc.org/mrs
- U.S. Committee for UNICEF   www.unicefusa.org
- Unitarian Universalist
  Service Committee   www.uusc.org
- Volunteers in Overseas
  Cooperative Assistance   www.acdivoca.org
- Volunteers in Technical
  Assistance   www.vita.org
- Winrock International
  Institute for Agricultural
  Development   winrock.org
- World Concern   worldconcern.org
- World Council of
  Credit Unions   woccu.org
- World Education   www.worlded.org
- World Relief Corporation   worldrelief.org
- World Resources Institute   www.wri.org
- World SHARE, Inc.   www.worldshare.org
- World Vision Relief and
  Development, Inc.   worldvision.org
- World Wildlife Fund   wwf.org
- Worldteach   worldteach.org
- Worldwatch Institute   www.worldwatch.org
- Y.M.C.A.   ymca.com
- Y.W.C.A.   www.ymca.org
- Zero Population Growth   zpg.org

The following nonprofit research, educational, and trade organizations and associations variously function as think tanks, lobbying groups, and training organizations. Most do a great deal of international work:

- **American Enterprise Institute (AEI)** — www.aei.org
- **Brookings Institution** — brook.edu
- **CATO Institute** — cato.org
- **Center for Strategic and International Studies** — www.csis.org
- **Chamber of Commerce** — www.uschamber.org
- **Council for International Exchange of Scholars** — www.cies.org
- **Council of the Americas** — counciloftheamericas.org
- **Council on Foreign Relations** — cfr.org
- **Council on International Educational Exchange** — www.ciee.org
- **Earthwatch Institute** — earthwatch.org
- **Foreign Policy Association** — fpa.org
- **Freedom House** — freedomhouse.org
- **Heritage Foundation** — heritage.org
- **Hoover Institute on War, Revolution, and Peace** — hoover.org
- **Human Rights Watch** — hrw.org
- **The International Center** — www.internationalcenter.com
- **International Food Policy Research Institute** — www.cgiar.org
- **International Schools Services** — iss.edu
- **Meridian International Center** — www.meridian.org
- **NAFSA/Association of International Educators** — nafsa.org
- **Near East Foundation** — neareast.org
- **Network for Change** — library.envirolink.org
- **Overseas Development Council** — odc.org

- RAND Corporation   www.rand.org
- U.S.-China Business Council www.uschina.org
- United States Olympic
  Committee   www.usoc.org
- The Urban Institute   urban.org
- World Learning   www.worldlearning.org
- World Neighbors   www.wn.org
- Youth for Understanding
  International Exchange   www.yfu.org

International Job Seekers

Individuals interested in international jobs tend to have a passion for working in the international arena. The passion is usually related to a particular region, country, or culture. Given the seeming difficulty in locating and communicating with international employers, the Internet has begun to play an increasingly important role in an international job search. Job seekers and employers can now quickly connect with each other and communicate by email and conduct online interviews. In addition to the many nonprofit international sites identified in the previous section, several other websites primarily focus on international jobs.

EscapeArtist.com escapeartist.com	International

This is the ultimate gateway site to the international arena. It's jam-packed with just about everything you ever wanted to know about moving, living, working, investing, and retiring abroad. It's a no-nonsense site that delivers lots of great content: *"We don't have a lot of nonsense about culture shock and 'how to keep in contact with home' chat-baloney. If you want to go, go; if you want to whimper, stay home. Home is where the heart's on fire."* The site includes extensive sections on international jobs. You can easily spend hours getting lost and found on this site. If there only is one international website you use, make sure it's this one.

Overseas Jobs   International
overseasjobs.com

This well organized site includes numerous international job listings as well as a resume database (through AboutJobs.com database). Offers company profiles, job search tips, mailing list, and links to related sites in its network.

Monster Work Abroad   International
international.monster.com

Another Monster.com specialty website, which includes a large database of international jobs, a huge resume database, expert advice, chats, boards, and articles. Includes job search tips and resources for improving an international job search. One of the best international job sites on the web. This site appeals to a wide range of international job seekers, from entry-level to senior level and consultants.

JobsAbroad.com   International
jobabroad.com

This site especially appeals to college students and recent graduates who want to work, study, and/or travel abroad. Includes information on internships, language schools, volunteering abroad, teaching abroad, and travel. Its jobs section includes job postings and linkages to country-specific sites.

Transitions Abroad   International
transitionabroad.com

A very popular site for students and others interested in work, study, and alternative travel. Packed with information and resources for anyone interested internships abroad, teaching English, volunteering abroad, and responsible travel. Publishes the popular *Transitions Abroad* magazine.

iAgora.com	International
iagora.com	

This site functions as an international community for exchanging information and advice on working, living, and studying abroad. Includes lots of useful job search tips, discussion groups, resources, and links. A great place to network with individuals from all over the world.

Other useful international employment-related sites include the following:

■ About.com	intljobs.about.com
■ AboutJobs.com	aboutjobs.com
■ ActiJob.com	actijob.com
■ Alliances Abroad	alliancesabroad.com
■ CareerWeb	careerweb.com
■ Dave's ESL Café	eslcafe.com
■ Expat Exchange	expatexchange.com
■ Global Career Center	globalcareercenter.com
■ Heidrick & Struggles	heidrick.com
■ International Jobs Center	internationaljobs.org
■ International Staffing Consultants	www.iscworld.com
■ International Resources (key resource site)	umich.edu/%7Eicenter/ overseas/work/workresources. html
■ Job Monkey.com	jobmonkey.com
■ Jobpilot.com	jobsadverts.com
■ Jobshark.com	jobshark.com
■ Jobs.Net	jobs.net
■ JobsDB.com	jobsdb.com
■ Jobware International	jobware.com

- **Korn/Ferry International**   ekornferry.com
- **Nicholson International**   nicholsonintl.com
- **Management Recruiters**
  International   brilliantpeople.com
- **PlanetRecruit**   planetrecruit.com
- **PricewaterhouseCoopers**   pwcglobal.com
- **Spencer Stuart**   spencerstuart.com
- **Teaching Jobs Overseas**   joyjobs.com
- **Top Jobs**   topjobs.net
- **WorldWorkz**   worldworkz.com

The largest number of websites for international job seekers are regional or country-specific, such as www.africajobs.net, asia-net.com, asiadragons.com, employment.com.au (Australia), jobscanada.com, eurojobs.com, www.southamericajobs.net, www.arabiajobs.net, and Monster.com's 15 country-specific websites. We outline hundreds of these and other international-related sites, including several international headhunter sites, in a separate companion volume, *The Directory of Websites For International Jobs Seekers* (Impact Publications).

Part-Time, Temporary, and Contract

During the past decade, the number of part-time, temporary, and contract employees has increased substantially. As a result, more and more staffing agencies have extended their services over the Internet. In addition to the temporary staffing agencies outlined in Chapter 13 (pages 183-184), the following websites are especially popular with individuals and employers interested in part-time, temporary, or contract work. Many of these sites specialize in IT workers who often prepare project-based contract arrangements to full-time jobs.

eLance	Free Agents
eLance.com	

Employers in need of project-by-project professional experience can use this site for identifying the right talent. Includes numerous project and professional categories. Job seekers can view various posted projects and apply online. Includes a search engine that employers can use to identify local expertise. Includes several special features, including tips on creating a profile, effective bidding, eLance Gallery, and eLanceDirect.

BrainBid.com   **Free Agents**
brainbid.com

If you enjoy being a free agent, working from project to project, and branding yourself as an expert, this may be the perfect site for marketing yourself to employers in search of such individuals. Job seekers bid on projects registered by employers. Site includes newsletters, recommended links, free agent resources, and community forums.

---

eWork   **Free Agents**
ework.com

Claiming more than 300,000 registered users in its talent market database, this site attempts to match the projects of hiring managers with independent professionals and small services firms that have the necessary skills. The site also includes newsletters, featured articles, and online courses. eWork also provides employers with payroll, benefits, and related personnel services.

Numerous other websites offer services for a wide range of free agents who want to work part-time or as contract workers:

- A2Zmoonlighter.com   a2zmoonlighter.com
- Aquent Talent Finder   aquent.com
- Consultants-On-Demand   consultants-on-demand.com
- ContractJobHunter   cjhunter.com
- Contract-Jobs.com   contract-jobs.com
- Contractorforum.com   contractorforum.com
- Dice.com   dice.com

▪ Do a Project	doaproject.com
▪ ePlaced.com	eplaced.com
▪ FreeAgent.com	freeagent.com
▪ Guru.com	guru.com
▪ Handyman.com	handyman.com
▪ Icplanet	icplanet.com
▪ Itmoonlighter.com	itmoonlighter.com
▪ MBA Free Agents.com	mbaglobalnet.com/freeagents.html
▪ Talentmarket.monster.com	talentmarket.monster.com
▪ Parttimejobstore.com	parttimejobstore.com
▪ Software Contractor's Guild	scguild.com
▪ Swiftwork	www.swiftwork.com
▪ TalentGateway	www.talentgateway.com
▪ Unicru	unicru.com

Freelancers and Telecommuters

Freelancers and telecommuters are a special type of free agents. Many of them are writers and designers who work on special stories and projects. Many also are work-at-home moms who create their own small businesses or acquire telecommuting jobs that range from telemarketing and customer service jobs operated from call centers to computer programming and online marketing conducted from homes. The following sites reveal numerous opportunities for these types of free agents who constitute a large segment of the working population. Indeed, some studies estimate that more than 20 million people in the United States may work in these nontraditional work settings.

MoneyFromHome.com **moneyfromhome.com**	**Home Work**

Posts jobs of interest to home-based workers. Screens legitimate versus scam operations that often plagued this employment arena. Includes a special section for moms, profiles of successful home workers, frequently asked questions. Individuals pay an annual membership fee of $35 to access this site.

Sologig.com   Freelancers
sologig.com

Designed for experienced freelancers, consultants, and independent professionals who wish to connect with some of the country's top employers and recruiters, this site includes a resume
database and project listings. The resource center includes
linkages to several resume writing and blasting services.

The following websites provide a wealth of information on free-
lancing, telecommuting, and home-based jobs:

- All Freelance   allfreelance.com
- Bullhorn   bullhorn.com
- FreelanceJobSearch.com   freelancejobsearch.com
- FreelanceOnline.com   freelanceonline.com
- FreelanceWriting.com   freelancewriting.com
- Freetimejobs.com   freetimejobs.com
- Homeworking.com   homeworking.com
- Institute of Management
  Consultants   imcusa.org
- MediaStreet.com   mediastreet.com
- Nationwide Consultants   nationwideconsultants.com
- OutSource 2000   outsource2000.com
- Outsourcing Jobs   outsourcingjobs.com
- PortaJobs   portajobs.com
- ProsForHire.com   prosforhire.com
- Smarterwork.com   www.smarterwork.com
- Telecommuting Jobs   tjobs.com
- Telework Connection   telework-connection.com
- Womans-Work.com   womans-work.com
- Work at Home Moms   wahm.com
- WorkOnLine   telecommute.hypermart.net

Spooks, Spies, and Intel Specialists

Even spies need jobs! Indeed, with the ending of the Cold War more than a decade ago, many individuals in the intelligence community found themselves in a very different job market. A very special group known for their unique technical skills, high levels of job satisfaction, and comradery, many of these individuals regularly leave the closed worlds, including the "black" services, of federal security agencies and the military and transition to the private sector. Many of the resources identified in the "Military Transition" section are relevant to this special group of job seekers who increasingly gravitate to intelligence and security jobs in the private sector. The following websites, many of which provide excellent networking opportunities for this closely knit community, are especially relevant to such job seekers:

Intelligence Careers	**Intelligence**
intelligencecareers.com	

Offers searchable job listings and a resume database for information and intelligence specialists. Includes news and linkages to other employment websites for career advice, internships, law enforcement jobs, intelligence topics, and newsletters.

Intelligence Briefs	**Intelligence**
intelbriefs.com/inteljobs.htm	

This site is designed to assist information specialists find jobs. Includes a resume database and job search resources through a linkage with Vault.com and job postings through other major employment sites, such as USJobBoard.com and FlipDog.com. Also includes employment news feeds and resume writing and blasting services.

Other websites of interest to anyone seeking a job in intelligence services includes:

- Armed Forces
  Communications Electronics
  Association   www.afcea.org
- Association of Former
  Intelligence Officers   www.afio.com
- Association of Old Crows   www.aochq.org
- Defense Advanced Research
  Project Agency   www.arpa.gov
- Central Intelligence Agency   www.cia.gov
- Competitive Intelligence   bidigitalcom/ci
- Federal Bureau of
  Investigation (FBI)   www.fbi.gov
- Infowar.com   infowar.com
- International Association of
  Counterterrorism and
  Security Personnel   iacsp.com
- International Association of
  Law Enforcement
  Intelligence Analysts   www.ialeia.org
- IT Toolbox Security   security.ittoolbox.com
- National Security Agency   www.nsa.gov
- National Security Institute   nsi.org
- Society of Competitive
  Intelligence Professionals   scip.org
- Society of Former Special
  Agents of the FBI   www.socxfbi.org
- Special Forces Association   sfadhq.org

Ex-Offenders in Transition

Each year nearly 500,000 individuals in the U.S. leave prisons or jails after having served time for various criminal acts. The majority or drug-related cases. In New York City alone nearly 125,000 individuals are released each year. At any one time nearly 4 million adults are on probation and 700,000 on parole. Not surprisingly, few employers are eager to assist this group of job seekers. Indeed, as soon as an ex-offender tells the truth on an application about his or her criminal record, many employers automatically disqualify them from further consideration. The number one problem for many ex-offenders upon being released is to find a steady and rewarding job. Often viewed as the dregs of society – the last hired and the first fired – nearly 70 percent of these individuals lose their jobs within the first 60 days after being released. Lacking employment and repeating past patterns of criminal behavior, many of these ex-offenders commit crimes and eventually return to prison or jail. Unfortunately, there are few community-based support services to help this tainted group of job seekers find employment. Local churches, shelters, and nonprofit organizations provide some assistance. Occasionally the Federal Bureau of Prisons and nonprofit organizations host special job fairs for ex-offenders. While there are even fewer websites designed to assist them with employment, a few sites try to assist this very special and difficult to place group of job seekers. If you are an ex-offender, or if you know someone with such a background, please visit these websites. They could possibly change lives

- American Correctional Association — corrections.com/aca
- American Jail Association — corrections.com/aja
- American Probation and Parole Association — www.appa-net.org
- Better People — betterpeople.org
- Correctional Education Company — prisonedu.bigstep.com
- Ex-Offender Resources — explore.cornell.edu/work/ex-offender.htm
- Family and Corrections Network — www.fcnetwork.org
- Goodwill Industries — goodwill.org
- Impact Publications (See "Ex-Offenders and Prison" section) — impactpublications.com
- Inmate Families Organization — inmatefamilies.org
- Labor Finders — laborfinders.com
- National Institute of Corrections — nicic.org

- Northern California   norcalserviceleague.org/
  Service League   jobplace.htm
- Open Inc.   openinc.org
- Osborne Association/   osborneny.org/south_forty.
  South Forty   htm
- Prison Fellowship Ministries prisonfellowshop.org
- Project RIO   www.workforcelin.com/html/
                               rio/default_no.html
- UNICOR Placement   unicor.gov/placement/
                               ippeopp.htm
- Vera Institute of Justice   vera.org

Index

A

Abbott-Langer.com, 156
Academia, 189-193
Academic360.com, 189-190
Academic Employment
    Network, 191-192
Accessjobs.org, 244
Accountantjobs.com, 201
Action Without Borders, 244
Advertising, 83-84
Airline Employment Assistance
    Corps, 194
Airlinecareer.com, 193
Airlines, 193-194
AIRSdirectory.com, 40
Allbusiness.com, 120
Alumni groups, 143-144
Alumni.net, 144
Americanjobs.com, 204
American Society of Association
    Executives, 123
America's CareerInfoNet, 113
America's Job Bank, 59-60
America's Learning Exchange,
    103
AnalyzeMyCareer.com, 90-91
Approach, 6-7

Architectjobs.com, 195
Architect Search, 195
Architecture, 195-197
Artjob.org, 198
Arts, 197-199
AskTheEmployer, 147
Assessment:
    importance of, 7
    instruments, 85
    online, 86-99
    problems with, 86
    sites, 83-99
Assessment.com, 87
Associations:
    networking, 141
    professional, 122-124
AssociationCentral, 123
Associations On the Net, 122
Attorneyjobsonline.com, 215
Aviationjobsonline.com,
    193-194
Avjobs.com, 194

B

Bankjobs.com, 200
Bear's Guides, 105
Benefitslink.com, 200

261

Bernard Haldane Associates,
 146, 167-168
BestJobsUSA, 71
Birkman Method, 90
Bioview.com, 218
Bizweb.com, 120
Bluettogray.com, 228-229
Boston Consulting Group,
 185-186
BrainBid.com, 254
Brassring.com, 75-76
BrilliantPeople.com, 72, 181
Brint.com, 119
Buddy finders, 145
Business, 189-202
Business.com, 120-121

C
Campuscareercenter.com, 225
Candidates, 175-177
Capella University, 106
Career:
    advice, 111-125, 147
    coaches, 146-147, 163-174
    counselors, 133, 137, 163-174
    information, 111-125
    management firms, 166
    professionals, 99, 137, 163-174
    research, 117-124
    writers, 117
Careerbuilder, 62
Careercity.com, 73
Career.com, 64
Careerexchange.com, 77
Careerexplorer.net, 110
CareerHub.com, 87-88
Career-Intelligence.com, 233
Careerjournal.com, 67-68
Career Key, 95
Careerkey.com, 31
CareerLab.com, 93-94
CareerLeader, 94
Careermag.com, 78
Career Masters Institute, 171
Careerperfect.com, 91

Career Planning and Adult
 Development Network, 174
Careerresources.net, 45
Careers-by-design.com, 95
Careershop.com, 72
Careers-in-business.com, 199
Careers.org, 46
CareerTV.net, 76
Careerweb.com, 67
Careerwomen.com, 233
CareerXroads.com, 41
Catapult, 45
CEOExpress.com, 118
Certified Career Coaches, 172
Chefs, 211
Chronicle of Higher Education,
 190
Classifieds, 50, 53-55
Clubs, 145
College Board (see Myroad.com)
Collegejobs.com, 226
College students, 223-227
CollegeView.com, 110
Communities:
    information, 27-29
    virtual, 27-35
Compensation (see Salary
 Negotiations)
Computerjobs.com203
Computerwork.com, 203-204
Computers, 202-205
Connections, 137
Contactors, 253-255
Construction, 205-206
Constructionjobs.com, 205
Constructionjobstore.com, 205
Coolworks.com, 220
Corporate Gray Online, 228-229
CorporateInformation, 119
Cover letters (see Resumes)
Cyberfiber.com, 32

D
Davideck.com, 91-92
Dcwebwomen.org, 142

Destinygroup.com, 229
Dice.com, 202
Directories:
   defining, 15
   major, 18-19
Disabled, 237-239
Disabledperson.com, 238
Distance learning, 101-105
Distance Learning on the Net, 104
Distance Education and Training Council, 105
Diversity, 234-237
DiversityLink.com, 235
Downsizing, 124-125
Drake Beam Morin, 169

E
EDGAR, 121-122, 157
Education:
   associations, 109
   online, 101-110
   programs, 105-108
   traditional, 109-110
   websites, 189-193
Educationamerica.net, 191
Effectiveness, 4
eLance.com, 253-254
Email, 12
Emode.com, 98
Emotional Intelligence Quotient, 97
Employers:
   benefits to, 57
   goals of, 50-53
   role of, 7
   sites, of, 175, 185-186
Employersonline.com, 78
Employmax.com, 65-66
Employment firms, 182-184
Employment sites:
   gateway, 37-47
   mega, 49-81
Employment911.com, 68
Employmentspot.com, 68-69
Employmentwizard.com, 79

Engineering, 206-208
Engineeremployment.com, 206
Engineeringjobs.com, 206
Entertainment, 197-199
Entertainmentcareers.net, 197
EscapeArtist.com, 250
Exeunet.com, 180
Executive:
   candidates, 231
   recruiters, 135, 175-182, 231
Executivesonly.com, 179
Ex-offenders, 258-260
Expectations, 2
eWork.com, 254

F
4Work.com, 71
40-Plus Clubs, 145
Fedjobs.com, 241
Financialjobs.com, 201
Fiveoclockclub.com, 145
Flipdog.com, 60-61
Focus, 5
Fortune.com, 92-93
Free agents, 253-256
Freelancers, 255-256
FutureStep.com, 96

G
Gateways, 37-47
Goals, 2
Gogettem.com, 14
Golfingcareers.com, 221
Google.com, 16, 31-32, 187
Government, 239-243
Greentogray.com, 228-229
GSIA Carnegie Mellon, 96
GuideStar.org, 123-124, 243-244

H
Harcourt-learning.com, 107-108
Harrisinof.com, 121
Headhunter.net, 62-63
Headhunters, 135, 175-182
Health care, 208-211

Healthcarejobsusa.com, 208-209
HERmail.net, 142
Higheredjobs.com, 190
Highlandsprogram.com, 97
Hirediversity.com, 235
Hollywoodweb.com, 198
Homefair.com, 160
Homescape.com, 161-162
Homestore.com, 160
Hoovers.com, 118-119
Hospitality, 211-214
Hospitalityadventures.com, 212
Hospitality Careers Online, 212
Hotjobs.com, 61-62
Hotresumes.com, 136
HR departments, 127-128
Humanmetrics.com, 98

I
iAgora.com, 252
Idealist.org, 244
Impressions, 151
Information technology, 202-204
Inner Self Personality Test, 98
Intel specialists, 257-258
Intelligence Briefs, 257
Intelligencecareers, 257
Interest Finder Quiz, 96
International Association of
Career Management
Professionals, 173-174
International:
    job seekers, 250-253
    nonprofits, 244-250
    research, 249-250
International Distance Learning
    Course Finder, 104
Internet:
    approaches to, 3
    resources, 13
Interviewcoach.com, 153
Interviews, 149-154
i-recruit.com, 177-178
Itcareers.com, 203
iVillage.com, 232-233

J
Jackson Vocational Interest
    Survey, 97
Jobaccess.org, 238
Job Accommodation Network,
    238
JobBankUSA.com, 32, 76
JobBoard.net, 47
Job boards, 49-50
Jobdirect.com, 80
JobExchange (see
    Employmentwizard.com)
JobFactory.com, 69, 124
Job-Hunt.com, 44
JobHuntersBible.com, 43-44
JobInterview.net, 151-152
Job interviews, 5
Jobmonkey.com, 212-213
Joboptions.com, 63-64
Job postings, 53-54
Jobrelocation.com, 161
JobReviews.com, 152
Jobs4sales.com, 201
Jobsfed.com, 241
Jobs.com, 63
Job seekers, 223-260
Jobsopps.net, 75
Job search:
    approach, 6, 50-55, 84-86, 134
    clubs, 145-146
    focus on, 4
    Internet in, 6
    organizing, 6
    steps in, 1, 83
    targeted, 134
JobsAbroad.com, 251
Job-search-engine.com, 124
Job seekers:
    frustrated, 3
    Internet savvy, 8
Jobsinsports.com, 220
Jobsleuth.com, 73
Jobsonline.com, 61
JobSourcenetwork.com, 46
Jobspectrum.org, 219
JobStar.org, 155

Jobtrak.com, 74-75, 226
Jobweb.com, 74, 225-226
Joyce Lain Kennedy, 153
Jumboclassifieds.com, 77

K
K-12jobs.com, 191
Kaplancollege.com, 106-107
Keirsey.com, 88
Kellyservices, 184
Keywords, 26, 50

L
Latpro.com, 235
Law, 214-217
Law enforcement, 239-243
Lawenforcementjob.com, 241
Lawjobs.com, 215
Legalstaff.com, 214
Library, 14
Locators:
    military, 145
    personal, 144-145

M
Mailing lists, 32-34, 140
Management Recruiters
    International (see
    BrilliantPeople.com)
Manpower.com, 184
MAPP (see Assessment.com)
Medcareers.com, 209
Medhunters.com, 209
Media, 197-199
Meetit.com, 153
Mega.JobSites.com, 47
Message boards, 34-35
Mega employment sites, 49-81
Mentors, 146-147
META tags, 26
Microsoft, 186
Microsoft eLearn, 108
Military:
    locators, 145
    transitioning, 227-231

MindEdge.com, 104
Mindfind.com, 79
Minorities, 234-237
MoneyFromHome.com, 255
Monster.com, 35, 58-59, 151,
    157, 179, 209, 251
Monster Work Abroad, 251
Mycollegeguide.org, 110
Myers-Briggs Type Indicator®,
    85-88, 91
MyJobSearch.com, 40, 65
Myroad.com, 94

N
National Board of Certified
    Counselors, 170
National Career Development
    Association, 170
Nationjob.com, 66
Netshare.com, 180
Net-Temps.com, 70, 183
NetWorker Career Services, 132
Networking, 139-147, 180
Networks:
    alumni, 143-144
    association, 141
    re-building, 144-145
    women's, 142
Nonprofits, 243-250

O
1-Page Multi Search, 17, 187
100hot.com, 25-26
Occupational sites, 187-223
Olsten.com, 184
OnlineProfiles.com, 97
Outplacement, 168-169
Overseasjobs.com, 251
Oya's Directory of Recruiters,
    177-178

P
Part-time jobs, 253-255
Personality Online, 89
Personalitytype.com, 88-89

Petersons.com, 102-103
Phoenix,edu, 106
Planetalumni.com, 144
Preferredjobs.com, 77
Prohire.com, 77
Professional Association of
    Resume Writers and Career
    Coaches, 173
Profiler.com, 93

Q
Queendom.com, 92
Quick Personality Test, 98
Quintcareers.com, 42, 114-115

R
R. L. Stevens and Associates,
    147, 169
Ranks.com, 24-25
Rebecca Smith's eResumes.com,
    131
Recreation, 220-222
Recruiters, 135
Recruitersonline.com, 178
Recruitusa.com, 79-80
Redundancy, 57
Relocation, 159-162
Relocationcentral.com, 160-161
Response rates, 133
Resume:
    associations, 131-132
    blasters, 130, 133-137, 181-182
    database, 53, 129
    distributors, 130, 133-137
    professionals, 131-133
    sites, 127-137
    tips, 130-131
    writers, 131-133
Resumes:
    costs of, 130-131, 134-135
    electronic, 127-129
    online, 1
    paper, 127-128
Resumesion.com, 133
Resumezapper.com, 181-182

Right Management Consultants,
    146, 168
Riley Guide, 42-43, 113-114
Robert Half International,
    156-157, 183
Runzheimer.com, 151

S
Salary negotiations, 154-158
Salary.com, 155
SalarySource.com, 158
Science, 217-220
Science Careers, 218
Search agents:
    defining, 15
    major, 18
Searchenginewatch.com, 22
Search engines:
    defining, 15
    number of, 14
    popular, 19-22
    using, 12, 16–17
Search Systems, 122
Securities and Exchange
    Commission, 157
Self-directed-search.com, 89
Self-starters, 165-166
Services, 55-57
Showbizjobs.com, 197
Sixfigurejobs.com, 179
Sologig.com, 256
Spies, 257-258
Sports, 220-222
Staffing.com, 182-183
Staffing firms, 182-184
State Vocational and
    Rehabilitation Agencies,
    237-238

T
"T" letter, 92
TAOnline.com. 230
Teachers, 189-193
Telecomcareers.net, 200-201
Telecommuters, 255-256

Temporary work, 253-255
Testing (see Assessment)
Tests on the Web, 92
Time:
    Internet, 11-12
    using, 11-12
Thomasregional.com, 121
Top9.com, 19, 22-24
Topica.com, 32
Traffic, 50, 52-53
Transitionsabroad.com, 251-252
Travel, 211-214

U

University of London, 46
University of Phoenix, 106
Usajobs.opm.gov, 239
Usenet newsgroups, 29-31, 139-140

V

Vault.com, 69, 115
VetJobs.com, 229
Virtual Relocation, 160
Virtualville.com, 154

W

Wageweb.com, 156
Wantedjobs.com, 78-79
Websites:
    benefits of, 7
    boutique, 2
    comparison of, 22-26
    effectiveness of, 4
    financing, 7-8, 50-53
    job seeker, 223-360
    niche, 2, 187-260
    number of, 1
    occupational, 187-222
    size of, 3
    structure of, 7-8, 52, 83-84
    top, 2, 58-81
Womans-work.com, 234
WetFeet.com, 70, 115-116
Women, 232-234

Women's Executive Network,
  147
WinningTheJob.com, 116-117
Wisdom, 12

The Authors

F OR NEARLY TWO DECADES DRS. RON AND CARYL
Krannich have pursued a passion – assisting hundreds of thousands of individuals, from students, the unemployed, and ex-
offenders to military personnel, international job seekers, and
CEOs, in making critical job and career transitions. Focusing on key job
search skills, career changes, and employment fields, their impressive
body of work has helped shape career thinking and behavior both in the
United States and abroad. Their sound advice has changed numerous
lives, including their own!

Ron and Caryl are two of America's leading career and travel writers
who have authored more than 60 books. A former Peace Corps Volunteer
and Fulbright Scholar, Ron received his Ph.D. in Political Science from
Northern Illinois University. Caryl received her Ph.D. in Speech Communication from Penn State University. Together they operate Development Concepts Incorporated, a training, consulting, and publishing firm
in Virginia.

The Krannichs are both former university professors, high school
teachers, management trainers, and consultants. As trainers and consultants, they have completed numerous projects on management, career
development, local government, population planning, and rural development in the United States and abroad. Their career books focus on key

job search skills, military and civilian career transitions, government and international careers, travel jobs, and nonprofit organizations. Their books represent one of today's most comprehensive collections of career writing. With over 2 million copies in print, their publications are widely available in bookstores, libraries, and career centers. No strangers to the Internet world, Ron and Caryl have been instrumental in publishing several Internet recruitment and job search books as well as developing career-related websites: www.impactpublications.com, www.winningthe job.com, www.contentforcareers.com, www.veteransworld.com, and www. greentogray.com. Many of their career tips, as well as excerpts from their books, appear on such major websites as monster.com, careerbuilder.com, careerweb.com, and campuscareercenter.com.

Ron and Caryl live a double life with travel being their best kept *"do what you love"* career secret. Authors of 19 travel-shopping guidebooks on various destinations around the world, they continue to pursue their international and travel interests through their innovative *Treasures and Pleasures of . . . Best of the Best* travel-shopping series and related websites: www.ishoparoundtheworld.com and www.contentfortravel.com. When not found at their home and business in Virginia, they are probably somewhere in Europe, Asia, Africa, the Middle East, the South Pacific, or the Caribbean and South America pursuing their other passion – researching and writing about quality arts and antiques as well as following the advice of their other Click and Easy™ volume designed for road warriors and other travel types: *Travel Planning on the Internet: The Click and Easy™ Guide. "We follow the same career and life-changing advice we give to others – pursue a passion that enables you to do what you really love to do,"* say the Krannichs.

As both career and travel experts, the Krannichs' work is frequently featured in major newspapers, magazines, and newsletters as well as on radio, television, and the Internet. Available for interviews, consultation, and presentations, they can be contacted as follows:

Ron and Caryl Krannich
krannich@impactpublications.com

Career Resources

THE FOLLOWING CAREER RESOURCES ARE AVAILABLE directly from Impact Publications. Complete the following form or list the titles, include postage (see formula at the end), enclose payment, and send your order to:

IMPACT PUBLICATIONS
9104 Manassas Drive, Suite N
Manassas Park, VA 20111-5211
1-800-361-1055 (orders only)
Tel. 703-361-7300 or Fax 703-335-9486
Email address: *orders@impactpublications.com*
Quick & easy online ordering: www.impactpublications.com

Orders from individuals must be prepaid by check, moneyorder, Visa, MasterCard, or American Express. We accept telephone, fax, and email orders.

Qty.	TITLES	Price	TOTAL
Internet			
___	100 Top Internet Job Sites	$12.95	___
___	America's Top Internet Job Sites	19.95	___
___	CareerXroads (annual)	26.95	___
___	Career Exploration On the Internet	24.95	___
___	Cyberspace Job Search Kit	18.95	___
___	Directory of Websites for Overseas Job Seekers	19.95	___
___	Guide to Internet Job Searching	14.95	___
___	Haldane's Best Employment Websites for Professionals	15.95	___
___	Job-Hunting On the Internet	8.95	___
___	Job Search Online For Dummies	24.99	___
___	Online Web Design	17.95	___
___	Sams Teach Yourself e-Job Hunting	17.99	___
___	Weddle's Job-Seeker's Guide to Employment Web Sites	12.95	___
Assessment			
___	Career Tests	12.95	___
___	Discover the Best Jobs For You	15.95	___
___	Discover What You're Best At	13.00	___

	Title	Price	
____	Do What You Are	18.95	_____
____	Finding Your Perfect Work	16.95	_____
____	Gifts Differing	14.95	_____
____	I Could Do Anything If Only I Knew What It Was	12.95	_____
____	Making Vocational Choices	29.95	_____
____	Pathfinder	14.00	_____
____	What Type Am I?	14.95	_____

Career Exploration and Job Strategies

____	100 Great Jobs and How to Get Them	17.95	_____
____	Best Jobs For the 21st Century	19.95	_____
____	Change Your Job, Change Your Life	17.95	_____
____	Complete Guide to Occupational Exploration	39.95	_____
____	Enhanced Guide For Occupational Exploration	34.95	_____
____	Enhanced Occupational Outlook Handbook	37.95	_____
____	Occupational Outlook Handbook	23.95	_____
____	O*NET Dictionary of Occupational Titles	49.95	_____
____	What Color Is Your Parachute?	16.95	_____

Networking

____	A Foot in the Door	14.95	_____
____	Great Connections	11.95	_____
____	How to Work a Room	14.00	_____
____	Masters of Networking	16.95	_____
____	Power Networking	14.95	_____
____	Power Schmoozing	12.95	_____
____	The Savvy Networker	14.95	_____

Resumes and Letters

____	Best Resumes For $100,000+ Jobs	24.95	_____
____	Best Cover Letters For $100,000+ Jobs	24.95	_____
____	Cover Letters For Dummies	14.99	_____
____	Cyberspace Resume Kit	18.95	_____
____	Dynamite Cover Letters	14.95	_____
____	Dynamite Resumes	14.95	_____
____	Electronic Resumes and Online Networking	13.99	_____
____	Haldane's Best Cover Letters For Professionals	15.95	_____
____	Haldane's Best Resumes For Professionals	15.95	_____
____	High Impact Resumes & Letters	19.95	_____
____	Military Resumes and Cover Letters	19.95	_____
____	Resumes For Dummies	14.99	_____
____	The Savvy Resume Writer	12.95	_____

Interviews

____	101 Dynamite Answers to Interview Questions	12.95	_____
____	101 Dynamite Questions to Ask At Your Job Interview	13.95	_____
____	Haldane's Best Answers to Tough Interview Questions	15.95	_____
____	Interview For Success	15.95	_____
____	Job Interviews For Dummies	14.99	_____
____	Proof of Performance	17.95	_____
____	The Savvy Interviewer	10.95	_____

Salary Negotiations

____	Better Than Money	18.95	_____
____	Dynamite Salary Negotiations	15.95	_____

___ Get a Raise in 7 Days	14.95	___
___ Get More Money On Your Next Job	14.95	___
___ Haldane's Best Salary Tips For Professionals	15.95	___

International and Travel Jobs

___ Global Resume and CV Guide	17.95	___
___ Inside Secrets to Finding a Career in Travel	14.95	___
___ International Jobs	18.00	___
___ International Jobs Directory	19.95	___
___ Jobs For People Who Love to Travel	15.95	___
___ Work Abroad	15.95	___

SUBTOTAL   ___

Virginia residents add 4½% sales tax   ___

POSTAGE/HANDLING ($5 for first
product and 8% of SUBTOTAL) $5.00

8% of SUBTOTAL -- ___

TOTAL ENCLOSED ---------------------------- ___

SHIP TO:

NAME _____

ADDRESS _____

_____

_____

PAYMENT METHOD:

❑ I enclose check/moneyorder for $ _____ made payable to
IMPACT PUBLICATIONS.

❑ Please charge $ _____ to my credit card:

❑ Visa   ❑ MasterCard   ❑ American Express   ❑ Discover

Card # _____

Expiration date: _____ / _____

Signature _____

The Click and Easy™ Online Resource Centers

Books, videos, software, training materials, articles, and advice for job seekers, employers, HR professionals, schools, and libraries

Visit us online for all your career and travel needs:

www.impactpublications.com
(career superstore and Impact Publications)

_____

www.winningthejob.com
(career articles, advice, and bookstore)

_____

www.contentforcareers.com
(syndicated career content for job seekers, employees, and Intranets)

_____

www.veteransworld.com
www.greentogray.com
www.bluetogray.com
(military transition databases and content)

_____

www.ishoparoundtheworld.com
(unique international travel-shopping center)

_____

www.contentfortravel.com
(syndicated travel content)